THE ILLUSTRATED WITNESS TO
WORLD WAR II

THE ILLUSTRATED WITNESS TO
WORLD WAR II

A HISTORY OF THE GREATEST CONFLICT THE WORLD HAS KNOWN WITH EYEWITNESS ACCOUNTS AND OVER 380 ARCHIVE IMAGES

KAREN FARRINGTON

southwater

This edition is published by Southwater, an imprint of Anness Publishing Ltd
108 Great Russell Street, London WC1B 3NA; info@anness.com

www.southwaterbooks.com; www.annesspublishing.com

Anness Publishing has a new picture agency outlet for images for publishing, promotions or advertising.
Please visit our website www.practicalpictures.com for more information.

Publisher: Joanna Lorenz
Editor: Joy Wotton
Jacket Design: Nigel Partridge
Production Controller: Wendy Lawson

© Anness Publishing Ltd 2014

Previously published as *Witness to World War II*

PUBLISHER'S NOTE
Although the advice and information in this book are believed to be accurate and true at the time of going to press, neither the authors
nor the publisher can accept any legal responsibility or liability for any errors or omissions that may have been made.

PICTURE CREDITS
The publisher would like to thank the following organisations for supplying photographs for use in this book. Every effort has been
made to trace the copyright holders for the pictures. In some cases they have been untraceable, for which we offer our apologies.
Imperial War Museum; Musée d'Histoire Contemporaine; US Marine Corp; US Coast Guard; US Library of Congress; US National
Archives; US Army Photo Services; USAF Photo; US Navy Photo Section; Smithsonian Institute; J. Baker Collection; Ford Motor Co;
Robert Hunt Library; Bundesarchiv; Bibliothek fur Zeitgeschichte; Public Records Office of Hong Kong; Kyodo News Services; Australian
High Commission, London; BFI; British Airways; The Scout Association; The Morning Star via The Marx Memorial Library, London;
Oxfam; Novosti; National Archives of Singapore; Daimler–Benz; RCA; London Transport Museum; National Museum of Labour History;
The Truman Library; VSEL Vickers; Ufficio Storico Fototeca; National Maritime Museum; Biggin Hill Archives; Stato Maggiore
Aeronautica; RAF Museum; The Boeing Co. Archives; Renault; Vickers; Los Alamos Scientific Lab; Polish Underground Movement;
Manx Museum; Red Cross Archives; Far East War Collection/Vic Brown.

CONTENTS

BATTLE FOR THE SKIES

INTRODUCTION

World War II was the most immense conflict mankind has ever known. This book shows exactly how it took shape, from its beginnings in the confused politics of the 1920s and 1930s to its apocalyptic end in the ruined and shattered cities of Germany and Japan in 1945.

Not only was this the largest conflict ever seen; it was also the militarily most complex, with events at sea and in the air having a defining effect on warfare on land. In order to unravel these complexities, war in the skies, on (and under) the oceans, and on land are treated separately, so that all the details can be fully examined. But the approach is far from being coldly technical: hundreds of moving eyewitness and contemporary accounts, many from interviews personally conducted by the author, show what the war meant to the individuals concerned. Commentary on its political and economic causes covers every key moment, and shows the impact of the new technologies and military strategies on the progress of the war.

This history of the greatest conflict the world has known contains over 380 archive images. Contemporary photographs record incidents as they happened, and specially commissioned battle plans and maps illuminate the development

Left: During World War II, the Home Army or *Armja Krajowa* became the dominant Polish resistance movement in German-occupied Poland.

Right: Thousands of British and Australian troops were captured when Singapore fell to Japan on 15 February 1942. This was probably Britain's worst defeat during the Second World War.

of the war. The major battles, on land, at sea and in the air are described, together with an expert analysis of the events and weaponry. A chronology of the period helps put all specific actions of the war into their historical context.

The first section of the book analyses the rise of Nazi Germany under Adolf Hitler in the 1930s. Tension rose throughout the period, and hopes for peace were dashed by Hitler's aggression, until, on 1 September 1939, Germany invaded Poland. Britain and France declared war on Germany on the 3rd. Polish resistance proved hopeless when the country was also attacked by Soviet Russia. The clampdown on Jews in Poland began almost as soon as the first shots of World War II were fired, leading to the Holocaust and the industrialized murder of over 6 million Jews including 1.5 million children.

Early in 1940 the Germans captured Denmark and Norway, and in May they launched a blitzkrieg of fast-moving armoured columns supported by aircraft, resulting in the defeat and occupation of France and the Low Countries and the evacuation of British forces from Dunkirk. In the summer of 1940, the Battle of Britain was fought in the skies over England, eventually forcing Germany to suffer its first defeat and abandon its plans to invade the UK. During the autumn London was subjected to nightly bombing in an action that became known as the Blitz. Britain obtained a victory over Italian forces in North Africa, but in June 1941 the war escalated when Hitler invaded Russia. In December, in one of the most notorious air actions of the war, Japan attacked Pearl Harbor and seized large parts of China and South East Asia leading the USA to enter the war and making global conflict a reality.

In June 1942 the war began turning in favour of the Allies with the US victory at the Battle of Midway in the Pacific and the loss of the German

Left: **On 7 December 1941, Japan's surprise attack on Pearl Harbor, Hawaii, led to the USA entering the war, opening the Pacific Theatre.**

Right: Hurricane pilots of 73 Squadron, in front of their desert-worn aircraft in north Africa in 1941.

Sixth Army at Stalingrad. To coordinate policy the leaders of Britain, Russia and America, Winston Churchill, Joseph Stalin and F.D. Roosevelt met during the war at conferences at Teheran, Yalta and Potsdam.

In 1943 the German Army under Rommel was ousted from North Africa, the Allies invaded Italy, and in July the Germans were defeated in Russia at the key battle of Kursk, involving 6,000 tanks, 2 million men and 4,000 aircraft. US and Australian forces gradually began clawing back Japanese-occupied territory.

On D-Day, 6 June 1944, in the largest ever sea-borne invasion, British and US forces landed in Normandy and started to break through the German defences. In a desperate attempt to stave off defeat, Hitler launched against Britain his 'secret weapons' of V1 flying bombs, nicknamed 'doodlebugs' and V2 long range rockets. However with the Allied armies deep in Germany and the Russians in Berlin, Hitler, on 30 April 1945, committed suicide and German forces surrendered shortly afterwards. Peace returned to Europe, the terrible concentration camps were liberated and on 20 November 1945, the Nuremberg Trials of the major war criminals began before the International Military Tribunal.

War in the Pacific continued and, as the Japanese refused to surrender, the Americans dropped atomic bombs on the Japanese cities of Hiroshima and Nagasaki on 6 and 9 August leading to Japan's surrender on 15 August and the end of the war.

This authoritative and accessible military history will enable the reader to understand the war more fully than ever before. It shows how and why the war was fought, and what happened to the ordinary men and women caught up in it. For some it became a terrifying inferno that led mankind to the depths of hell, but others found it brought out reserves of courage and endurance that they never knew they possessed.

THE SOLDIER'S WAR

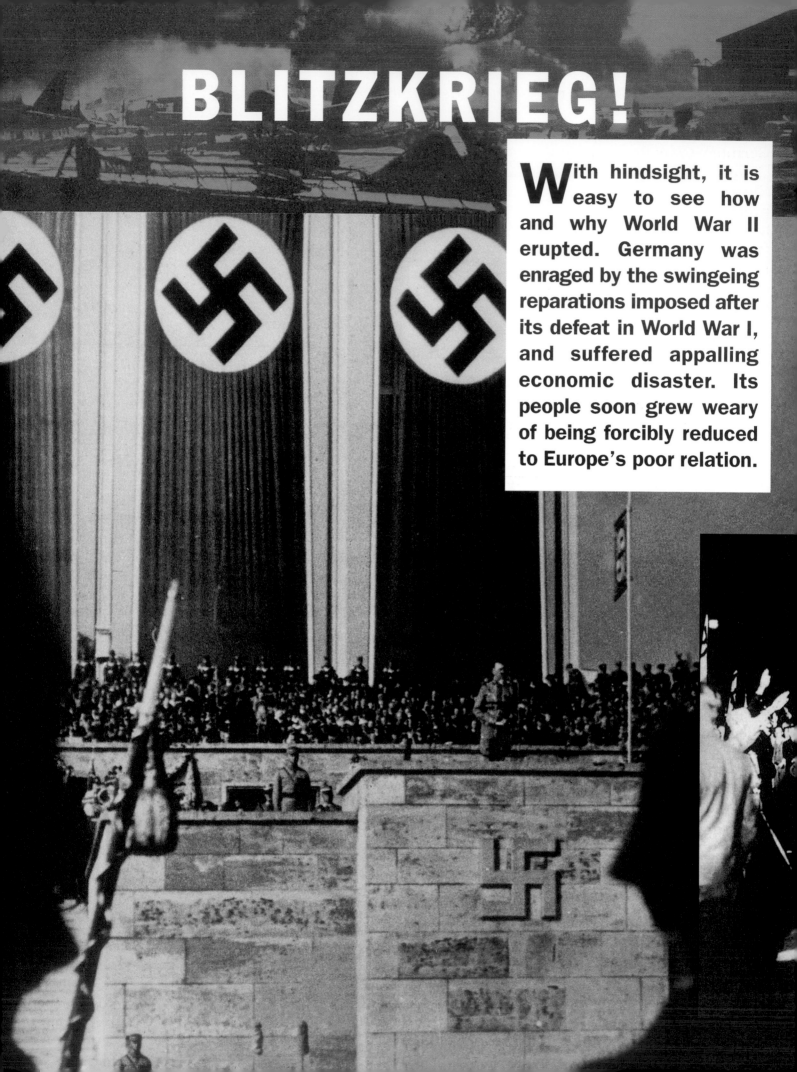

BLITZKRIEG!

With hindsight, it is easy to see how and why World War II erupted. Germany was enraged by the swingeing reparations imposed after its defeat in World War I, and suffered appalling economic disaster. Its people soon grew weary of being forcibly reduced to Europe's poor relation.

The time was ripe for a charismatic leader to sweep into power with the promise of returning Germany to its former glory. Unfortunately for the rest of Europe, those pledges for prosperity at home went hand in hand with an aggressive foreign policy. Nevertheless, Hitler offered the Germans an irresistible chance of stability, vitality and solidarity.

The only difficulty with which to wrestle is just how Britain and France missed the warning signs – catapulting them into a war in September 1939 for which they were ill-prepared and poorly armed.

Both countries were weary of war, still reeling from the enormous loss of manpower. At home they were too preoccupied with domestic problems to heed the warnings of the few who witnessed what was really happening in Hitler's Germany. Violent anti-semitism was put down to the work of a few extremists. Many in power had an admiration for Hitler who achieved so much by cutting unemployment and building prestigious new 'autobahns'. His admirers overlooked the fact that Germany had concentration camps, no free press and no free parliament. And few outside the Reich had any idea of the military strength and firepower that the Führer was amassing.

When Hitler marched into the demilitarised Rhineland in 1936, many considered he was only taking back what rightfully belonged to Germany. The annexation of Austria in 1938 was looked upon virtually as an internal matter. Only with Hitler's demands for land from Czechoslovakia later that same year did Britain and France begin to sense the threat.

Hitler relished the chance to 'free' fellow Germans from 'Polish barbarism'

A negotiated agreement with Hitler was designed to end his expansionism, but when Hitler marched into Prague in the face of that agreement, Britain and France finally realised the folly of their actions.

All thoughts turned to Danzig, the free city in a Polish-held corridor which split Germany from East Prussia, and which Hitler believed was part of Germany. He relished the chance to 'free' fellow Germans who he claimed were being subjected to Polish barbarism.

CARDBOARD TANKS

Much of Germany's rearmament had gone on covertly. Even when war broke out many British people were convinced that their former enemy had tanks made of cardboard. Indeed, the Germans did carry out military manoeuvres with

Left: Nazi book-burning ceremony. Only works regarded as acceptable to the fascist dictatorship were tolerated.
Far left: Hitler addresses a Nazi party rally at Nuremberg in 1938.

cardboard tanks in the early 1920s before secretly importing and building their own real ones. Meanwhile, France had the largest army and the most impressive air force in the world. Most of its citizens prided themselves on the fact that Germany was unlikely to begin hostilities against such a superior force. As England viewed the Channel as an impregnable wall

Hitler unleashed a new and frightening brand of warfare called 'Blitzkrieg'

of defence, so France had the much-vaunted Maginot line. It took nine years to construct the frontier defences, the brainchild of French minister André Maginot. The network of towers and tunnels was remarkable enough in itself. Had the Germans attacked the line directly, it might have served its purpose

BRITAIN'S FASCIST LEADER

Oswald Mosley became the creator of the British Union of Fascists in the early 1930s after having been a member of both Conservative and Labour parties and having been linked for a while with the Liberals.

He had a lively, sharp mind and a clarity of vision. He was even branded the best political thinker of the age. But his frustration at the confines of the accepted political doctrines cast him to the margins where he hit upon the fascism sweeping Europe.

The British, however, were not entranced with uniforms and salutes in the same way as the Germans, Italians or Spanish, among whom fascism flourished. He became a figure of fun, never taken seriously even after the outbreak of war. He was nevertheless jailed in 1940 for four years. Following his release, he was vilified in Britain and finally moved with his wife Diana Mitford and two small sons to France. He continued to exercise his mind around political problems but failed to find a platform for his views. He died in 1980.

well, albeit that it stretched only as far as the Belgian border, and not beyond it.

Static trench warfare, which had claimed so many lives, was now an outdated concept – yet France and Britain didn't realise it. When Hitler invaded Poland in September 1939, he unleashed a new and frightening brand of warfare into the world called 'Blitzkrieg'.

First to feel the heat of this 'lightning war', Poland lurched back in helpless horror when the German army crossed its borders at dawn on 1 September 1939. It took only a few hours for the invading force to quell Polish defences. As the German troops and tanks rolled through the Polish countryside, the country's major cities were being bombed by the Luftwaffe

Left: German soldiers survey the results of their fast-moving campaign in Poland.
Top: Britain was braced for attack months before it actually came.

Above: Germany used its tanks to thrust ahead during the Blitzkrieg. They were unleashed with great success against Poland, France and the Low Countries.

and its ports were being shelled by German ships.

Key to the success of Blitzkrieg was the use of tanks in large numbers and innovative style – they were still thought by Britain and France to be valid only as infantry support. The Panzer forces charged ahead independent of the troops, and wreaked havoc among defenders. Bursting through defensive lines, they harried the Poles from the rear, creating confusion and smashing supply lines.

The German air force had learned much by aiding Franco during the Spanish Civil War, which ended in May 1939. Now pilots were putting this knowledge to good use and after a month Poland capitulated.

Poland's capital Warsaw held out for a few weeks longer than the rest of the country against the Third Reich. Heavy bombardment turned this once grand city to rubble. As it surrendered, the Germans were triumphant. The hated Treaty of Versailles, which had condemned them to international servitude since 1919, was at last eradicated.

This time Britain and France refused to sit back and watch their ally being dismembered by Hitler. Both declared war on Germany almost immediately – although failed to do anything which would materially assist Poland – and braced themselves for the onslaught. Thankfully, it never came.

Despite the success of the Polish campaign, many German officers were concerned about taking on the might of the French army backed by Britain. Hitler was persuaded to abandon thoughts of an immediate push through the Low Countries into France, in favour of launching a spring campaign.

REALITY OF WAR

The reality of war was slow to strike home in Britain. When the feared air raids and gas attacks failed to materialise, there was an almost euphoric mood as people busied themselves sandbagging homes and putting up blackout screens in windows. The casualties in road traffic accidents caused by the rigorously enforced blackout far exceeded those caused in the war. Phrases full of mock indignation like 'put that light out' and 'don't you know there's a war on' typified the bureaucracy pervading the country. Unemployment stayed high,

Above: A French cottage is destroyed by advancing German troops, who put French and British defenders to flight.

war production lamentably low. Reservists were being signed up for army duty surely but slowly, performing drills with bayonets and gas masks and sometimes wooden 'rifles'.

Nearly 200,000 soldiers in the British Expeditionary Force were sent to France where they dug in on the Belgian border. By this time, Germany had mobilised six million men.

Hitler was concerned at the ease with which the British navy had managed to raid a German ship in Norwegian waters. On 9 April 1940 Hitler's troops moved into Denmark and Norway for another short, sharp campaign. Denmark was without an army and acquiesced the following day.

Norway, deeply anti-militarist by tradition, nevertheless put up a fight despite the evident popularity with which the Germans were greeted in some quarters. Churchill himself was looking at the possibility of occupying Norway to reap the rewards of its strategic position. The government would do no more than lay mines in Norwegian waters to disrupt a vital German supply line. In fact, the Royal Navy was doing just that when some of the invasion force from Germany sailed up. There was a skirmish in which some damage was inflicted on German ships. That was the only glimmer of optimism in what turned into an otherwise disastrous escapade.

Churchill himself was looking at the possibility of occupying Norway

Britain sent landing parties to key points, but the small-scale campaign was ill-planned and improvised. The poorly equipped troops had no artillery and no air cover, whereas the Luftwaffe was in control of many Norwegian airstrips and was making full use of them. It wasn't long before the British, and the French forces with them, were forced to withdraw in disarray.

The debacle outraged many people and MPs in Britain, who feared the country was only making a half-hearted attempt at war. On 7 May there was a debate in the House of Commons in which Prime Minister Chamberlain made a statement on the Norwegian affair. The government won a vote of confidence by only 81 votes, too few for Chamberlain to continue.

BLITZKRIEG IN THE WEST

From 14 May 1940, German Panzer forces bridged the River Meuse and poured into Belgium and northern France, driving all before them. The XIX Panzer Corps under Guderian crossed at Sedan, the XLI Panzer Corps (Reinhardt) at Monthermé, the XV Panzer Corps (Hoth) at Dinant, while Höpner's XVI Panzer Corps swept down from the north east. Within days, the German tanks were at the English Channel, but then paused. The British attempted a counter-attack at Arras, while the French planned a similar move from the south. These efforts came to little, however, and by the end of May, with the German forces once again on the move, the British Expeditionary Force had its back to the sea at Dunkirk, awaiting rescue.

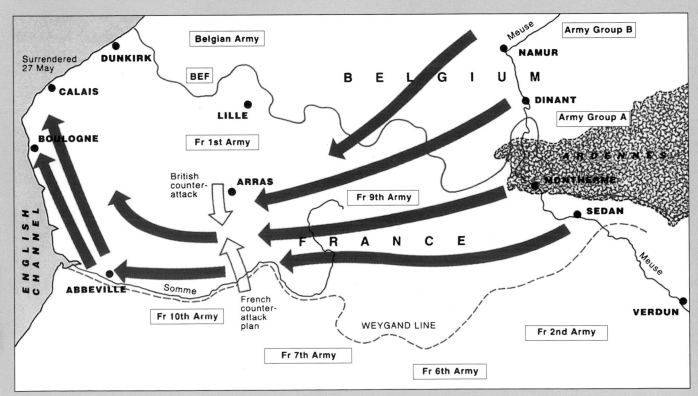

He resigned on 10 May, the same day that German troops made their first forays into Holland and Belgium. The

The spring campaign got underway with a vengeance in western Europe

spring campaign got underway with a vengeance as the horrors of Hitler's Blitzkrieg came to western Europe.

Airborne troops took the Belgian fortress of Eben Emael, chasing out the petrified defenders. At the same time in Rotterdam, 12 floatplanes landed on the River Maas. Out of each of them came an inflatable dinghy and a clutch of German troops ready to swarm over essential vantage points throughout the city.

HOLLAND FALLS

There were also more orthodox methods of invasion, by Panzer forces over the borders. The French army and the British Expeditionary Force prepared themselves for a surge of German troops coming through northern Belgium. To their surprise, Panzer divisions had crossed the Ardennes, condemned as impassable by Allied commanders. Amid confusion, a division led by Rommel began a headlong rush westwards.

Holland capitulated on 14 May. It was another hammerblow to the morale of the French. Without a dynamic leader – their Commander-in-Chief Gamelin was inaudible, indecisive and thought to be suffering acutely from the

---

EYE WITNESS

Alf Turner joined a Territorial Army battalion in his home town of Barnstaple, North Devon, when he was 19.

'In September 1940 we were stationed at Battle. Following Dunkirk it wasn't a case of "if the Germans invade", it was "when the Germans invade". So we had to put a minefield along the beach at Battle.

Not many people knew much about laying minefields. I was with a captain on the beach. We laid about four minefields and were starting on the fifth one. Our driver asked if he could help. The captain allowed him to lay a couple. The driver must have trodden on one and the explosion set lots of the mines off.

The captain and I were lucky to escape. A few days later our brigadier told us it was a vital area and asked us to go back to re-lay the minefield. I told the captain the chances of us coming out alive were only five percent. Still, we had a job to do.

We re-laid about four and I was leading the way when the captain said he should go first. Soon after he took over he pointed to his right. In the middle of a crater lay the head of the dead driver. The shock must have unbalanced him.

Then the ground seemed to open up and I felt I was going into a great big pit. Yet actually I was being blown upwards. Our new driver was waiting on a shelf some 40 feet above the beach. He saw me go into the air above him and go back down again.

I was cross-eyed, had a perforated ear-drum and an injured arm. Still, I managed to get out of there. I was put under sedation for 24 hours, during which time I jumped out of bed three times. They even asked me to go down to the minefield again. I went – but this time they decided it was too dangerous to tackle again.

I was given a week's leave. The medical officer said if I had had any more, I wouldn't have come back. Going home in the blackout was hard. I had to race across pools of darkness, imagining all the time that parts of a body were coming out at me.

A fellow lance corporal blamed himself for the captain's death. He was a religious man and prayed very hard for me, knowing it was a dangerous job. But he didn't pray for the captain and he felt guilty about that.'

Left: Crammed onto the decks of a small steamer, weary troops of the BEF reach a British port.

ravages of venereal disease – the French army fell away, their lack of commitment a world away from the fighting spirit they showed so often during World War I.

The British forces found themselves racing back to the French coast, barely keeping a step ahead of the German advance. Despite an attempt to counter-attack at Arras in northern France, it soon became clear the situation was hopeless. Their commander, General Lord Gort, ordered his men to Dunkirk where they would await evacuation.

DUNKIRK

Hitler ordered his most advanced Panzer divisions to halt, conserving his troops for the invasion of Paris. It gave the British time to install a defensive shell around Dunkirk, behind which they could stage a daring, dangerous and vital evacuation.

Courageous rearguard campaigners held off the German advance while the Royal Navy sent in ship after ship to remove the stricken forces. By 31 May the news blackout on 'Operation Dynamo', the code name for the operation to save British servicemen, was lifted and scores of small boats set sail for France to give aid to the Royal Navy. Experienced mariners set off alongside weekend sailors to pluck as many men as they could from the beach. It was a tough voyage on small craft but each skipper was imbued with a grim determination.

Before the surrender of the remaining defenders of Dunkirk on 4 June, 338,226 men – from Britain, France and Belgium – had been carried to safety. It was no mean feat, given that the official estimates for the evacuation were 45,000. Disastrously, most of Britain's armoury was left behind. There were too few guns remaining in Britain to arm the country's soldiers.

PARIS OCCUPIED

French soldiers, supported in the west by some British fighters, continued to retreat. Two weeks following Dunkirk, Paris was occupied and region after region continued to fall. When French Prime Minister Reynaud resigned on 16 June, his successor Marshal Pétain immediately sued for peace.

The final humiliation for France came on 21 June when Hitler had its leaders sign an armistice in the same railway coach where the German surrender was authorised following World War I. Britain stood alone against the might of the Third Reich with only 21 miles of English Channel to save it from invasion.

Left: Bewildered soldiers and frightened civilians roam the streets of Dunkirk as the Germans close in.

THE WAR
IN AFRICA

When Italian dictator Mussolini dreamed of expanding his empire, he set his sights on Africa. Already the proud possessor of rich colonies, he yearned for more. Those held by the beleaguered British seemed to be ripe for the taking.

Far left: *A British six-pounder gun comes under attack from long-range artillery.*
Left: *The Italian fascist dictator Benito Mussolini rallies his people.*

British found him a surprising and bold adversary after the easy pickings of the Italians. But with the aid of troops from the Dominions, the British were determined to keep their vital foothold in Africa.

SEESAW WAR

It was the start of an indecisive seesaw war which lasted for three years and cost thousands of lives. Celebrated triumphs quickly turned to desert dust, as both sides discovered to their cost. British, Australian, New Zealand and South African soldiers got used to digging slit trenches in gritty, rock-hard ground, much as their

Below: *Thousands of Italian prisoners of war were taken as the British and Commonwealth troops made their initial push across the North African sands.*

Germany, which had been stripped of its African possessions at the end of the World War I, had no business on the continent. In any case, Hitler was preoccupied with conquering Russia. If the Axis powers had got their way, Italy would have swept through Africa and the oil-rich Middle East and Persian Gulf, kicked out the British and set up a vast empire whilst Germany would have concentrated on changing the face of Europe.

It was not to be. The Italians soon suffered a humiliating defeat at the hands of the British defenders of Egypt and were on the verge of being run into the sea when Hitler intervened. The Führer wanted Allied troops tied up in Africa, while he made progress with his plans elsewhere in the world. And he was mindful that whoever held North Africa had the key to the oil riches of the Middle East, a tempting trump card. He chose to take part in

the North African conflict as a potentially profitable diversion.

So, in early 1941, the irrepressible General Erwin Rommel, who had been so successful in western Europe, was dispatched to save the Italians from annihilation, with the aim of securing a new front for the Third Reich. Rommel was a talented leader who prided himself on getting results. The

predecessors had in World War I.

Italy didn't declare war on Britain and France until June 1940 when Hitler's troops were at the gates of Paris and plans to invade Britain were a reality.

The Italian strongholds in North Africa were Ethiopia and Libya. In August Mussolini sent troops into British Somaliland in East Africa and the colony fell to him within a fortnight. Boosted by success, Italian troops stationed in Libya began to menace Egypt, in British hands.

Italian forces crossed the border between the two countries on Friday 13 September and began a five-day advance which ended with them digging into their positions some distance from their goal.

OPERATION COMPASS

Egyptian ports became collection points for Commonwealth troops. British soldiers were joined by Australians, New Zealanders, Indians and South Africans for a mighty push against the Italians, code-named 'Operation Compass'.

On Monday 9 December British Commander-in-Chief General Sir Archibald Wavell began the offensive. Before the week was out, 2,000 Italian prisoners were taken at Sidi Barrani. The Australian 6th Division took a further 30,000 prisoners when it overran Bardia on 5 January 1941.

The pattern was set. Sticking to the coast road, the Australians bagged another 27,000 prisoners on taking the strategically important port of Tobruk. Meanwhile, British troops dipped inland to by-pass a large mountain range.

By now the allies were moving

MONTY – DESERT MAGICIAN

Pride of Britain's armed forces, Bernard Law Montgomery, was born in London in 1887, although his ancestors were from Ulster. When he was two his father Henry was appointed Bishop of Tasmania. The island became his home until he reached his teenage years.

In later life, he often told how his childhood was an unhappy one. His mother Maud was strict and administered terrible beatings. He resented her greatly throughout his adult life.

After distinguishing himself as a soldier in World War I, it appeared he was married to the army. But to the surprise of all, in 1927 this difficult and irritable character married an artist and mother of two who had been widowed at Gallipoli. Warm and affectionate, they were a happy couple and had a son, David, in 1928.

In 1937, Betty died suddenly in a freak tragedy after being stung on the foot. Monty was desolate and threw himself once more into his profession. In the earliest days of World War II he led a division of the British Expeditionary Force in France.

Following the evacuation at Dunkirk, he was based in Britain until August 1942 when Prime Minister Winston Churchill made him head of the British 8th Army in North Africa. British troops, despite early successes, had been on the run from Rommel's Afrika Korps. It was Monty's job to turn the tide of the conflict – and it was one which he relished.

Just months after taking command of the Desert Rats, he scored a significant victory at the second Battle of El Alamein before chasing the German troops across North Africa into Tunisia where they finally surrendered in May 1943.

His next port of call was Sicily and he successfully led his forces up the foot of fascist Italy before being recalled to London. Before him was the most crucial command of his service life. Promoted to the rank of Field-Marshal, he was to help lead the Allied invasion of France. In charge of the key offensive was General Dwight D. Eisenhower with whom Monty clashed on many occasions. Later, Monty was criticised for his thoroughness. Accused of being too cautious, he frustrated his colleagues by refusing to commit his men to action until he was satisfied every small detail of the battle plan had been scrutinised and double-checked. However, his policy, which made for steady but slow progress, won the hearts and minds of his men.

Britain's hero soldier led the British and Canadian 21st Army Group across France, Belgium, The Netherlands and northern Germany to eventual victory.

After the war he held a series of high-ranking posts, including deputy commander of the North Atlantic Treaty Organisation. He was made a Knight of the Garter, and was created a Viscount in 1946. He died in 1976, aged 88.

across the Libyan region of Cyrenaica, capturing Derna, Beda Fomm and finally, on 6 February 1941, Benghazi.

It was by any standard a whirlwind campaign. Allied troops travelled across 440 miles in just 60 days and dwarfed the Italian offensive which prompted the action. They were travelling across inhospitable terrain and even attacked Benghazi in a sand-storm. The retreating Italians who threw up token resistance were then caught in a masterful pincer movement by the British and Australian forces.

With Allied action against the Italians in Ethiopia making excellent progress too, Churchill must have revelled in the rout of the Duce. The British Prime Minister's satisfaction, however, was to be short-lived.

Churchill must have revelled in the rout of the Duce

Six days after the fall of Benghazi, Rommel arrived in Africa with his keen troops from the 5th Light Division and the 15th Panzer Division. He was welcomed by many resident Arabs who had long resented the British presence in North Africa. Within two weeks Rommel attacked El Agheila, the southernmost tip of the Allied gains.

Despite his lack of experience in desert warfare and a recurring mystery stomach complaint,

Above right: *Australians march ashore at Suez in May 1940.*
Right: *The capture of Benghazi was an important first victory.*

EYE WITNESS

Bill Jenkins, a sergeant in the Australian infantry throughout the war, explains why so many Australians were keen to fight the Allied corner.

'At the time we had a population of seven million. We recruited in the first six months of the war over 200,000 volunteers. During the whole of the war, 750,000 people were involved. So percentage-wise I think we did reasonably well for the mother country. The old Australians were very much involved in Empire and considered a trip to England as "going home" even if they were not born there. World War I was still in our memory, too. We were going off to finish the job that the soldiers then had started. There was the adventurous spirit, the deep feelings of patriotism that ran through many of us. And most Australians love a fight!'

Left: Tobruk was a vital port which Rommel fought hard to win. But the besieged Australian forces held fast despite terrible hardships.

Rommel was soon making big gains. Unpredictable and single-minded, Rommel was an inspiration to the men of his Afrika Korps. Contrary to common belief, they were not specially trained for the tropics but underwent only a standard medical. Like their leader, they were professional soldiers who earned the respect of their enemy during the North African campaigns.

TOBRUK BESIEGED

Churchill had risked British, Australian and New Zealand troops from North Africa for the tandem campaign in Greece. It meant Wavell had been unable to crown his glorious advance by taking Tripoli. Now the Allies were paying for this.

By 3 April 1941, Benghazi had fallen once again. Soon Tobruk was under siege. The town was manned by a stoic Australian division integrated with straggling British and Indian troops that had become split from their units in the overwhelming German advance.

Australian commander Major General Leslie Morshead organised sturdy defences around the town, installing every bit of artillery he could lay his hands on. The bombardment from Tobruk took its toll on the attacking German and Italian forces. Rommel was by now far from his Tripoli supply base with its crucial stocks of water, food, fuel and ammunition. He

---

EYE WITNESS

Arthur Stephenson, of the Royal Artillery, was 21 when he joined up in 1939. He served in Africa and Normandy.

❛I've got a lighter at home with a Canadian badge on it. In the desert I was trying to light my pipe. This Canadian came up and went to light it for me.

He was there one minute and gone the next. A shell-burst killed him outright. All that was left was his lighter. He was only three yards away from me and I was completely unscathed. ❜

---

needed the port as an alternative. The Australians held fast. If Rommel made mistakes, it was here when his hand was forced by the Australians. His efforts to capture Tobruk cost him dearly.

Britain was able to receive new supplies from a Mediterranean convoy which delivered to Alexandria in Egypt. Tobruk was given support from the Royal Navy and the efficient Desert Air Force. Wavell launched a counter-offensive known as 'Operation Battleaxe' to relieve Tobruk overland. His golden touch deserted him, however, and thanks to the wit of his opponent it failed.

Rommel, who earned his 'Desert Fox' nickname through his cunning, now lured the British forward

Rommel, who earned his 'Desert Fox' nickname through his cunning, lured the British forward by feigning retreat. When the armoured units came within range, the superior German anti-tank guns opened fire causing devastation.

It was a costly lesson to the British and one which lost Wavell his job. In his place came General Sir Claude Auchinleck, who arrived to find a stalemate as both sides sought to rearm. He orchestrated 'Operation Crusader' in November, once again with the aim of relieving Tobruk. During the eight months they spent holed up in the port, the Australians had delivered some severe blows to Rommel from their fortress, targeting tanks in particular. Now Auchinleck found a corridor for Allied forces to link up by December.

Both sides benefited from aerial support. The Luftwaffe had easy access to North Africa from its bases in southern Italy while the RAF Desert Air Force proved crucial to the success of Allied troops on the ground. Rommel beat Auchinleck to a counter-attack which he made in January 1942 and forced the Allies back once more. There followed a fierce exchange in May at Gazala in which Rommel led a charge through enemy minefields and lines. Auchinleck was squeezed out of Libya, back into Egypt. The retreat was compounded when Tobruk was surrendered in June by the South African

garrison then holding it, after only a week under seige, and 25,000 prisoners were taken. Rommel was promoted to the rank of Field-Marshall by a delighted Hitler. Without pausing to celebrate, he pressed ahead with his campaign.

From intercepted messages from Rommel, Churchill believed the German commander was in dire need of assistance

Churchill was devastated by the Allied armies' swift reversal of fortunes. From decoded intercepted messages from Rommel to Berlin, he believed the German commander was in need of assistance and on the verge of capitulation. Churchill failed to understand that this sob story was a device used by Rommel to win more supplies

and men – which were rarely forthcoming.

Rommel's men were, however, weary. Auchinleck's air and artillery bombardment as they advanced towards El Alamein had the desired effect and stopped them in their tracks. A brigade from the 9th Australian Division broke out of El Alamein and swept forward. But the efforts of the Australians and the 8th Army failed to do much more than dent the Afrika Korps.

Now it was Auchinleck's turn to feel the wrath of the British Prime Minister. While defending El Alamein in Egypt, he was replaced by General Bernard Montgomery.

Although calculating and methodical, Montgomery had

Below: Sir Claude Auchinleck served in Norway and India before succeeding Wavell in North Africa.

the same fire for victory inside him that drove his rival Rommel. With powerful Sherman tanks from America, Monty regrouped his British, Australian and New Zealand forces and prepared his battle plan.

Monty preferred a confrontation rather than the lightning manoeuvres perfected by the Germans. It was his aim to destroy as much of the enemy army and artillery as possible. In his words, it would be a 'dog-fight' and by his standards it was an almost reckless campaign in its intensity.

Arguably still medically unfit for command, Rommel found himself overwhelmed

The second Battle of El Alamein began on 23 October, the day Rommel returned to his post after a spell of sick leave in Germany. Arguably still medically unfit for command, Rommel found himself overwhelmed by the reinforced Allied army which for the first time now substantially outnumbered his own. He soon found that, even if he had wanted to, he was unable to adhere to Hitler's orders not to retreat.

Allied firepower rained down on the Afrika Korps. There was some disarray in Allied lines and the thrust forward was belated. Finally a bold brigade of Australians drove north, at immense cost in terms of personnel. Montgomery regrouped and came forward again in 'Operation Supercharge', with New Zealand and British

EYE WITNESS

Stanislaw Lachoda was an 18-year-old signalman in the 2nd Battalion of the Polish Carpathian Brigade, a volunteer group made up of Poles who had escaped Nazi and Soviet occupation. In August 1941 the brigade was taken from Alexandria to Tobruk by the Royal Navy to replace Australian troops at Tobruk.

Soon after 'Operation Crusader' got underway, I was seconded with two other signalmen for an operation to mislead and disorientate the enemy in the western sector.

Well armed with Brens, Tommy guns and a plethora of hand grenades, attacking squads wearing desert boots and overalls silently crept behind the Italian positions and, on a given signal, let everything go at the enemy.

It was only when the mission was accomplished that the Italians recovered from the shock of being fired on from the rear and it was then their turn to lay a heavy barrage of machine-gun and artillery fire on us retreating along the narrow wadi towards the safety of our own positions. Despite the failure of communication due to the destruction of our radio's antenna, our own artillery laid protective fire for us at the right time when we were clear of the enemy's positions.

In situations as fluid as desert mirages, those who dared and took risks were the gainers and the timid ones got what they deserved.

By 8 December neither side scored a resounding victory despite heavy human and material losses but there appeared signs that the battle-weary Afrika Korps was contemplating disengagement. Our own patrols confirmed that the western sector based on the hill Ras El Medauar was still held by Italians. It was our next target.

The attack on the southern slope of the hill was spearheaded by 2nd company to which I was attached as one of the signal patrol. Our job was to provide telephone links with the battalion HQ. We moved silently step by step through the treacherous minefields, along a cleared narrow lane marked by white tape.

There was chaotic fire from Italian Breda guns as well as flares as we edged along. The last obstacle, a thick concertina of barbed wire, was dealt with and a final jump into noisy heaps of empty tin cans covering the slope led us into an elaborate system of concrete pill-boxes and bunkers. Most of the Italians surrendered after token resistance, the stubborn ones were dragged out from murky and smelly hideouts. Before sunrise the white and red Polish flag was hoisted up. The capture of Ras El Medauar was celebrated with fireworks, using up a huge stock of captured flares.

infantry going into the jaws of battle under cover of artillery fire. Rommel, who had been ordered not to retreat, replied in kind. But while the British had healthy supplies of arms and men, Rommel was far from his base. The creeping successes of Allied troops forced his hand.

ROMMEL ON THE RUN

Rommel's army fled back along the coast road, the scene of so many retreating marches, with Monty's 8th Army and the 2nd New Zealand Division led by the courageous and skilled General Freyberg at its heels. The Desert Air Force inflicted terrible damage. Monty refrained from trying to outflank his enemy, guessing that British troops would not

carry out this by-now familiar German tactic so ably. He favoured a set-piece move against Rommel and his confidence in old-fashioned textbook battlecraft paid dividends. There was another factor for him to consider, too. In November the combined Anglo-American forces began landing in North Africa in the territory of Vichy France. These were the 'Torch' landings, the first slice of action seen by many American soldiers and British reserves.

While Vichy rulers were implacably opposed to Britain, their attitude towards the Americans was ambivalent. The local Vichy commander was persuaded to switch sides from Germany to the Allies in November 1942 after the Allies easily managed to gain the upper hand. This left the path clear for the fresh forces to take on the cornered German Afrika Korps.

Left: A pensive Monty displays his famed taste for unconventional battledress.
Below: American troops stride ashore unopposed during the 'Torch' landings, November 1942. They soon met fierce German defenders.

Hitler in turn provided reinforcements at last, bolstering the defences of Vichy-held Tunisia where Rommel headed from Libya. He was not ready to seize an opportunity for a counter-attack. His troops were short on supplies and still in the minority. Despite the excellent defensive position offered by the mountainous borders of Tunisia, he realised the situation was hopeless.

AXIS SURRENDER

Rommel was recalled in March 1943. His men continued the fight until May when Tunis fell. The surrender of the Axis forces in North Africa came on 13 May, with the capture of 275,000 soldiers. It was a relief to the Allied army, which had by now known the very worst of desert warfare. Montgomery was hailed a national hero, and Rommel, although the loser, was in turn hailed a military master.

BARBAROSSA– TARGET RUSSIA

Hitler has become infamous in history for his hatred of Jews. Yet he also singled out the Russians as a worthless, reviled race: he called them 'sub-humans'. It became his avowed aim to see the people in chains and Communism eradicated once and for all.

Before the war between Hitler's Germany and Stalin's USSR began, the German Führer laid down the ground rules to his generals. In essence, there were none:

'The war against Russia will be such that it cannot be conducted in a knightly fashion. The struggle is one of ideologies and racial differences and will have to be conducted with unprecedented, unmerciful and unrelenting harshness. The commissars are the bearers of ideologies directly opposed to National Socialism. Therefore the commissars will be liquidated. German soldiers guilty of breaking international law . . . will be excused. Russia has not participated in the Hague Convention and therefore has no rights under it.'

Left: Joseph Stalin. Hitler feared and detested Communism and all other left wing ideologies. Stalin's regime in the USSR embodied all that Nazism opposed.

These words set the tone for a brutal and bloody conflict, far exceeding the ruthlessness shown so far by invading Nazi forces in western Europe.

Hitler's first problem, however, was how to bring the Russian Bear to battle at all. For months during 1939 the USSR's tyrant leader Stalin had been courted by Britain and France, both anxious to get Soviet support for the forthcoming hostilities with Germany. Hitler's disparaging views of Russia were very well documented, not least among the Soviet people themselves. In the

Above right: 'Barbarossa' unleashed the fury of Germany's erstwhile ally. Below: Hitler and Soviet Foreign Minister Molotov (left) reach an uneasy peace, 1939.

circumstances, it seemed Stalin was a natural ally of Britain and France.

FRAGILE PACT

Suddenly, however, the carefully wrought diplomacy collapsed like a house of cards. Out of the blue came the Berlin-Moscow Non-Aggression Pact, signed at the Kremlin by Ribbentrop, for Hitler, and Molotov, for Stalin, in August 1939. Hitler found himself the closest ally of his hated adversary. Stalin guessed it would at least buy him time before his country became involved in a war it neither wanted nor could afford.

'The war against Russia... cannot be conducted in a knightly fashion'

And the reason behind the gleam in Stalin's eyes at the signing of the pact was revealed just a month later. Two weeks after German forces marched into Poland, Russian forces invaded from the east. The two countries proceeded to partition the helpless Poland as they pleased. If Stalin was concerned that he was dancing with the Devil, he comforted himself that

fight, using superior tactics and winning some impressive victories. It wasn't until March 1940 that the war was finally over with the surrender of little Finland, time enough for the Finns to have inflicted humiliation on their giant neighbour, which lost an estimated one million fighting men. Hitler noted the failings and flailings of the Red Army with more than a passing interest.

uprising against him. Whether the threat was imagined or real, no one can say. What is certain is that Stalin wrecked a terrible revenge to defend his lordly position.

By the end of 1938 three out of every five of the Red Army's

Below: General Heinz Guderian, architect of Blitzkreig in the west, keeping up morale in Russia in 1941.

Britain and France would tie up sufficient numbers of German troops on the Western front to make the opening of a second front an act of idiocy by Hitler.

In November, encouraged by his easy success, Stalin engineered a war with Finland. When the Finns flatly refused to hand over disputed territory, the Red Army marched in, anticipating another quick victory.

Six weeks later their hopes had been dashed. The vastly outnumbered Finns put up a fierce

Stalin was livid with the poor performance of his army. But there was no one to blame but himself for the debacle – as he

Stalin wreaked a terrible revenge to defend his lordly position

himself had ordered the deaths of many of his leading commanders during a devastating purge of the army in 1937. It happened after whispers of a military

marshals were dead as well as 13 out of 15 army commanders. More than a quarter of the army's brigadiers and more than half of the divisional commanders had been executed, too. There was also bloodletting among the politicos involved with defence. Those that remained were untalented and uninspiring. They hampered the progress of the fighting force with outdated ideas, which included the abandonment of automatic weapons and the

halting of the comprehensive tank programme in favour of horsedrawn artillery. So the army was left woefully lacking in experience, for which it paid a terrible penalty.

Nevertheless it was still the largest army in the world, although Hitler had other considerations than this in preparing his battle plan.

GREEK DIVERSION

By 1941 he was convinced he could overwhelm the Soviet Union and kill off Communism there for good. But he was compelled to delay the invasion due to the German involvement in Greece, an unexpected diversion which cost the Reich valuable men and time.

It was a late spring that year, too, leaving roads clogged with mud and rivers swollen by the slow thaw. Germany needed the best possible weather to make a clean, quick strike into the heart of its foe.

By the beginning of June, all the indications were that Hitler was ready to pounce. As many as 76 different warnings came

to Stalin to that effect. Churchill gleaned top secret information from his Ultra decodes, telling of the proposed invasion. Spies stationed around the Axis world delivered similar warnings. One German soldier, a secret Communist, escaped across the border to warn Stalin of the impending attack.

Still the inscrutable leader refused to believe Hitler would wage war on him. He remained primarily concerned about his frontier with Japan, the growing menace in the east. Even the rapid and unexpected fall of France failed to persuade him that Russia would be next on the German Führer's hit list.

Stubbornly, Stalin dismissed the international warnings sent to Moscow as scandalous rumour-mongering and barred his top army commanders from mounting defences along the border, for fear of provoking Hitler. He even had the run-away German soldier shot.

His policy of appeasement designed to keep Russia out of the war stretched as far as sending train loads of oil, grain and metals to the Third Reich even while its troops were congregating

Left: The summer offensive against Russia progressed rapidly at first, until the German invaders ran out of good weather.

Below: A Red Army observer on the lookout for enemy aircraft in Moscow, 1941. The Soviets were ill-prepared for a German attack.

THE GREAT DEBATE

By 1940, America was caught up in 'The Great Debate', about whether or not it should enter the war.

The largest body of isolationists campaigning to keep America out of the conflict was the America First Committee, centred in the Mid-West where anti-British and pro-German sentiments were strongest. Fascists united with Communists and radical Irish Americans in wanting to keep America neutral. In opposition was the Committee to Defend America by Aiding the Allies, founded in May 1940.

Among those contributing to the debate was Colonel Charles A. Lindbergh, who in 1927 became the first aviator to cross the Atlantic non-stop, and whose two-year-old son was kidnapped and murdered in 1932. He had visited Nazi Germany, inspected the Luftwaffe and declared the force was invincible.

to allow his men to retreat.

Hundreds of planes in the sizeable Red Air Force were immediately knocked out. All was going according to plan for Germany. It seemed like the army would be at the gates of Moscow in six weeks as forecast.

Yet within a month the Soviets began fighting back. Their resolve began stiffening, their exploits became harder to contain. In fact, the Russian soldier was a formidable enemy in combat because he was prepared to fight to the death. Their

on the borders.

On 22 June 'Operation Barbarossa' got underway with 165 divisions trundling into Russia in a three-pronged attack. The 2,500,000 Germans in the invasion force were not alone. Lining up with them were divisions of Italians, Romanians, Hungarians, and Finns and one Spanish unit. Before the attack was launched there was no formal declaration of war.

Initially it was the familiar story of Blitzkrieg. The Panzer divisions ploughed through the Russian countryside heading for Kiev, Leningrad and Moscow. Occasionally the dirt track roads

Above: Farm workers and factory hands were called on to defend their country alongside Russia's soldiers, as the German onslaught swept in from the west.

were difficult to pass. Yet nothing could stop the motorised units for very long. In their wake the infantry marched at a pelt, straining to keep up with the successful advance and mopping up resistance along the way

They picked up thousands of prisoners, many caught by the rear sweep of the advance unit which snared them in a bag. Stalin engineered some of the major military disasters of the entire conflict when he refused

readiness to make the ultimate sacrifice became particularly apparent as the war progressed. The Germans treated their Soviet prisoners with callous contempt. They were given fewer rations than other Allied prisoners of war and there was a catalogue of cruelty and atrocities. During the war, a staggering 3,300,000 Soviet prisoners of war died in German custody.

DEATH SQUADS

When the Russians got to hear of the treatment being meted out to their comrades they fought harder than ever. There was also increased incentive to fight to the last, as they knew that imprisonment would be worse than death. Equally, anything construed as cowardice by the soldiers and failure by their commanding officers led to execution by death squads of their fellow countrymen.

At the end of July Hitler made a controversial decision which perhaps cost him the war in Russia. Concerned at the rapid pace of the Panzers compared with the slow-moving infantry, he ordered a change in tack which had the advance units of his campaign veering off in another direction. The effect of this was to give the big cities valuable time to defend themselves.

His leaders in the field were mystified and outraged. In particular, General Heinz Guderian, who stood only 220 miles from Moscow, sought to disentangle himself from the order.

But despite some initial hesitation, Hitler was convinced

When the surge forward began the first winter chill crept into the air

Above: In 1941, before winter set in, Third Reich forces were entrenched in battles on the outskirts of Moscow, shaking the foundations of the Kremlin itself.

he was right. It caused a flurry of resignations from his senior commanders, who knew instinctively that the time was right to press forward for Moscow. With the shelter the city offered to an army, the icy arctic winter might just be tolerable. Without it, the German hierarchy – who could only guess at the ravages such a winter would hold – gave an involuntary shiver.

When the surge forward began again, the first winter chill began to creep into the air. By September, Riga, Minsk, Smolensk and Kiev had fallen. A record 665,000 soldiers were taken prisoner when Kiev collapsed, the most ever taken during a single wartime operation. Leningrad, like Sevastopol

Left: German soldiers quickly realised the perils of fighting in a Russian winter when thick snow disabled much of their machinery.

in the Crimea, was under siege. Western Russia was pock-marked with destruction. Stalin had ordered a 'scorched earth' policy among his men which meant retreating armies torched everything in their wake to both hinder the enemy and deprive them of possible supplies.

The residents of Moscow and Leningrad had not wasted their unexpected breathing space that summer. An army of women, old men and children spent their every waking hour digging in. Between them they provided the key spots with miles of earthworks, anti-tank ditches, barbed-wire walls and pill-boxes.

TRENCHFOOT

During their labours, their spirits must have lifted with the first deluge of autumn. The Germans, now wearying, depleted in numbers and burdened by casualties, looked up to same endless grey skies in despair. The rains brought about cases of 'trenchfoot' – the vile affliction the Americans call 'immersion-foot'. The condition occurred when wet

> *An army of women, old men and children spent their every waking hour digging in*

feet were not dried out for days or weeks on end. Numbed and uncomfortable, the infected feet frequently turned purple and, in severe cases, the nerve endings died and gangrene set in.

The Russian roads now turned into mires of mud. The German Panzers were literally bogged down and progressed at a painfully slow pace. Mechanical failures began to haunt each division as its desperate soldiers fought to keep the wheels turning.

The frosts of October came

HITLER'S LONELY LOVER

Eva Braun spent 12 years as mistress to the hypnotic German Führer and no more than a few hours as his wife.

Braun probably began her bizarre relationship with Hitler as early as 1931. Yet he refused to accord her the public recognition she desired despite his apparent regard for her.

Much of their relationship was spent apart, with the sporty, attractive Braun, born in 1910, waiting for Hitler to finish his state commitments before squeezing in some time with her. Hitler's chauffeur described her afterwards as 'the unhappiest woman in Germany. She spent most of her life waiting for Hitler.'

Even after her sister married General Fegelein, a member of Himmler's staff, she was unable to persuade Hitler to formalise their relationship. She attempted suicide twice, in 1932 and 1935, on account of Hitler's involvement with other women.

On 15 April 1945 Eva Braun arrived in Berlin to join Hitler for what were clearly his final days. In the early hours of 29 April they were wed. The following afternoon they were dead, Hitler having shot himself and Braun having taken poison. Her body, clad in a dark dress, was placed in a shell hole at the rear of the Berlin bunker and set ablaze alongside that of her husband.

as a relief to the Germans. At least the ground was hard enough to support the tank tracks.

Haunted by the fate of the French Emperor Napoleon who had made mighty advances into Russia only to be crippled by the winter freeze, Hitler declared that Moscow was to be taken.

OPERATION TYPHOON

The final thrust of 'Operation Typhoon' brought German troops tantalisingly close to their goal. Some reports insist the leading units penetrated a suburb of the capital and saw sunlight glinting on the roof of the Kremlin itself. Even now they were able to take 660,000 more Russian prisoners. But their progress slowed and finally halted.

By now 200,000 members of the Germany army had been killed. The surviving German

Below: It wasn't just the weather that was bitter. Fighting between Russia and Germany on the Eastern front was some of the bloodiest of the entire conflict.

soldiers were no longer energetic. Five months of fighting had taken its toll. The resistance they found among the defenders of Moscow was fierce, the military machinery they relied on for spearheading their attack was failing. And now the relentless winter had set in, bringing with it snow storms and temperatures of minus 20 degrees Celsius.

German soldiers were inadequately clothed for the biting cold. The greatcoats they wore were scarcely thick enough to protect them from the bitter winds. In a feeble attempt to insulate themselves, they tore up paper and stuffed it inside their clothes. For snow camouflage they used bed sheets which again offered precious little warmth. Now frostbite was the worst enemy, claiming many more victims among the demoralised Germans than the fighting itself.

Vehicle oil froze unless it was kept warm, so the Germans were unable to move at all. The fine German horses used to pull artillery and supplies perished

by the thousand. Hitler had ordered 'no retreat', perhaps realising that any movement forward or backwards posed a danger to his troops. It would be three years before the supplies of winter clothing to German troops from the Reich were adequate.

The Soviet army was well used to the harsh weather. Sheepskins and furs were standard issue. Greatest among their assets were heavy-duty felt

---

Now frostbite was the worst enemy, claiming many more victims than the fighting

---

boots soon supplied in bulk by America where they were made to Russian specification. The Russians knew how to care for their animals throughout the coldest weather. A squad of crack Siberian troops was being called in, experts at winter warfare and at home on a pair of skis. The fate of Moscow hung in the balance.

JAPAN'S LIGHTNING WAR

With the success of Pearl Harbor under their belts, the Japanese were eager to capitalise on the supreme advantage of surprise. Defending British, Australian and American forces were caught off-guard throughout South East Asia and the Pacific as Japan began a 'Blitzkrieg' of its own.

Key targets were Hong Kong, the Philippines, Malaya, Singapore, Burma, Thailand, the Dutch East Indies and the stepping stone islands of Wake and Guam. Each offered the new Japanese empire mineral or agricultural wealth that was badly needed, or was a necessary land-base to protect precious cargoes.

Hong Kong was the first of the British domains to fall. Only 400 miles from Japanese air bases in Formosa (now Taiwan), it was vulnerable from the outset. The defence of Hong Kong and other British outposts had suffered thanks to the war effort in other parts of the world. During 1939 and 1940, troops, ships and aircraft were sent to trouble-spots like North Africa and the Mediterranean at the expense of the far-flung colonies, which appeared to be in no imminent danger.

By August 1940, Churchill accepted the view held by service chiefs that Hong Kong was practically indefensible and that the garrison on the island could be better used elsewhere. Japanese intentions were far from clear at this point. However, with growing indications that Japan was possibly hostile, no one acted further on the recommendation. The following year the Hong Kong garrison was strengthened by the addition of two Canadian battalions.

An initial strike made by the Japanese on 8 December proved to be devastating. The Allied troops were driven back to Hong Kong city within a matter of days. For a week, the Japanese were held at bay across the water barrier. Under the cover of darkness on 18 December, the inevitable Japanese landings on Hong Kong island began. Following Churchill's declared policy, resistance was slight. On Christmas Day one arm surrendered. Their comrades gave up the fight a day later. For the loss of 3,000 dead and wounded the Japanese had captured Hong Kong, together with its force of nearly 12,000 men.

The Philippines were to have suffered their first Japanese air bombardment on 8 December Although not an American possession, they were reliant on US support before becoming independent. In fact, morning fog grounded the aircraft based in Formosa, delaying take-off.

The Americans, meanwhile, were debating whether or not to carry out a bombing mission in Formosa. This indecision was to prove fatal. In the early afternoon, when the US B-17s were finally being prepared for a sortie, the overdue Japanese air craft finally arrived. With the American planes presented on an airfield, the Japanese pilots did their destructive worst. A number of the planes intended to protect the Philippines were wrecked.

For the loss of 3,000 dead and wounded the Japanese had captured Hong Kong

Left: *Victorious Japanese troops enter Rangoon after quickly annihilating opposition troops in Burma. The Burmese people gave them an indifferent welcome.*

Above: *Dejected British soldiers file through the streets of Singapore after the disastrous fall of the colony to the Emperor's forces.*

RATIONS

Rations were boosted – and cut – for Britons on the home front throughout the war. Here is a typical weekly allowance per person.

8oz sugar, 3oz cheese, 3oz cooking fat, 4oz bacon or ham, 2oz jam, 2oz sweets, 2oz tea or coffee 1 egg, 3 pints milk, 1lb meat
Bread, fish and sausages, although not rationed, were scarce. Although there was no restriction on fruit and vegetables, many were impossible to get. Lemons, bananas, onions and even pepper were rarely, if ever, seen during the war years in Britain. Inventive housewives made chocolate truffle cake from potatoes, and banana pudding from parsnips.

Right: General-Marshal Homma makes an assisted landing on Luzon in the Philippines on 24 December 1941, ousting defending American troops.

The Japanese 14th Army quickly captured off-islands and made landings on Luzon, the largest Philippine island, as early as 10 December. There were continuing probes until the main landings, which took place on 22 December.

Coastal defences, comprising poorly trained and fearful Filipinos soon crumbled. A core of American troops was kept in the capital, Manila, by commander General MacArthur until it became clear that the defence of the island was an impossibility. He then ordered a withdrawal into the Bataan Peninsula in the hope the 31,000 troops could mount an adequate defence.

The Americans did manage to repel a number of raids. Then both sides became severely weakened through rampant malaria. Morale sank further in the American ranks when it became clear that little effort was being made to evacuate them. When the Japanese offensive began again on 3 April it took only six days to force a surrender.

Coastal defences, with poorly trained and fearful Filipinos, soon crumbled

There remained almost 15,000 Americans on the nearby island of Corregidor. The fight for this scrap of an island was to be fierce. The Japanese carried out daily artillery bombardments across the straits from Luzon as well as waves of air attacks. When much of the American artillery had been knocked out, the Japanese mounted an invasion with 2,000 troops. More than half were lost in the battle that ensued during the night of 5 May. But despite their losses, the Japanese managed to land some tanks, enough to crush the remaining resistance.

A surrender bid by American General Wainwright was hampered by guerrilla action adopted by the Americans. By 9 June all resistance was crushed.

The loss to the Americans had been considerable; likewise to the native forces. A combined total of 95,000 were taken captive by the Japanese. Yet the defenders had held out for six months with no outside assistance, a significant achievement given the domino fall of islands in the rest of the area.

On paper, it appeared the

British defenders of Malaya and neighbouring Singapore were more than a match for the invaders. There were about 100,000 Allied troops taking on just 30,000 incoming Japanese. In Britain there was confidence that Singapore particularly was a fortress with stout defences. It was unthinkable that the stronghold would be overrun. As so often happens during wars the unthinkable happened – at speed.

The defeat of the British and Allied forces at the hands of the Japanese was a shocking one for which few at home were prepared. Yet there were shortcomings in the defences of the countries invaded which allowed the enthusiastic Japanese to run rampant.

Despite the signs of militarism evident in Japan, the British government remained convinced this small country would not take on the combined might of America, Britain and Russia. After the war, Churchill admitted he among others had underestimated the threat posed by Japan, particularly in its air power.

The Allies had no tanks with which to blast the enemy while the Japanese rolled over the inhospitable terrain with something in the order of 300. And while the Allies possessed more than twice the amount of artillery, much of it was in Singapore facing seawards to repel a southerly invasion. The Japanese flooded in from the opposite direction.

OPPRESSIVE HEAT

As for aircraft, the Allies had only a sixth of the number of aircraft that the Japanese had at their disposal. In a war which proved air might was imperative, the British were left seriously under-equipped.

Japanese troops were trained for jungle warfare. The British and Australians were quickly wearied by the oppressive heat.

In command of the Japanese troops was General Tomoyuki Yamashita, a devoted servant of Emperor Hirohito and a military marvel. Among his troops, he was known as 'the tiger'. The Allies, meanwhile, were under General Arthur Percival, held with such low regard by his men that he was called 'the rabbit'.

On the day that the prize British capital ships *Prince of Wales* and *Repulse* were sent to the bottom of the sea, Japanese forces marched into Malaya. With waves of air cover, they were quickly able to force the British down the Malay Peninsula in a rolling retreat. The highly organised invaders cut quickly through any defences they encountered. About 4,000 British troops and their equipment were stranded in central Malaya when Japanese tanks broke through their lines and seized a road bridge, curtailing

Below: *Seasoned jungle warriors, the Japanese troops found far less difficulty operating in the tropics than their beleaguered enemies did.*

WAVELL VICTORIOUS

When British and Commonwealth troops under the command of General Sir Archibald Wavell drove Italian troops into a spectacular retreat early in 1941, there was rejoicing at home at the first glimpse of meaningful victory. The News Chronicle wrote:

'It is still too early for any complete estimate of General Wavell's happy and glorious achievement; but from what we already know two factors stand out and demand the most generous praise: the perfect co-ordination of land, sea and air forces and the superb Staff work that preceded the attack and made the co-ordination possible.'

Somewhat prematurely, it ended:
'Rapidly the Axis is becoming a meaningless phrase: an axis requires two ends, and, if it is to function, each end must perform an equal task. Otherwise the whole thing crumbles away. One day that will happen, and General Wavell, by his care and genius, has brought that day nearer than two months ago we dared hope.'

their withdrawal. The capital, Kuala Lumpur, was abandoned by the Allies on 11 January and still the retreat continued to gather pace.

MALAYA FALLS

It took the Japanese just 54 days to overcome the resistance in Malaya. Their casualties amounted to around 4,600, compared with the loss of 25,000 Allied troops, many of whom were now prisoners of war. Thousands of Indians recruited to fight for the Empire already had doubts about the wisdom of risking their lives for the country which oppressed their own. Now many took the opportunity to join brigades organised by the Japanese and were fighting against former comrades.

Fleeing British and Australian forces made a dash for Singapore and blew up the bridge connecting the island

Right: A Japanese artillery detachment making its way through the jungle in late 1941 during the Singapore campaign. They met little resistance.

with Malaya as they went. Japanese forces mustered threateningly on the other side. Singapore was bombed on the day the war with Japan began. The casualties were mostly among the civilian population. Perhaps for the first time, Churchill realised the folly of leaving the island of Singapore so woefully lacking in defences.

In January 1942, he declared: 'Not only must the defence of Singapore Island be maintained by every means but the whole island must be fought for until

every single unit and every single strongpoint has been separately destroyed. Finally, the city of Singapore must be converted into a citadel and defended to the death. No surrender can be contemplated.' On 8 February the Japanese troops put his words to the test by swarming across the Johore Strait which had so far barred them from the island. Some used small boats and dinghies. Others simply swam across. The Australian defenders in the region might have been expected to use the spotlights especially installed to light up their targets and blast the invaders out of the water.

The soldiers were left firing at darkened objects in the night

Yet the order to switch on the lights never came. The soldiers were left firing at darkened objects in the night. Not only that, the troops were soon ordered to fall back rather than to counter-attack. It was a symptom of the faulty lines of communication

EYE WITNESS

Bill Jenkins, from New South Wales, served in the Australian infantry from the outbreak of World War II to its close.

'My battalion and another one from Victoria were probably the only Allied units to have fought all its enemies. We were up against the Italians in the desert, the Germans in Greece, the Vichy French in Syria and the Japanese in New Guinea.

The Japanese were the worst. They were a different culture – you didn't know what to expect next from them. No prisoners were taken on either side and they were very vicious. Yet the Japanese were good soldiers. I have got much respect for them but not for their culture which allows them to do such terrible things.'

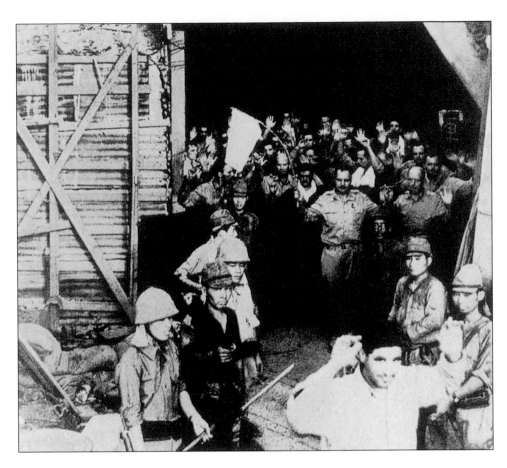

Above: US soldiers surrender to Japanese troops. Ahead of them is a gruelling march to a harsh prison camp.

that dogged the short campaign by the Allies to keep Singapore. The standard of leadership among the Allies was also continually poor, with tactical blunders being made time and again. Ill-thought-out orders to withdraw from strongly held positions around the coast gave the Japanese an open door.

SINGAPORE SHAME

Nor did the sight of thick black smoke rising over Singapore city do much to improve their state of mind. It plumed from oil tanks set alight by the British themselves in the harbour area to keep them from falling into Japanese hands. From it came a pungent black rain which fell across a wide area. A flurry of activity by Japan's supporters in Singapore added to the chaos and confusion in the city.

Food stocks were running low and the water supply was under threat by the time street battles commenced. Percival

realised that to proceed with the fight was futile. A package air-dropped to his headquarters in a cascade of red and white ribbons invited him to surrender. It bore the following sinister sentence from Yamashita: 'If you continue resistance, it will be difficult to bear with patience, from a humanitarian point of view.'

He chose to ignore Churchill's orders to fight to the bitter end. Percival marched to meet the triumphant Yamashita with a Union Jack and a white flag, held aloft side-by-side. This did little to endear him to the establishment at home. His signature ended the British domination of Singapore at a conference held in the Ford factory on Bukit Timah hill. Some 80,000 British, Indian and Australian troops were forced to face four years of captivity under the harsh Japanese regime

With the loss of Singapore came the realisation that Britain's proud boast of being able to defend its colonies no matter where they were in the world was now a sham.

It was later described as 'the greatest military disaster in [British] history'. For years Percival was an outcast and was held personally responsible. While his leadership was certainly flawed, he was only one of many Allied commanders who found themselves bowled over by the Japanese steamroller.

The extent of the Singapore debacle was only revealed fully after the war. Yamashita had considered himself on the brink of losing the vital campaign : 'My attack on Singapore was a bluff. I

had 30,000 men and was outnumbered more than three to one. I knew that if I had been made to fight longer for Singapore I would have been beaten. That was why the surrender had to be immediate. I was frightened that the British would discover our numerical weakness and lack of supplies and force me into disastrous street fighting. But they never did. My bluff worked.'

December 1941 also saw the invasion of Burma. It was inadequately protected, with Malaya and Singapore seen as having greater requirement for military resources.

Once again, Japan had by far the most effective air force. It would become another story of inglorious retreat, this time over 1,000 miles into India.

The Burmese capital Rangoon was being bombed by Christmas. The British forces were once again forced back under the onslaught of the 35,000 invading Japanese troops, who proved themselves faster and more adept in jungle warfare. On 6 March 1942 the order came to evacuate Rangoon.

MONSOON SEASON

After both sides had reinforced, the British, assisted now by Chinese forces, defended a 150-mile line south of Mandalay. The Japanese sidestepped the line and enveloped the troops manning it. By April, the British troops not only had to consider the advance of the enemy but also the onset of the monsoon season, due in May, which would turn the roads vital for retreat into mires.

Burmese soldiers were deserting in droves to join the new national army that was fighting with the Japanese invaders.

> **Burmese soldiers, always unhappy about the colonial control of their country, were deserting in droves to join the new national army**

British rearguard forces held up the Japanese advance before making the final dash for safety themselves. The tanks of the 7th Armoured Brigade made repeated counter-attacks to delay the enemy campaign.

A week before the monsoon season began, the majority of the British forces fell back behind the Indian frontier. They had lost much of their equipment and had suffered three times the number of casualties that the Japanese had incurred. It was a miracle that any succeeded in escaping at all.

The Dutch East Indies came

EYE WITNESS

Hugh Trebble, a local newspaper journalist, joined the Civil Air Guard before the war when it offered the chance to learn to fly for one penny per minute. In 1940 he was recruited into the Royal Air Force, in which he was a clerk.

'I was posted overseas in June 1941 and got to Singapore by August. From there I went to RAF Butterworth, overlooking Penang Island in north west Malaya.

There was a lot of personnel in Malaya and Singapore but no equipment. At Butterworth we were still flying Bristol Blenheims. I never saw any combat aircraft the entire time I was there.

After the Japanese invaded down the east coast we were pulled back to Kuala Lumpur to a base called Sungeibesi. A few weeks later General Wavell flew in to assess the situation. As soon as his Hudson took off we blew it [the base] up. We retreated via a rubber plantation down to Singapore.

There, we were put in a camp at RAF Seletar. The last flight of so-called bombers that set off from there was made up of obsolete Vickers Wildebeest, twin-engined bi-planes. They took off but they never landed. They were destroyed before they could put down.

There was a desperate atmosphere in Singapore, even more so after the battleships *Prince of Wales* and *Repulse* were sunk. When they left port it was with a total absence of air cover and destroyer cover. They should never have been sent out in the first place.

In Singapore there were fixed guns facing over the sea – when the Japanese came overland. They Japanese soldiers easily overpowered anything we had. Some Allied soldiers got off troop ships and were taken prisoner virtually straightaway. They never fired a shot in anger. They had nothing to fight with anyway.

On 13 January 1942 I was among many who were evacuated from Kepple Harbour on the *Empire Star*, a Blue Funnel ship, heading for Java. Clearly, we were sent to Singapore for propaganda purposes – nothing else.'

under attack in December 1941. These islands were rich in oil and thus an important target for the oil-starved Japanese. In a bid to halt the Japanese, the defending Dutch, Australian, British and American forces were put under a single command, known as ABDA, led by Britain's General Archibald Wavell.

Although the Dutch resistance was soon annihilated, the Australians proved a more formidable foe. Yet there was little they could do to protect the scores of tiny islands from Japanese occupation.

After the disastrous Battle of the Java Sea, which the Allies lost in February 1942, the Japanese could count the Dutch East Indies as their own.

EYES ON CEYLON

Other casualties in the Japanese war were Guam, Wake Island and the Gilbert Islands, which fell before the end of 1941. In the spring of 1942, the Bismarck Archipelago, the Solomon Islands and north eastern New Guinea all succumbed to Japanese forces.

Britain now feared attack from the Japanese navy in the Indian Ocean, where Ceylon was a prime target

Britain feared an attack from the Japanese navy in the Indian Ocean where Ceylon was a prime target. On 5 April 1942 the British braced themselves for attack following an air strike by more than 1,000 planes at Colombo the capital of Ceylon. Two British cruisers were sunk and the port was badly damaged. The distances were too great for an invasion to be sustainable, and the Japanese knew it. They withdrew behind the lines of their expanded empire and concentrated on defence.

THE EASTERN FRONT

Winter weather had brought the German advance in Russia to a complete standstill. Yet Stalin knew that freezing temperatures and snow flurries alone would not be enough to defeat the might of the Third Reich's army.

He was neither a gifted tactician nor a seasoned campaigner, unlike his enemy Hitler. In personal command of his army, Stalin was isolated at the top. The blunders he made as the campaign against his country got underway cost millions of lives. He would soon learn by bitter experience about how to run a war.

He enjoyed a certain degree of good luck and, in time, he used it well. To his advantage, he had a seemingly inexhaustible supply of men.

After Pearl Harbor, Stalin realised Japan was too embroiled with its actions against America to threaten Russia now. So the men tied up with defending its eastern rear were at last free to man the German front. In addition, there were countless thousands of reservists, recruited from all over the Soviet Union, to replace fallen comrades.

It was this perpetual sacrifice of men above all other factors that changed the course of the war. If Stalin had found his people with less resolve and more ready to capitulate, Hitler might have won on the Eastern front.

D-Day could not have gone ahead without the Russian front diverting German resources

A victory there would have ensured him triumph in the west. D-Day, the most decisive action of the entire war, could not have gone ahead without the Russian front diverting so

many German resources.

Somehow this massive country survived its appalling casualty rate. It prompted the frustrated German chief of staff Halder to comment: 'We estimated that we should contend with 180 Russian divisions; we have already counted 360.'

Above: *The half-frozen mud is littered with the bodies of dead Russian soldiers. Total Soviet losses, military and civilian, in the war may have exceeded 20 million.*

Left: *Resignation is etched on the face of a German soldier on the Eastern front, more than two years after 'Barbarossa'.*

Left: A smouldering tank is stopped in its tracks during the campaign.

World War I, aged 18, winning two medals before the Bolshevik revolution. By 1919 he was in the Red Army and a Communist Party member. Personal rapport with Stalin saved him during the military purge of 1937. He remained one of the few generals who was able to speak his mind to the Soviet dictator, although on at least one occasion he was demoted as a result of doing so.

Wherever possible, the Soviet Union's heavy industry was moved nut by nut and bolt by bolt to the east of the country to prevent it being swallowed up in the German advance – from here productivity was now stepped up. While the Germans suffered from privation, with inadequate supplies being ferried along overstretched lines beginning in occupied Poland and beyond, the Russian forces had their needs seen to swiftly and without hindrance along railway tracks still running into Moscow despite the conflict.

Key among the Russian supplies was the new T-34 tank, heavily armoured, fast and tough. It was equal if not superior to the tanks being driven by the Germans. By 1943 Russian industry was able to produce twice as many tanks as its German counterpart.

MARSHAL ZHUKOV

Russia also received fresh stocks from the Allies. Perhaps the most significant of these was a mammoth consignment of trucks from America. It enabled Stalin to move men around his huge country at increased speed. He

had a fine commander in the field in Georgi Zhukov, whose military genius shone out from the floundering incompetents left at the top of what remained of the Red Army.

Zhukov joined the Tsar's army as a conscript at the outbreak of

When they arrived they would face a quick court martial before being shot

Below: Marshal Zhukov (left) pores over a battle plan as high-ranking Russians grapple with modern warfare techniques.

RETREAT AND DIG

Not all the other Russian generals were so lucky. After war broke out, Stalin habitually telephoned commanders who had been compelled to pull back their armies and summoned them to Moscow. When they arrived they would face a quick court martial before being shot for dereliction of duty. Stalin was the only leader of World War II who continued with the outdated notion of shooting generals for failure in the field.

Russian generals were forced on the offensive by Stalin no matter what the odds, as it was the only

RICKY

In the treacherous task of clearing minefields, the British invasion force used specially trained dogs. When the dog sat down it was clear to his handler that a mine had been sniffed out.

Welsh sheepdog Ricky was clearing a canal bank in Holland when a mine blew up just three feet away from him. Ricky was wounded in the face while the blast killed the section commander. Regardless of his injuries, Ricky returned to his duties and found several more mines before retiring for treatment.

His courage won him the Dickin Medal, created by the People's Dispensary for Sick Animals, to recognise the courage of animals in the front line. Inscribed on it are the words 'For gallantry, we also serve'. Ribbons attached to the disc are green, brown and blue to represent sea, land and sky.

way he knew of achieving victory. Devoid of any inspiration until the arrival of Zhukov and his protégés, they would send waves of men 'over the top' to hurl themselves at the Germans, much as soldiers did during the trench warfare of 1914-18.

It took Stalin at least a year to realise that his strategies were fatally flawed. When he began lending an ear to the new breed of generals he finally realised that technique was everything in modern warfare. It was then that Russia began to turn the tables on its foe.

MOSCOW REPRIEVED

After an inconclusive Russian counter-offensive out of Moscow in December 1941, both sides suspended operations until May 1942 to give themselves time to recoup men and hardware. Moscow was saved from occupation but its people still suffered the deprivations of war.

While Stalin was convinced Moscow remained the Third Reich's prime target Hitler had other ideas. The need for more resources for his spiralling war effort became more pressing. He eyed the Soviet oilfields in

Below: Prepared for invasion. Moscow was lined with anti-tank devices to halt Hitler's progress.

the Caucasus greedily, knowing that success in capturing such prized assets would deprive Stalin of precious fuel resources as well.

Code-named 'Operation Blue', Hitler's drive east began at the beginning of May. In characteristic style the thrust was dynamic and 170,000 Russians were taken prisoner in the first week. Two Russian counter-attacks ended in disarray. The first German objective to take the tank-making town of Kharkov was achieved by the end of June.

But frustration followed victory as the Germans lost the initiative

when they became involved in a battle for the city of Voronezh. Russian fighters, released from the order to stay their ground by Stalin, could finally strike and then melt away, causing maximum damage and nuisance to the Germans.

It delayed the German stab towards Stalingrad, the gateway to the Caucasus, which Hitler had earmarked as his own.

In October the German 6th Army reached Stalingrad and launched a bloody offensive with the aid of endless strikes by the Luftwaffe. Russian defenders of the city adopted the tactics of guerrilla warfare, going underground to snipe at the oncoming Germans.

OPERATION URANUS

Even as the winter set in, German commander Paulus braced himself and his men for a final effort, during November 1942. Although the killing went on, he achieved little.

The Russians were to use some of the devastating tactics they had learned the hard way, at the hands of the invading Germans. Paulus found his flanks surrounded by a mighty Russian force ready to put a

---

EYE WITNESS

Dennis Goading, of Gosport near Portsmouth, England, was a British rifleman with the King's Royal Rifle Corps. As a light infantryman he was engaged in hand-to-hand combat with German troops throughout the 1944 advance across western Europe.

❝There are still so many myths about the war. If one of our men was wounded in an attack we didn't all stop and gather around him like you see in the movies. We didn't have time to think about it. We just carried on and completed our assignment.

Of course, you would help if you could. But it took four men to deal with one man wounded and you could end up going nowhere.

Then again I saw soldiers who didn't even realise they had been hit. It was only when one of their mates pointed out blood seeping through their uniform that they felt the pain.

Cracking up under fire is another aspect surrounded in mythology. Everybody thinks of these guys running away. I saw one lance corporal who just got up and wandered, babbling straight into enemy fire. He was what we called bomb happy, or shell-shocked. We never found his body.

I came across the same symptoms affecting Germans who surrendered to us after we took the Falaise Gap. Almost an entire German division was wiped out there and there were thousands of bodies and animal carcasses just heaped up in the streets. That was a sight no man should ever have to see.

The German troops had been shelled and bombed for days without end. By the time the Canadians and ourselves got to them, they had no fight left. You could tap them on the shoulder and they would follow you; they didn't know or care where you were taking them.

We always had to be alert. Once when we were clearing a forest a German infantryman popped out of his fox-hole a few yards away and levelled his gun at me. I heard one of my mates shout 'Look out Den' and then that man opened up on the German and killed him.

I'll never forget staring at his body and watching this very pale white cloud emerging from his chest, so faint you could hardly see it. Some soldiers later told me I'd seen the man's soul departing.❞

---

noose around the weakened 6th Army. This was Stalin's 'Operation Uranus', devised between himself, Zhukov and Chief of Staff General Vasilevsky.

When he heard about the disaster, Hitler was furious. He pledged supplies would be dropped by the Luftwaffe to the beleaguered Paulus and organised a relief column. But he refused to give Paulus the lifeline he needed for himself and his men – the order to break out of the encirclement or retreat.

GERMANS BESIEGED

At Stalingrad, only a fraction of the food and medical supplies needed were arriving. Injury or sickness accounted for as much as one fifth of the 100,000-strong force.

Left: German pilots notched up some stunning successes on the Eastern front despite facing grim flying conditions.

The Russian commanders were confident enough to offer Paulus an opportunity to surrender as early as 8 January 1943. Paulus knew the Führer would be maddened so he stood fast.

Another heavy bombardment rained down on Stalingrad a few days later, leaving the depleted fighting force even more demoralised and desperate. In a last-minute frantic gesture, Hitler promoted Paulus to the rank of Field-Marshal. Paulus knew well enough the politics behind the honour. No German Field-Marshal had ever surrendered. The message was clear, fight to the death.

In the misery of snow and ice, Paulus must have glanced at some of the bodies of the German soldiers who died in those weeks and wondered why.

Now Paulus found the courage to be the first Field-Marshal to wave a white flag. At the close of January his headquarters was overrun and he surrendered to the elated Russians. He went on to join a turncoat regiment of Germans who, following capture, fought for the Russians. For the victors there was the prize of 110,000 prisoners. For the defeated, it was unmitigated disaster.

Germans were on the run elsewhere in Russia as well, chased by an increasingly confident Red Army who were at their best in winter. It was far from the end of the war at the Eastern front. But it was the beginning of the end for Germany even though Hitler remained blind to the fact for months to come.

Now Paulus found the courage to be the first Field-Marshal to wave a white flag

The subsequent drive by the Russian army between January and March was fruitless. Crack German Commander Field-Marshal Erich von Manstein staged a determined recovery. Hitler's morale was broken by the Stalingrad debacle, losing his self-confidence and intuition.

Fighting continued in explosive spats until the scene was set for a major confrontation at Kursk. Hitler allowed the planned offensive, 'Operation Citadel', to be delayed time and again while his commanders struggled to get sufficient numbers of tanks in position.

It was 5 July before the battle commenced. By 12 July there were some 2,700 German tanks and 1,800 German aircraft ranged against almost 4,000 Soviet tanks. It was the largest head-on tank battle in history, an epic test of firepower which would leave both sides battered and worn. Tank after tank went up in flames, its crew having little chance of escaping the inferno. At the end of the day there were 300 German tanks smouldering. The German advance had been halted. It spelled defeat once more for the Reich. The dramatic loss of so many tanks would take Germany many more weeks to recover than it would Russia, leaving their armoured divisions sorely lacking in firepower and mobility.

Now it was for Hitler to contemplate withdrawal. It was alien to his nature to pull out of territory fought over and won two years before. But the Red Army was flexing its muscles and was already chasing the German army out of the Crimea and the Baltic lands. The plan favoured

Below: *The tank battle at Kursk was an epic trial of strength. In the end it was the Russians who triumphed.*

DIEPPE

Twenty-one years after the disastrous raid at Dieppe which cost the lives of hundreds of Canadian servicemen an investigation was launched to probe whether an advertisement for soap flakes gave the enemy vital advance information.

The commando raid at Dieppe in August 1942 involved 5,000 Canadians, 1,000 British, 50 American Rangers and some Free French fighters. Only half returned. The rest were killed or captured after being pinned down on the beach by the Germans. A week before it took place English newspapers carried an advertisement for Sylvan soap flakes under the title 'Beach Coat from Dieppe'. The copy afterwards read: 'How could you have known when you bought it that sunny day before the war that such a flippant little coat would be so useful about the house in war-time?'

There was speculation that in the advertisement was hidden the message 'Beach Combined Operations at Dieppe'. The woman pictured carried secateurs. Were they in fact wire cutters? Scotland Yard and MI5 swooped on the advertising agency Graham and Gillies and on the manufacturers of the soap flakes. They were persuaded it was a horrible coincidence. But no one knows whether the Germans had read the advertisement and seen secret codes where none in fact existed.

by commanders like Manstein, to pull back to a single defensive line, soon became the only option. With sufficient supplies and men to build defences, Hitler may have held on to the gains he had made for longer. The Germans were unable to dig in along the 2,000-mile front and provide an effective defence. Hitler's dream to take Russia had turned into the same nightmare that afflicted Napoleon 150 years before.

By January 1944 the Red Army was at last able to lift the siege of Leningrad. The city had been encircled since November 1941, suffering months of artillery bombardment. When liberation came after 900 days, only one third of the original population of three million were left alive.

Just as the winter of 1941/42 caused devastation among the invaders, so it brought misery to the hemmed-in people of Leningrad.

Rationing was down to just nine ounces of bread per day for working people and half that amount for those too young or too old to be employed. Cats, dogs, even rats, were eaten in a bid to stave off starvation. In front of the desperate people lay the no-man's land of defences against the Germans. Behind them lay frozen Lake Ladoga, over which there was a narrow trail into free Russia.

When liberation came after 900 days, only one third of the original population of three million were left alive

Minimal supplies found their way across the trail at first and even the smallest relief attempts were harried by German aircraft. By the spring, residents

Above: The sight of Russian tanks lying uselessly by the roadside provides a grim spectacle for passing troops.
Right: Many German soldiers died as they vainly struggled to repair vehicles frozen in the snow.

had learned a harsh lesson.

Every available inch of land was cultivated and there were fresh vegetables available throughout the rest of their imprisonment. Electricity was also rationed, the sewers were brim full and clean water was in short supply.

When the saviour army lifted the blockade, they were greeted with a weary relief by the Leningraders.

Between March and April the Red Army reclaimed 165 miles of territory. Their greatest push was yet to come, however, in the form of 'Operation Bagration', which began in June, just as Hitler came under acute pressure from the D-Day landings in Normandy. Before it began, the partisans working for the Russians behind German lines set to work by

setting off a series of disabling explosions.

The operation was characterised by now-familiar tactics employed by the Red Army. A burst of artillery fire to 'soften up' the enemy followed by the rapid advance of the infantry. Thousands of German soldiers were taken prisoner as Minsk fell once again to the Russians. Their humiliation was to walk down the silent streets of Moscow on their way to prison camps, watched by the eyes of the city residents. Now the German forces in the east were

stretched to breaking point. Hitler refused to let his troops pull back even when they had been overrun. The Führer's behaviour only offered more to the Russians by way of enemy casualties and prisoners.

By August, the Russian troops were on the Polish border. They had been forced to contend with more than three times the number of troops facing the Allies in Normandy and had proved themselves equal to the task. For the first time, the war was to be carried into Reich territory.

A FORGOTTEN ARMY

Just like the British fighters in Burma and the American soldiers assisting the Chinese, the troops who fought to regain Italy believed they were 'a forgotten army'.

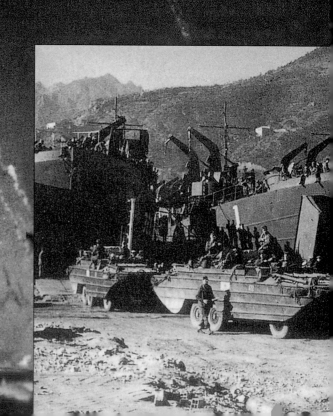

Theirs was a protracted campaign remembered mostly for its mud, miscalculation and unexpectedly high casualty rate. Churchill had described the Italian peninsula as 'the soft underbelly' of the Third Reich. Fierce German resistance proved his judgement to be wildly awry.

After nearly a year of strenuous fighting, the Allies took Rome on 4 June 1944. The trumpeted D-Day operations which began the following night swallowed the limelight. Forces who felt they had lost the recognition they deserved joked wryly thereafter about themselves being 'D-Day dodgers in sunny Italy'.

The opportunity to open a second front in Europe occurred when the fighting in North Africa was brought to a close in 1943. For months, the Americans had been pushing for a campaign in northern France. But Churchill and his commanders felt it was premature, preferring instead to squeeze the Germans from the south.

By July 1943, the invasion of Sicily, code-named 'Operation Husky', was in readiness. Montgomery was to lead his weary but able 8th Army in one assault while General Patton, heading the US 7th Army, came via a different route. The aim was to trap the defending German forces in a pincer movement.

Little did they know that the resolve of the Germans was harder than ever

During the course of the invasion, Italy swapped sides in the war, having overthrown the dictator Mussolini. A staggering 40,000 were able to slip through the British and American trap and escape to the mainland.

Sicily was in Allied possession by 17 August. An armistice was signed on 3 September as the 8th Army crossed the Straits of Messina to land in Calabria, in 'Operation Baytown'. The effect of the revelation of the Italian *volte face* on the troops poised to continue with the invasion of the mainland was disastrous. There were cheers and celebrations before the operation had even begun. The

Far left: The sky is decorated by a fireball, following a German dive-bomber attack on an American cargo ship during the invasion of Sicily.
Left, inset: Allied DUKW amphibious vehicles, nicknamed 'ducks', are loaded aboard a landing ship at Salerno harbour in preparation for the next phase of the invasion of Italy.

Above: Weary from a foot slog in Sicily, US soldiers prop themselves up at the foot of an Italian memorial to the soldiers of World War I.

men believed southern Italy was theirs for the taking and they were mentally ill-prepared for the brutal fighting which awaited them.

SALERNO LANDINGS

On 9 September, 165,000 British and American servicemen from 500 ships were engaged in a large-scale amphibious landing. The landings at Salerno, code-named 'Operation Avalanche', were scheduled by US commander General Mark Clark to last three days. He had confidence in the ability of the troops to secure a quick victory. Within just 72 hours he expected Naples to have fallen, giving the Allies a crucial harbour facility.

In fact, it took 21 days of gruelling battle. An attack staged at Taranto designed to divert the Germans failed. Crack German troops held the British and Americans at Salerno until reinforcements had been brought forward.

Above: *Allied artillery in action against Italian targets. The gunners, from 97 Heavy AA Regiment, Royal Artillery, feel the heat.*

Montgomery expressed doubts about the planning of the campaign from the outset, and encountered tough resistance as he and his men tried to rendezvous with the rest of the invasion force. He was horrified to find the German positions had been reinforced. Clark's and Montgomery's troops finally made the planned link up on 16 September. In those weeks 25,000 soldiers and civilians died.

Although a first vital foothold in Italy had been carved out, the fighting didn't get any easier. The terrain of rocky peaks and steep escarpments favoured defensive positions, all of which were held by the Germans. Time and again, the

Allied soldiers found themselves fatally exposed.

By 15 November the campaign was halted by winter weather. Relations between the British and American commanders were equally chilly.

The next tactic to bring about a breakthrough took the form of the Allied landings at Anzio in January 1944. In 'Operation Shingle', the beachheads were quickly secured, yet the Allies had difficulty spearheading an advance. Indeed, they only narrowly missed being driven back into the sea by a determined German counter-offensive. Soon Anzio was under seige. Conflicts there were bitter. The Allies were desperately seeking routes to push forward.

By now the Allied reinforcements consisted of British, American, French, Canadian,

New Zealand, South African, Greek and Brazilian troops. Even the Japanese were playing their part. The Nisei-Americans, Japanese settlers in America who had been reviled at home after Pearl Harbor, made several vital strikes on behalf of the Allies.

MONTE CASSINO

The road to Rome was marked by the architectural treasure of Monte Cassino, a sacred Christian site founded in 529 by Saint Benedict. It was filled with cultural riches gathered through the centuries, kept lovingly in archives by the monks who lived and worked at the abbey.

Perched high on a mountainous ridge, Monte Cassino looked down into the town of Cassino. Monastery and town were connected by a funicular railway which climbed the sheer rocky face of the peak with ease.

Cassino was in the hands of the Germans in January 1944, a major strength in its defences known as 'the Gustav line'. It was the target of Allied plane attacks but even a heavy pounding failed to eradicate the defenders. Soon, it became clear the Germans were using the abbey as a defensive stronghold, unassailable at the mountain top.

The Americans then took one of the most controversial decisions of the conflict – to bomb the delightful monastery which was consequently smashed to smithereens.

Little was achieved. Allied forces were left clinging to the mountainside, scrambling forward a few yards whenever they

Right: The German forces in Italy finally surrendered to the Allies on 2 May 1945.

could. It wasn't until May that the Allies by-passed the hazard, leaving the ruins of the abbey to fall to the Polish army in the rear. With heavy casualties, the Polish, assisted by a British contingent, took 1,500 prisoners – men of the German 4th Parachute Regiment.

To capture Monte Cassino, the Allies used 27 divisions with 1,900 tanks, together with 4,000 aircraft. Casualties on both sides were appalling, with some 105,000 Allied soldiers killed or wounded alongside 80,000 Germans.

FALL OF ROME

Although Rome fell soon afterwards and the incoming troops received a tumultuous welcome from its citizens, it was not the end of fighting in Italy. Still Germany threw men and ammunition at the advancing Allies. Pockets of resistance around Rimini and Bologna held the advance until the winter months, when by necessity it all but ground to a halt. Allied troops were forced to dig in during the inclement weather, experiencing the same dreadful conditions that faced their forebears in the trenches of World War I.

Right: The fierce battle at Monte Cassino left the monastery a shattered wreck.

As late as 9 April 1945, the Allies were compelled to begin another offensive. It wasn't until 2 May that a surrender was negotiated with the weary and disillusioned Germans.

EYE WITNESS

Lieutenant-Colonel Alex Borrie was in a New Zealand brigade involved in the battle for Italy and later wrote *Escapades around Cassino*. In his diary dated 18 March 1944, he wrote:

❝Our C Company moved past Castle Hill to attack Cassino. Their main objectives were 'Hotel des Roses' and 'Hotel Continental'. They were to retreat to a cave above part of the Monastery Road at 6pm. I was sent up the hill with a team of soldiers carrying food and medical supplies. The 4th Indian Division was beyond our Company on Hangman's Hill. Passing from Castle Hill to the road, the Germans put up many flares. We felt most conspicuous but the experienced soldiers said: "Stand still!" No shots were fired. At 9.10pm we reached the cave spot on time. I called out "Any Kiwis here?" "Ssh, quiet, we just arrived ten minutes ago. There are Germans everywhere."❞

OVERLORD!

It was the day that Europe had been waiting for, when Allied soldiers would tread again on French soil. In the event, many had to step over the bodies of fallen comrades lying lifeless in the Normandy surf before their feet touched Nazi-occupied France.

The Americans had been pressing for an assault on occupied Europe virtually since their entry into the war. Cautious British commanders, stung by heavy losses during the foray at Dieppe two years previously, at last thought the time was right to begin the liberation of the continent. A defeat could have been a death-blow to Britain's war effort, leaving her without an army. The commanders were finally convinced that victory was likely to be theirs.

The Germans, too, had been waiting with trepidation for the day that their enemies would try to get a foothold once more in Europe and had fortified the French coastline accordingly. Construction on the lines of tunnels, guns and bunkers to protect Hitler's Europe stretching 3,000 miles from Holland to the south of France began in September 1941 and got underway in earnest when Rommel took charge of the huge task in 1943.

German intelligence was good yet they still had no idea when and how the invasion would come. Norway, the Balkans and Calais were all strong possibilities. The imminence of the invasion, however, was beyond doubt in anyone's mind.

Hitler hoped it would be Disaster-Day for the Allies, with the German defenders casting the invaders back into the sea. He guessed rightly that the outcome of the attack would

Left: When Utah beach was secured, troops and supplies flooded ashore from the scores of ships in the Channel.

Right: Dwight Eisenhower sent a 'good luck' message to all those who took part in 'Operation Overlord', the Allied invasion of occupied France.

decide the war. Fulfiling everybody's expectations, the invasion came in early June. 'Operation Overlord' was the culmination of more than a year's work. It was an elaborate plan involving thousands of soldiers, sailors and airmen. The troops who would be scrambling up the shores and overwhelming the German opposition could only guess at what fate held in store for them when they set sail across the Channel for France. The shortest route from Britain would have been from Dover to Calais, where German and British troops could already spy each other on clear days. German defences were tight on that section of the French coast in readiness for an Allied invasion.

Despite the advantage of the brief crossing, the beaches around Calais posed too great a threat to the troops. Allied commanders had to look elsewhere. Further west, they found the answer to their conundrum – the long, golden beaches of Normandy. Here the German defences were comparatively thin.

Before 'Operation Overlord' got underway, there were key factors to consider which would help the Allies triumph in the war. First was the training of the men involved. Although amphibious landings had been

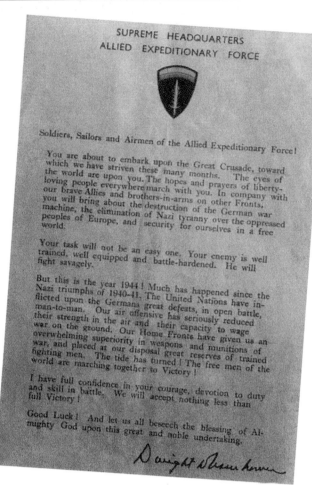

tried and tested during the war, nothing of the same magnitude had ever been attempted. British, American and Canadian soldiers were posted around Britain for rehearsals.

Coastal resorts such as Woolacombe, Gosport, Westward Ho!, Salcombe, Studland Bay and Slapton Sands played host to hundreds of soldiers sent to practise beach landings in an environment similar to that which they would encounter in France.

Slapton became a scene of disaster when live ammunition killed some of the soldiers taking part. Then, On 28 April 1944, mass devastation was wrecked when German E-boats slunk into a convoy in training off the coast, sinking two landing craft and killing 749 soldiers and sailors.

'OPERATION OVERLORD'

During the night of 5/6 June 1944, the armada carrying 21st Army Group – the 'Operation Overlord' strike force – approached the coast of Normandy. The assault was to be concentrated on five beaches: the two in the west (code-named 'Utah' and 'Omaha') were the responsibility of the Americans under Bradley; the three in the east ('Gold', 'Juno' and 'Sword') were the target of the British under Dempsey. The army group was under the overall command of Montgomery. Early in the morning of the 6th, the reconquest of continental Europe began as the first Allied forces hit the beaches and struggled to establish beachheads. German resistance was tough, but the liberation was underway.

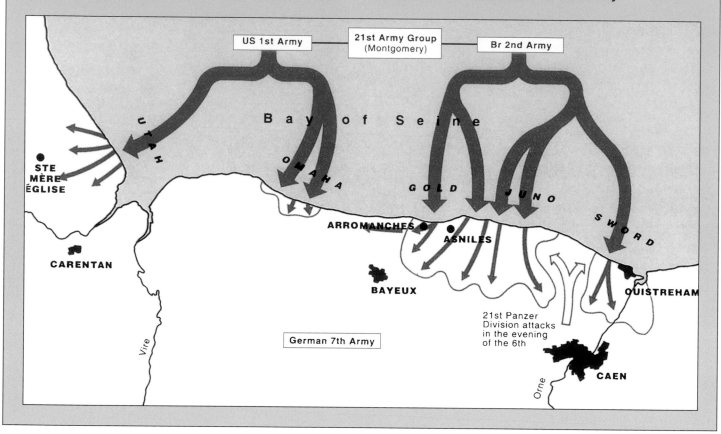

Support for the soldiers and sailors promised to be greater than anything known before. Construction firms all over the United Kingdom set to work on a top secret engineering project, each company manufacturing a different component for a giant concrete jigsaw. Few of the workers involved could guess that they were building massive harbours called 'Mulberries', to be towed across to France for docking purposes by 150 tugs. Now the invading forces didn't have to capture a ready-built harbour, always a costly exercise in terms of human lives. Tanks, trucks, big guns and supplies would roll along the Mulberries with ease.

PLUTO

A pipeline under the ocean (codenamed 'Pluto'), made from steel or sometimes steel and lead, was installed to bring essential fuel quickly from Britain to France; it was laid on the sea bed by slow-moving tugs. After the war, it was salvaged to provide plumbing for 50,000 houses.

Reconnaissance was meticulously detailed. Air force pilots flying Spitfires stripped of ammunition to make them as speedy as possible photographed as much of the coastline as they could. In addition, an appeal for holiday photographs and postcards of the region reaped thousands of pictures of the area. Further aided by maps provided by the French Resistance, cartographers began to build up a three-dimensional impression of the targeted Normandy beaches.

Midget submarines went on dangerous nightly missions to the Normandy coast. Their occupants braved the water and the German patrols to bring back soil and sand samples and up-to-date information on the position of German defences.

The British authorities began a highly detailed decoy campaign to fool the Germans, who were equally involved in reconnaissance.

Along the Kent coast, some 150 miles from the British heart of 'Overlord', there was an impressive collection of armour and shipping being prepared. Only on close inspection was it revealed that the tanks were rubber and the ships were made from plywood. Lines of tents were empty apart from army cookers puffing smoke through the chimneys to make them appear authentic. The oil depots, planes and jetties that

Only on close inspection was it revealed that the tanks were rubber

mushroomed in the area were also shams, designed to convince the Germans that the Allied thrust would be launched against Calais.

'Operation Fortitude' was vital to the success of the invasion. The Allied forces could still be driven back if the Third Reich descended on them within the first few days of the assault. With a variety of bogus intelligence messages, the commanders behind 'Fortitude' managed to convince the Germans that the invasion in Normandy was only a diversion and that the real attack was coming at Calais. Given that information, the Germans refused to move their forces from Calais, thereby saving the Allies from an onslaught.

EYE WITNESS

William Ryan, of the US 16th Infantry Regiment, was in the first wave to land at Omaha beach. At 18, it was his first action. He went on to serve 30 years in the army and is a veteran of the Korean and Vietnam wars.

'We loaded up the transports at Portland, Weymouth, about 2 June. We were supposed to attack on 5 June. They cancelled it due to weather. We were on the ship all those days.

Everyone was sea-sick. At about 2am on 6 June we loaded on to small 36ft LCVPs, we were 12 miles out. They wanted to surprise the enemy. The seas were six or eight feet high. By now most of the men were so sick they didn't care whether they lived or died. They were too sick to be scared. Even coxswain was sick. I ran the boat for five miles until he started to feel better.

My company was assigned six boats. We lost two boats almost immediately – they were swamped with heavy waves. Heading for the beach the coxswain lost his bearings. When he realised we were off course he had to try again. The guys from the next sector blew over into our beach – their boats filled the beach so we couldn't get in. We had to circle around like sitting ducks. When we finally started into the beach we lost all four boats with the fire from the German 88s.

I was blown over the side and knocked unconscious. I was told later that two of the men in the boat with me dragged me through the water and propped me up against an embankment. Otherwise I would have drowned. At first there were five or six wounded with me. Then there were hundreds. I laid on the beach in that same position from about 8am until 10pm when they evacuated us. I had concussion in addition to shell fragments in my head, shoulder and leg. All this time I was going in and out of consciousness, looking down on Omaha beach. It was just a madhouse.

Troops were pinned down by the gun emplacements. Eventually a US Navy destroyer came in as close to the beach as possible without running aground and started firing at all the German emplacements. In a little while two or three other destroyers started shelling as well. In my opinion, that is what saved Omaha beach from defeat.

I heard afterwards the skipper on the ship was ordered to go back to a safe position. Apparently he said he wasn't leaving while US soldiers were pinned down on the beach. He could have been court martialled for what he did. But he should have got a medal.

I didn't have anything to eat all day. In the afternoon a US soldier came over the hill with a couple of bottles of French red wine which he gave to us. You are never going to beat Americans in war. They are crazy.'

Right: D-Day would not have succeeded had the Allies not had mastery of the skies. A B-26 Marauder returns home after carrying out a bombing mission unchallenged over Normandy.

A double stood in for Monty and made a public departure for Algiers – when the real Monty was safely ensconced in 'Overlord' headquarters, which was based at Southwick House, Portsmouth.

The initial landings were to be made by 156,000 men, mostly Britons, Americans and Canadians. The line-up included an armoured division from France, one Belgian brigade, one Dutch brigade, one Polish division, as well as multi-national seaborne forces. In the skies, the main air forces were joined by squadrons from Norway, Czechoslovakia, France, Poland, Australia and New Zealand.

More men and equipment were held in reserve for future operations in Europe. It took an armada to ferry the men for the first action across the Channel. By late May, 359 warships, 1,000 minesweepers and associated vessels, 4,000 landing craft, 805 merchantmen, 59 blockships and 300 other small craft were at the ready.

Local people became used to the sight of tanks and trucks lining the streets, as major military traffic jams built up

Overhead, more than 11,000 aircraft were assembled. Some would be towing gliders to be released over France. Each of these carried some 30 troops, tasked with tackling inland enemy positions, including vital landmarks which would halt a German advance, like Pegasus Bridge. The seas and the skies both belonged to the Allies. Montgomery had promised his men that the invasion would not go ahead until that umbrella of protection was firmly in place.

Anyone living on the south coast of England could have had no doubt that an invasion was poised to go ahead. Local people became used to the sight of tanks and trucks lining the streets, as major military traffic jams built up on the main roads to Portsmouth. Now there were 1,500,000 American troops alone massed on British shores. Then, one morning, they were gone.

Beginning on 2 June, the hordes of men and machinery bound for Normandy boarded their ships. The weather had been unseasonably poor, putting the entire operation at risk. It had to be postponed once from 5 June. General Dwight Eisenhower, supreme Allied commander, considered a further postponement in the face of the driving winds and rains which could wreak havoc with a seaborne landing force. The next date in June when the tides and the light were compatible was not for almost another two weeks. Some commanders favoured waiting. Others, like Montgomery, believed the strike should go ahead. It would, after all, be impossible to keep aboard ship those men already embarked. Each soldier and marine had already been interned in a camp for at least three weeks and was primed and ready for action. Any postponement could only

Above: A US ship returns to a British port loaded with 'Overlord' casualties, while in France the action continues.

have led to a deterioration in their mental and physical fitness.

Eisenhower smoked and read Westerns while he pondered the dilemma. Finally he made his decision. Heartened by predictions of a break in the weather, he signalled the go-ahead for 6 June, with the words 'OK, let's go'.

IKE SPEAKS

Eisenhower, fondly known as 'Ike', gave this message to the departing men of the Allied Expeditionary Force: 'You are about to embark upon the Great Crusade, toward which we have striven these many months. The eyes of the world are upon you. The hopes and prayers of liberty-loving people everywhere march with you. In company with our brave Allies and brothers-in-arms on other Fronts, you will bring about the destruction of the German war machine, the elimination of Nazi tyranny over the oppressed peoples of Europe and security for ourselves in a free world.

'Your task will not be an easy one. Your enemy is well equipped, well trained and battle-hardened. He will fight savagely.

'But this is the year 1944! Much has happened since the Nazi triumphs of 1940-41. The United Nations have inflicted upon the Germans great defeats, in open battle, man-to-man... The tide has turned! The free men of the world are marching together to Victory.'

The only message to reach the expectant public that day was a short, sharp statement, reading: 'Under the command of General Eisenhower, Allied naval forces, supported by strong air forces, began landing Allied armies this morning on the northern coast of France.'

As the soldiers and sailors bobbed in darkness on a choppy sea, they were nervous, tense, euphoric and excitable. Some were sea-sick, some prayed, many fought an overwhelming feeling of doom. Still more found enough spirit to tell jokes.

The huge size of the armada involved in 'Operation Neptune', which got them across the Channels only served to inflate their confidence.

The troops heard the drone of aircraft overhead – a big boost to their morale. Not only were the planes going to bombard enemy positions along the coast in preparation for the landings. Some were carrying paratroopers who, in the first leg of 'Overlord', were being

EYE WITNESS

Henry 'Marty' Martin, from Chicopee, Massachusetts, USA, witnessed the tragedy of 'Operation Tiger' at Slapton Sands while training for D-Day.

❛When the German E-boats attacked we just thought it was just part of the exercise. I was right in that exercise and I didn't find out for another 43 years that 749 men had drowned. These guys were wearing their life jackets around their waists when they should have been up around their armpits. With 30-35lb packs on their backs they were just tipped upside down in the water and couldn't right themselves.

I can understand why the government kept it secret at the time because the news would have been a terrible blow to morale. I only question why it took so long for the facts to come out.❜

Right: Allied soldiers pause to inspect a French memorial to those who died in the carnage of World War I, before continuing with the liberation of western Europe.

dropped at 2am into east and west flanks of the landings.

When they approached the beach, they saw what appeared to be men walking on water. These were crew members of the midget submarines used to guide in the flotillas of landing craft. Men lashed themselves to the masts of their tiny submarines, which floated low in the water to signal to the captains of much larger vessels.

H-HOUR, D-DAY

Just a few hours later, naval guns were joining the aircraft in the pounding of enemy positions. Before 6am, the first men were ashore, putting months of rigorous training to the test.

British and Canadian troops were destined for the easterly beaches between Arromanches and Ouistreham. The three beaches earmarked for landings were code-named Gold, Juno and Sword.

In the west, the Americans tackled beaches Utah and Omaha, stretching between Les Dunes de Varreville and Colleville. On each beach there were barbed-wire hazards, anti-tank stumps entrenched in the sand and other menaces. First to come off the boats were the commandos who were to knock out the pill-boxes, and the sappers, charged with clearing a safe path up the beach.

The operation surprised the Germans, who at first believed the landings were a diversionary

tactic. Rommel was unprepared for the Allied arrival and was in Germany celebrating his wife's 50th birthday when the landings occurred. After Rommel heard of the invasion at 10.15am, he began a frantic drive back from Germany to his post.

After the war, Rommel's son Manfred recalled how his father had told Hitler many times that the invasion battle could not be won. Hitler refused to listen. 'All my father could do was to pull the front further and further back and, until he was wounded, carry out his duty.'

When he was told of the early morning events of 6 June, Hitler ordered his troops to clean

---

The Führer refused to release two Panzer divisions from the east of France

---

up the beachheads before nightfall. He knew the only way to save his extended empire was to throw the Allies back into the sea. But convinced it was a false alarm, the Führer refused to release two Panzer divisions from the east of France to counter the Allied attack until 3.40pm.

Troops on Sword, Juno and

Gold made solid progress in spite of casualties, although many soldiers landed without their guns and ammunition, which were lost in the water. They had to wait in huddles until the beach was taken before resuming their war. On Utah beach, the German defences found it impossible to keep the swarms of Americans at bay. It was speedily taken with fewer than 200 lives lost.

HELL OF OMAHA

On Omaha beach, bad weather, combined with strong currents and fierce resistance, made the landings a nightmare.

More than 2,000 men lost their lives. They were drowned when they were swept away by a changing tide with heavy equipment strapped to their backs. Some died when they trod on mines. Others perished from artillery, machine-gun, mortar and rifle fire from beach pill-boxes and from positions on cliffs above the beach. Wounded men strewn on the beach were in danger of being run over by tanks. There was little shelter and no escape.

Lieutenant-General Omar Bradley considered a withdrawal. It would have been disastrous

EYE WITNESS

George Ross, from Glasgow, was called up in 1939 when he was 19 years old. He recalls how as Sergeant Major of 101 Company, 5th Beach Group, he landed on Sword beach in the early hours of D-Day.

'We didn't know what we were going to come up against. The crossing was rough. Our craft was led by a chief petty officer. He had been at sea 25 years and never been sea-sick. But he was sick as a dog that morning.

Coming ashore, the first thing we noticed was a camouflaged pill-box. We got underneath the slits and launched a grenade attack. Our job was to establish a route where our tanks could come through. I honestly cannot say I was nervous. I was anxious but I had been warned about what to expect during six months of lectures beforehand.

There were bodies in the water of both British and Germans. One of the officers told us afterwards how, when he was walking up the beach, he felt he was walking on cushions. It was bodies of dead soldiers he was walking on.'

for the invasion, offering an opening for the Germans to attack both British and American flanks. Yet hardy US Rangers finally scaled the coastal heights to tackle the guns and alleviate the problems on the beach.

LONGEST DAY

Some of the men on the beaches were battle-hardened veterans. There was, however, a large contingent of raw soldiers, particularly among the Americans. They were pitched into the most intense, violent battleground, and forced to pick their way among the dead and dying amid the roar of big guns overhead and the sensation of small-

arms fire whizzing past their ears. The air was filled with the pungent smell of flesh, blood and cordite.

Particularly on Omaha but also true of the other beaches, the first wave of men forced to fight their way ashore were cut down. Preparing to take to the beaches, the second wave witnessed the carnage then ran past the bodies of their comrades.

Each flash of cowardice displayed by frightened, confused men was matched ten times by instances of heroism and stoicism. Each man was focused only on surviving for the next minute, the next hour and into the following day.

Ahead of them lay the task of capturing German-held towns, some of which fell more quickly than others. Russians who had been forced into German uniforms after being captured on the Eastern front were eager to lay down their arms. The French people rushed out to greet the

Below: A Sherman tank, nick-named 'Bessie', goes ashore to fight the battle of Normandy.

liberating Allies, offering drinks, flowers and greetings. Residents near the beaches braved the conflict to aid the wounded.

Tales of outstanding courage filled the newspapers for months and years afterwards. One commando corporal led his men up the beach past enemy pill-boxes, bellowing encouragement. He fell only when he had passed the pill-boxes – he had received more than 50 wounds.

The defending Germans were mostly in chaos. One senior commander reported that American gliders were landing Volkswagen cars in Normandy which were driven by American troops in German uniforms. The confusion and indecision that paralysed many Germans was countered by the heroic efforts of the Allied troops.

By the end of the longest day, 10,000 Allied soldiers had fallen. The figure was a third of that estimated by Allied command. But there was no turning back. The Allies had achieved the Normandy landings. Nothing and nobody was going to force them out of France again.

TANKS COME OF AGE

The tank came of age during World War II and proved to be a battle winner – or loser. The first tanks had been designed by Sir Ernest Swinton and saw action in the Somme offensive of World War I in 1916. Caterpillar tracks enabled them to cross treacherous terrain where no other vehicle could go. They were equipped with one or more guns, the crew sitting behind armour plating and firing off salvos at the enemy.

Now German General Heinz Guderian used the outbreak of World War II to put his own theories about the use of tanks to the test. Tanks should not be pinned down to flanking foot soldiers, he argued. Their purpose was to break out against the enemy, putting a speed into land-based warfare which it had never known before.

With that in mind, he formed his highly efficient Panzer divisions. The tanks were fast but lacked adequate protective armour. Nevertheless, they were an integral part of 'Blitzkrieg', the lightning war, a tactic with which Hitler easily won Poland, France, Holland and Belgium.

The technique took Britain and France by surprise. Although France had 2,475 tanks at its disposal their effectiveness was muted because of the way in which they were deployed. Instead of combining the fire-power as Guderian did, each tank was evenly spaced down a long defensive line. In time Allied commanders mimicked Guderian to get the best out of their tanks. Used individually, they were easy targets.

When a tank 'brewed up', the escape hatches were wholly inadequate, or blocked

If tankmen in World War I were better protected than their colleagues in the infantry, the same could not be said of their counterparts 20 years on. In fact, there were few infantrymen who would willingly change places with tankmen. For while

tanks stole a march on the enemy in the the killing fields of Flanders, technology had now caught up. Now there was a wide range of anti-armour artillery designed to knock tanks out. Men inside a stricken tank had little or no chance of escape.

And for the first three years of the war, German tanks and anti-tank weapons were better than their British counterparts. For example, the Mark II Matilda was known for its weak steering clutches, the Valentine offered only limited vision to its commander, the Crusader was mechanically unreliable. It took only an armour-piercing shell from one of the new breed of anti-tank guns used by the Germans to finish them.

That's when infantrymen remained glad they had the job they did. For when a tank caught fire, or 'brewed up', the tiny escape hatches on the tanks were wholly inadequate and were often blocked. Sometimes there was a matter of seconds

Above: *Tank crews during World War I were rightly delighted with the new hardware, which provided them with ample protection. But in World War II, a variety of anti-armour weapons existed to make life hell for the tankman.*
Far left: *The men of an armoured division running through the smoke-filled streets of the German town of Wernberg.*

before fire took a hold and the tank's ammunition began to explode. Sometimes there was not. Nicknames for tanks during the war included 'steel coffins', 'tommy cookers' and 'Ronson burners', because, like the products of the same name, they would always 'light first time'.

BLACKENED DOLLS

One witness gruesomely detailed the effects on the men trapped inside: 'Little blackened dolls about two feet high have been found in tanks. Once these were men.'

As the war progressed, the Germans learned about the short-comings of their tanks, which

Left: *Matilda tanks were favoured by the British military but they failed to match the firepower of German Tigers, pictured below.*

some – but not all – of the difficulties. Yet no design, no matter how superior, could compensate for the problems thrown up by the terrain the tanks were working in. Every theatre of war offered its pitfalls to tanks. In Europe

were lacking in firepower and suffered from flimsy armour. Their most painful lesson came on the Eastern front when their troops encountered the fearsome T-34 tanks of the Russian armoured divisions.

They introduced the Panther, in July 1943, and the Tiger, in September 1942, which were battle winners thanks to the enormous range of their guns, quite outstripping the British models, which were unable to get close enough to counter-attack effectively.

THE DEADLY 88

By the time the British developed the six-pounder gun, the Germans had in their armoury the heavier 75 mm weapon. As the Americans caught up, with their own 75 mm gun, the Germans leaped ahead again, fitting the deadly 88 mm guns, which were originally designed as anti-aircraft guns but wreaked havoc when mounted on the Tiger tank.

As an illustration of the immense advantage kept in hand by the Germans in terms of tank technology, a single Tiger tank operating in

Normandy knocked out 25 British tanks, 28 armoured vehicles and killed an additional 80 infantrymen.

It seemed as if the British had learned nothing from their experiences in the desert a full two years earlier. The poor state of British and American tank

The poor state of Allied tank technology was little short of a scandal

technology was little short of a scandal and left Allied tank crews disheartened.

A later generation of Allied tanks, including Shermans and Churchills, began to overcome

the rain made the earth unacceptably boggy; in North Africa the desert dust clogged engines and sharp stones tore the tracks; in Asia, where there were few tanks, the humidity affected the engineering. In nine days of fighting in Germany in 1945 the 9th Royal Tank Regiment and the 147th Regiment suffered 85 tank casualties. 17 were due to enemy action, 36 succumbed to mechanical problems, while 32 got stuck in the mud. This time the innovators were the British. A series of modified tanks were used to breach the beaches at Normandy. Witnesses reported that some German soldiers threw down their guns and ran at the sight of this bizarre new breed.

Behind them was Major-General Sir Percival Hobart. Like

A series of modified tanks were used to breach the beaches at Normandy

his brother-in-law Montgomery, Hobart was outspoken and did not suffer fools gladly. His forthright manner won him few friends at the War Office and by 1940 he was retired. It was the personal intervention of Winston Churchill which installed Hobart back in the fight against Hitler.

HOBART'S FUNNIES

Mindful that Allied troops would encounter all manner of defences during the landings, his priority was to install tough armour to protect the troops. Then he looked at ways of tackling an amphibious landing, crossing a minefield, blasting a well-fortified pill-box and travelling with heavy vehicles across boggy ground.

To get hefty tanks ashore from landing craft, he came up with the Duplex Drive, an amphibious tank with propellers and a canvas skirt to protect it from the water. When the tank made it to the shore, the canvas was lowered.

An adaptation of the Churchill tank helped to combat the threat of minefields. On the front a large rotating drum hung with heavyweight chains, was turned by power from the engines. This 'Crab' would explode the hidden mines without causing damage. The 'Ark', a tank with four long

ROMMEL – DESERT FOX

Erwin Rommel, courageous soldier and gifted leader of men, became known as the Desert Fox thanks to his cunning in North Africa.

The son of a teacher, Rommel joined the army from his home town of Württemberg as an officer cadet and proved his early promise during World War I. Between the wars he taught at Germany's military academies and authored a book about infantry strategies which was published in 1937.

When war broke out, Colonel Rommel was put in charge of the troops guarding Hitler. Frustrated with his behind-the-lines role, he seized the opportunity early in 1940 to command the 7th Panzer Division which he took into action in France before it was occupied, striking as far north as the Channel coast.

A year later he was put in charge of the German troops sent by Hitler to bail out the beleaguered Italians in North Africa. He shone in his new role, despite his misgivings about his wavering Italian allies. His impressive early victories won him the rank of Field-Marshal.

He was held in high esteem by his men for his initiative and bravery. In an example of his charismatic leadership, he once leapt from a car to address a division of men: 'There is an English Armoured Brigade getting ready to attack you from the north and in the south there is an English mixed force which is advancing. Take care that you are finished with the first before the second arrives!' Yet he was all but ready to pull out his exhausted men when Hitler ordered a strike on Cairo in Egypt. Once again, he found remarkable success until his supply lines became hopelessly overstretched as he ventured further into British-held territory. Weakened by lack of essentials and wearied by months of fighting, he was finally defeated and pursued out of Africa.

In 1944 Rommel was ordered by Hitler to secure the French coastline against Allied invasion. Even though he was already convinced the war was unwinnable, he tackled the unenviable task with a deep professional pride. Yet he received little practical support from the Führer despite his warnings that all would be lost if the enemy penetrated the insubstantial coastal defences.

Although at heart he was non-political, Rommel was recruited by plotters who wanted Hitler replaced. The popular and realistic Rommel was their chosen leader. It is unlikely, however, that he knew about plans to assassinate the Führer for he was deeply opposed to killing for political ends.

In any event, an attack by British bombers put Rommel in hospital with serious injuries when the abortive coup took place. Hitler himself was reluctant to expose Rommel as part of the plot against him. He knew only too well that he was vulnerable to the grass-roots affection won by Rommel. So he dispatched two generals to see his reluctant adversary to offer a deal. Rommel and his family would escape the shame of public exposure if he would take poison and eliminate himself as a threat to Hitler. On 14 October 1944 Rommel did as his leader asked and was buried with full military honours.

Right: Rommel (left) confers with a subordinate during the desert campaign.

beams at each corner, became a bridge to span small ravines and enable troops and armoured cars to cross.

Providing a roadway for troops and vehicles through soft ground became the job of the 'Bobbin' tank. It had a large, rolled, heavy-duty canvas roadway attached to its front. As the tank trundled along, it unfurled the roadway for following traffic. But perhaps the most fearsome of his designs was the 'Crocodile' another modified Churchill tank, designed to throw a scorching flame for 120 yards. Attached behind was its own fuel depot on wheels. So feared was this flame-thrower that when SS troops captured the crew of a Crocodile, they would shoot them straightaway.

RIFLES AND GUNS

In just four years, the advances in gun capabilities had been enormous. When the war started, the Allied stock of rifles dated mostly from the previous world war or before.

Rifles were smaller and lighter than ever before and fired faster too. Rates of fire were up in the machine guns as well. The

---

When SS troops captured the crew of a Crocodile, they would shoot them

---

British Bren could now dispense around 500 rounds a minute, the same as the US Browning. New mortars were light enough for infantrymen to carry with them into battle.

The pack of equipment loaded onto the back of the infantryman was very heavy. Soldiers had to rely on mules in some cases to transport the guns to the top of high, hostile escarpments in rugged terrain.

Even then the pre-prepared defences installed by the enemy were strong enough to resist the firepower of such weapons. Only bombs would have a sufficiently devastating effect and that required air support.

Given the firepower, the men used it, expending thousands of rounds of ammunition daily. The prospect of any shortages of fuel or ammunition, was a daunting one. World War II showed that a fighting force was only as good as its supply line.

Left: Jeeps were put through their paces in Normandy during the autumn of 1944. These rugged, four-wheel-drive vehicles were used to transport the wounded.

Left: Allied soldiers in Burma used newer, more powerful weapons to get the better of their enemy.

the thousand in America to reach the battle fronts and replenish the men.

WILLYS JEEP

Transport had to be reliable and tough to be of any use. In 1940, the Jeep made its debut, its name derives from the full name first given it general purpose (i.e. 'GP') vehicle. First constructed by the Willys Overland Company, this legendary creation had speed and agility and was an instant hit with the army. It could tackle even the roughest terrain and was useful for transporting troops, small arms and other light loads. It further helped to make horses redundant on the battlefield.

In Burma the Chindits had an advantage over their Japanese enemy through the regular supplies dropped in by aircraft. In Europe and Africa improving methods of amphibian landings allowed the trucks which were being turned out by

---

EYE WITNESS

Sydney Hartley suffered a badly injured leg when he was in the third of three tanks sent forward to pin-point the whereabouts of the enemy during a battle in the Tunisian campaign. It was later amputated just above the knee. He was 28 years old.

❮I knew the dangers of crossing open ground on enemy territory but I clearly remember thinking that, with a bit of luck, we might again just get out of this unscathed with us being the last tank in a line of three.'

After about 150 yards I heard the voice of the squadron leader come through my headphones. "Third troop, halt. Turn right and engage the enemy tanks." As we turned we realised we had run into a trap. Just coming into their final positions were two German tanks or self-propelled guns. We were all taken by surprise.

I knew this was the moment of truth, life or death. I quickly estimated the range, our big 75 mm gun was loaded, I put the sights on the target and fired. It was impossible to follow the tracer bullet because the sun was lying just behind the target. Then it didn't matter as I saw the German tank's gun flash and a split second afterwards our world exploded. Everything suddenly went black and I felt what seemed like a red-hot poker against my right leg.

Flames were rising and I knew I had to get out quickly. I tried to pull myself out of the turret but at waist high I realised something was holding me back,

because I was still wearing my headphones. Then I made a superhuman effort and flung myself the eight-foot drop to the ground. I knew something was terribly wrong with me. I heard this soul-destroying scream – it could have been any one of us. I dragged myself away. Looking at my right leg, the shock was more mental than physical. The armour-piercing shot had taken away half of my calf and broken up the calf bone. The foot was dangling from what flesh remained.

I took out a large field-dressing from my pocket and made a tourniquet. It looked like the driver and co-driver hadn't made it out of the tank. The next tank in line was burning although the crew got out safely. Mortar bombs were dropping all around. The troop corporal carried me to the rest of the men which was excruciatingly painful. I had morphine tablets but felt faint from blood loss. I didn't know which was most painful, my leg or the burns on my hands and face. The top skin of my hands peeled back like roller blinds. I had a very bumpy ride on a Bren-gun carrier back to the echelon along-side an injured German soldier and his friend.

I was laid out on a stretcher, looking up at the sky, when I saw a Messerschmitt 109 come into view. It appeared to be heading straight for me. He started machine-gunning us. It was the first of three aircraft attacks before I was put in the ambulance and driven away.❯

THE PACIFIC

Sweeping Japanese gains left the Allies with their work cut out, yet there was a grim resolve among them to push the invaders back. The rocky road to triumph over the extended empire of the Rising Sun began in New Guinea.

Japanese plans to take the unoccupied sector of New Guinea with a seaborne invasion were dashed following the Battle of the Coral Sea in May 1942. But they had not given up hope of seizing the island. Another offensive was planned, this time overland.

On 21 July 1942 an advance party of 2,000 Japanese soldiers landed at Buna, Papua, without a shot being fired. Their aim was to take Port Moresby, still in Allied hands. Ahead of them was a choice of two jungle tracks across the 1,200 ft Owen Stanley mountains – hostile and steamy terrain. They chose the most accessible or least impassable.

Defensive forces on New Guinea at the time comprised some scattered Australian brigades backed up by a limited number of indigenous New Guinea riflemen.

The Japanese forces seized the interior in little more than a week, scaling the rocky heights of the mountain range. Racing against time, the Australians rushed through reinforcements. By 12 August Lieutenant-General F. Rowell, in command at Port Moresby, decided he had enough troops at his disposal to send an expedition into the mountains.

PORT MORESBY

Another Japanese force, numbering about 11,500, was landed, enabling a significant thrust to take place against the Australians. The prospects looked bleak for the Allies as the Australians fell back and back. The Australian commandos were swallowed up in the Japanese advances.

But by now the Japanese were encountering some difficulties of their own. Allied aircraft were making a fine job of disrupting the already treacherous lines of supply. It meant soldiers fighting in the most torrid conditions were left without adequate food and medical supplies.

In addition, the spectre of dysentery and other debilitating diseases loomed. Troops were

Troops were weakened by highly infectious wasting diseases in jungle conditions

weakened by highly infectious wasting diseases which medics were unable to counter in jungle conditions. By September their advance had run out of steam. They were brought to a halt just 32 miles from Port Moresby.

The Australians had little time to even draw breath. More Japanese troops had landed at Milne Bay, to the east, with orders to occupy the all-important airfield there. Approximately 2,000 Japanese soldiers fought fiercely to reach the edge of

Above: *Japanese marines begin their march on New Guinea, confident of yet another victory.*
Left: *One of the Emperor's vessels lies wrecked off Guadalcanal, which became a graveyard for ships.*

the airstrip. Then the tide of battle turned against them. The Japanese had thought the Australian presence there was depleted. In fact there were nearly two brigades of men, two fighter squadrons and plenty of established artillery.

In a counter-attack at the end of August by the 18th Australian Brigade, the Japanese were chased back to the sea. Finally, on 6 September, the remnants of the landing force were withdrawn.

Now the focus was back on the Japanese holed up in the mountain range. Australian troops reinforced by Americans forged up the Kokoda trail, the same route the invading Japanese had followed but in the opposite direction. A parallel force hoping to outflank the enemy embarked up the Kapa Kapa trail, even more remote and difficult.

Ahead of them lay the Japanese, securely dug into three defensive positions at the peak of the Kokoda trail. On 16 October the first Japanese post was taken by an Australian brigade. Yet the supreme effort in the face of determined opposition sapped what little strength the Australian soldiers had left.

Without the help of their trusted Melanesian porters, The Australians were equally vulnerable to disease. The main cause of dysentery in New Guinea was polluted water. Springs were fouled by natives and the fighting men themselves, who were often too far away from their latrines to use them.

JAPANESE ROUT

It took fresh troops, who finally relieved the exhausted astray, the Allies were better off than their Japanese counterparts, who were still dependant on supplies coming in by sea and being passed up country. Australian troops found the bodies of their foe were emaciated and diseased. There were signs of cannibalism as no doubt starving soldiers had resorted to eating human flesh to stay alive.

Below: US marines heading for Japanese front lines at Guadalcanal. *Right:* US soldiers resting after action on New Guinea.

EYE WITNESS

Bob Cartwright, from Wimbledon, south west London, was a lance corporal in the Royal Army Medical Corps who saw action in North Africa before being posted to the Far East. He served as a Chindit in the 44th Recce Regiment on the force's second foray.

'There were 400 men in every column. The men from the medical corps like me travelled either at the front or the back. Conditions were ruddy awful. The recce men had to tackle unmapped mountains with gradients of one in one. They were so steep that men had to crawl on their hands and knees. Even the mules fell by the wayside. They plunged down ravines and couldn't get out.

On my back was a 60 lb first aid bag. For six weeks we were living on bully beef and biscuits and on any rice we could scrounge from local Burmese people, which wasn't much. Then US 'K' rations were airdropped to us. In one of the daily meals there was usually a bar of chocolate. We used to melt it on to the rice to make a pudding.
We were on our way to Kohima to relieve the siege there when we were ambushed in a teak forest. The leaves of teak trees are very big and crisp. We had to wait until it rained before we could get out without the Japanese hearing our every footstep.

We had to take malaria and salt tablets. If you weren't wet from perspiration you were wet with the rain. Men suffered from malaria, tick bites and ulcers. I don't know anyone who didn't lose weight. Everyone thought the world of Orde Wingate, the man behind the Chindits, even though he wasn't liked by the big shots in India. All they did was criticise him.

He had eyes that looked right through you and a really magnetic personality. I met him on two occasions. He inspired the troops.
We marched 600 miles through the jungle. I was out there about six months before they flew us out. The men were in excellent spirits. I don't think I heard anybody moan about what we were doing. It was only the weather that bothered us.

There must be many unmarked and unknown graves in Burma.'

---

who carried their equipment and sometimes the men themselves, they would not have got so far. Try as they might, they could not budge the invaders from the other two dug-outs. Casualties mounted from sniper fire, with the Japanese apparently secure in their fox-holes.

Australians, to add impetus to the assault. After intense fighting in swampy insect-ridden undergrowth the Japanese were finally routed. All the while, the Australian and American troops were benefiting from supplies dropped by air in the jungle. While some consignments went

Every mile of the jungle was bitterly contested by the two sides. The stop-start campaign was at its most deadly when the Japanese were cornered in well-built defences, with their backs to the sea. Both prongs of the Allied forces joined up but there was stalemate as the Japanese sat tight in their well-dug positions.

Even the arrival of new Allied troops to wage the battle brought piecemeal results. For

every fighting soldier, the conditions were nothing short of appalling. Allied troops were forced to pick off Japanese men and guns one by one as the doomed and diminishing force refused to capitulate. It wasn't until 3 January 1943 that the last of the Japanese resistance was ended. It had taken six months and cost an estimated 5,700 Australian, 2,800 American and 12,000 Japanese casualties.

As Australians and Americans fought to free Papua New Guinea, so US Marines were battling to liberate Guadalcanal, an island in the Solomons crucial in importance because of its airfield, Henderson Field. Frequent rain squalls in the sauna heat made it a perfect breeding ground for mosquitoes. Malaria was rife among soldiers already weakened by the humidity. Documents from Japan's high command captured later revealed the immense importance they attached to the island. 'Success or failure in recapturing Guadalcanal is the fork in the road which leads to victory for them or us.'

GUADALCANAL

On 7 August 1942 11,000 US Marines landed on Guadalcanal, surprisingly, without opposition. It would take a long time before Japan's soldiers on the island were eradicated, however. Japanese forces on neighbouring islands gave a more rousing reception to landing parties. On Tulagi, there was a hectic battle. At the end of it, the Marines were victorious. Tulagi was theirs. In total 108 US Marines had died while the Japanese force of an estimated 1,500 was wiped out.

Frequent rain squalls in the sauna heat made it a perfect breeding ground for mosquitoes

Like the Australians and the British, the American forces fighting the Japanese in the Pacific discovered that jungle warfare was a battle of nerves. The vegetation was host to scores of unusual animals making terrifying noises. Sounds of birds, lizards and insects echoed through the night, each one sounding like an approaching sniper. And sometimes it was indeed the enemy, creeping in the dark before moving in for a kill. It was vital for guns to remain quiet unless there was an attack, since a burst of fire pinpointed a soldier's position for the enemy.

The Japanese, throughout the Pacific and South east Asia, displayed a mastery of cunning jungle warfare tactics. They knew a grenade thrown from somewhere in the night would result in havoc in an Allied camp. Startled and confused, the Allied soldiers would fire wildly and draw their knives, often injuring their comrades in the subsequent chaos. Meanwhile, the Japanese melted back into the darkness.

There were reports of Japanese soldiers leaping

Below: *A tense moment as US soldiers, with guns at the ready, probe a jungle hideout in search of Japanese snipers.*

suddenly into Allied foxholes brandishing knives – then quickly jumping out again.

The Allied soldiers were left tussling among themselves in panic with weapons drawn. In the darkness, a voice might sound: 'Please, Johnny, help me.' It was tempting for the soldiers to rise up and respond to a

The Japanese displayed a mastery of cunning jungle warfare tactics

call for help. If they did so, it would spell their doom. Here was yet another technique used by the Japanese to get the enemy to reveal itself. The US occupation of Guadalcanal sparked some vital sea battles. But the first land-based reprisals from the Japanese came on 18 August when 1,000 Japanese troops were landed on

Guadalcanal. All were killed and their commander Colonel Ichiki committed suicide.

Aircraft from the US carriers patrolling in the region deterred further large-scale landings although there were numerous small-scale attacks mounted by Japanese units, all successfully repulsed. Japanese commanders had grossly underestimated the number of American troops stationed on Guadalcanal. The American garrison, now numbering 19,000, was able to prevent wholesale Japanese landings with naval and air support even though the empire gathered 20,000 men from around the region for an October offensive.

The Americans were, however, handicapped by the frequent attacks on Henderson Field made by battleships and aircraft, as well as by the nuisance raids led by the Japanese who had made successful landings on

Guadalcanal. It wasn't until the three-day Battle of Guadalcanal at sea that the hard-pressed American defenders enjoyed some respite.

It was then that the Japanese navy decided to pull back from Guadalcanal and defend a different line. Senior navy commanders recognised the increasing strength of the Americans reduced the chances of taking Guadalcanal to virtually nil.

CHINDITS

The army was keen to continue the campaign, confident that the 30,000 troops based on the island would eventually triumph. But without naval co-operation, transporting reinforcements or supplies to the island, would be impossible.

Here was a chance at last for the Marines to withdraw for some recuperation after four months of jungle warfare. Their replacements finally totalled about 50,000 men, who were fit enough to drive the remaining Japanese forces from the island with relative ease. By February 1943, all had been evacuated by sea.

In Burma, the Japanese were still holding their own. The British had one card left, which may not have been a winner but certainly kept them in the game. This was the first ever deployment of Long Range Penetration Groups, later known as the Chindits.

Behind the Chindits was Orde Wingate, an unorthodox soldier with broad experience of organising guerrilla operations. His men from the 77th Indian Brigade derived their name from the mythical Burmese temple guardian, the chinthe, half lion and half eagle.

Above: B-25 Mitchell medium bombers of the US 5th Air Force deliver destruction to a Japanese airstrip on New Guinea in March 1944.

Earlier in the war, Wingate had attempted suicide by stabbing himself in the neck while suffering from malaria and depression. He was saved and a year later brought his charismatic brand of leadership to an enthusiastic bunch of men.

INTO BURMA

Their aim was to operate behind enemy lines, causing disruption and damage. They had to be skilled jungle fighters, able to fade away quickly into the forested landscape. Those in demand for the first Chindit expedition in February 1943 were men who were masters of demolition skills and also able radio operators. The radio operators were vital to the success of the mission as they were responsible for contacting base and requesting supplies. These were dropped by air, giving the Chindits an essential advantage of endurance.

EYE WITNESS

Bill Jenkins joined the Australian armed forces in 1939 when he was 18 years old and served until 1945, seeing action on the infamous Kokoda trail in New Guinea.

❛We had just come back from the Middle East. I had three days' leave after two and a half years at war when I was recalled and put on a boat headed for New Guinea. Things were getting pretty desperate. The Japanese were in rowing distance of Australia itself. The pitifully small forces there to meet them were militiamen or home guard members who were decimated. We joined them and gradually drove the Japanese back over the Owen Stanley range of mountains. Sickness was terrible, with scrub typhoid, malaria and malnutrition claiming many lives. It was difficult for the planes to spot us and drop supplies. My brigade began with about 2,500 men. Less than 200 were evacuated at the close of the campaign. I returned weighing less than seven stones instead of 12 stones.❜

Together with elephants, mules and buffaloes, two groups comprising 3,200 men set off into occupied Burma, each ready to sub-divide into columns to achieve its aim. They set off with the poetic words of Orde Wingate ringing in their ears:

WINGATE'S WORDS

'It is always a minority that occupies the front line. It is a still smaller minority that accepts with a good heart tasks like this that we have chosen to carry out. We need not, as we go forward into conflict, suspect ourselves of selfish or interested motives. We have all had the opportunity of withdrawing and we are here because we have chosen to be here; that is, we have chosen to bear the burden and heat of the day. Men who make this choice are above the average in courage. We need therefore have no fear for the staunchness and guts of our comrades.

Our motive may be taken to be the desire to serve our day and generation in the way that seems nearest to our hand. The

EYE WITNESS

Alf Turner was a member of the 6th Battalion, The Devonshire Regiment, when he was posted to the Far East in 1943.

❝Our sergeant major told us it was the best draft of all and that we wouldn't do anything for six months. That was a load of tripe. After arriving at a reinforcement camp we were sent up to Bhopal to do a month's jungle training. Then we set off for Burma.

All you can see around you in the jungle are trees. If somebody fires, you don't know which way it is coming from. Being a country boy, I found it a bit easier than the Londoners out there who weren't used to night-time noises and wildlife.

The Japanese soldiers would shout out in the night: "Tommy, where are you?" And they would beat bamboo sticks to unnerve us. They tried to get us to give away our positions. After one attack an apparently wounded Japanese soldier was calling: "Tommy, help me, help me". One of our officers who couldn't stick it any more went out to him. We told him not to go. When he got near, the soldier jumped up and threw a grenade at him. The officer lost his leg.

The Japanese put grenades under dead bodies in the hope you would turn them over. Near-the Irrawaddy river we came across a village where all the men had been beheaded by the Japanese and all the women were hung up by their hands and disembowelled. They were cruel fighters.

We took very few prisoners. Those who were wounded would rip their bandages off after being treated. They wanted to die in battle.

We belonged to the 20th Indian Division and I was a technical sergeant in charge of transport. I had to use sticky tape to repair tyres. We came across some Japanese supplies and used those to keep the trucks going.

There were giant ant hills. In the monsoon season they would collapse and you could find yourself knee deep in earth with ants crawling all over your legs. Then there were the leeches. The only way to get them off was with a lighted cigarette butt. We also had snakes slithering over our legs, jungle sores and prickly heat.

In France and Germany the troops had fleets of invasion craft. When they liberated towns, the people came out to cheer them. In Burma we had a few 'ducks' but mostly we had to make our own rafts to see us across the rivers. And we were never welcomed by the people. They didn't seem to care if it was us or the Japanese.❞

Left: British troops of the 14th Army advance cautiously on the mud huts in the newly taken prize of Meiktila in Burma, March 1945.

battle is not always to the strong nor the race to the swift. Victory in war cannot be counted upon but what can be counted upon is that we shall go forward determined to do what we can to bring this war to the end which we believe best for our friends and comrades in arms, without boastfulness or forgetting our duty, resolved to do the right so far as we can see the right.'

Wingate's bold and unexpected plan took the Japanese by surprise. When forces crossing the main Irrawaddy and Chindwin rivers were spotted, commanders believed these were small groups on reconnaissance who would be easily dispatched. Only when major railway bridges were blown

That the Japanese were now aware of their presence made life increasingly difficult

up did the Japanese suspect an orchestrated attack against them. At that stage, two divisions were sent to flush the British out of the jungle.

By now, the Chindits were dispersed into smaller, isolated groups, some faring better than others. That the Japanese were now aware of their presence made life increasingly difficult for the jungle warriors, who became trapped in the dense vegetation while their enemies had the rule of the roads and tracks. Inevitably, the tightly planned operation began to fall apart. When food ran short, they ate their mules. But then they had no transport.

BAREFOOT TO INDIA

Four months later, some 2,200 men returned to India, hungry, physically frail and many with bare feet, veterans of a remarkable physical trial and fully conversant with both jungle and guerrilla

Above: *Gurkha troops march past giant statues of chinthe — after which the Chindits were named – having liberated a key Burmese city.*

tactics. The important principles of warfare had been tried and tested by them, including that of air-dropping supplies. The soldiers rarely visited local villages for food and drink, where they might have been captured.

The Chindits were a difficult enemy for the Japanese to pin down, moving as they did under cover of darkness. So concerned were the Japanese army by the exploits of the Chindits that they revised their defensive policies in upper Burma, which not only tied up forces but ultimately laid them open to defeat.

REICH IN RUINS

By the end of 1943, the Germans were on the run from Stalin's forces. The Battle of the Atlantic had ended in their defeat and U-boats were being systematically blown out of the water. Germany itself was suffering a barrage of bombing campaigns, Italy had changed sides and, to many in the Nazi hierarchy, it seemed the war was already lost.

The following year brought little by way of relief. The long-awaited landings of thousands of Allied soldiers finally occurred in Normandy in June. When German soldiers were unable to defend the beaches, it was clear the destination for the Allies was nothing short of the German Fatherland itself.

During their first few weeks on French soil, the Allied armies encountered some strong resistance, particularly centred at Caen. Here was a professional SS division and a green German unit culled from the Hitler youth. Some fighters were as young as 16, they proved to be formidable opponents.

The British forces failed to capitalise on their surprise attack to gain their D-Day objectives and paid the penalty for their short delay while regrouping, as the Germans dug in with a vengeance. It took two major pushes, code-named 'Epsom' and 'Goodwood' to oust the few hundred Germans,

costing hundreds of Allied lives.

Countless numbers of French civilians died, mostly in the enormous air raids launched by the Allies which reduced the historic town of Caen to rubble. Fires raged in Caen for 11 days after the main bombing attack. Estimates put the number of French dead as high as 10,000. Still the German resistance held fast. The net effect of the air raids was simply to provide new hazards, like blocked roads, for the Allied ground forces.

TANK BATTLES

There were bitter tank battles between the British and Canadian forces and the Panzer units which rushed to the area from eastern France and Poland. Supplies began to falter when a gale blew up in the Channel on 19 June, wrecking the Mulberry harbours, onto which the Allies were unloading.

There was talk of sacking Montgomery for his failure to move forward. While German reserves were embroiled in the battle,

other Allied divisions were given a free hand elsewhere on the coast.

The American troops, having captured the Cherbourg peninsula, broke out to make a sweep through central Normandy and discovered too the horrors of fighting in the Normandy bocages. This was the ancient hedgerow and field system which covered the countryside providing havens for German snipers and hazards for Allied tanks and infantrymen.

Churchill and the American leaders were filled with angry frustration

The German reinforcements, which had at last made their way to Normandy, created more firmly held pockets of resistance, which were tough to shift. Falaise, Metz and a number of other towns formed serious blockages in the arteries of the Allied invasion.

Soldiers who on D-Day had never fired a shot in anger or seen a dead body were within a matter of weeks brutalised by the harshness of conflict. If they were fearful, they hid their feelings. Many were overwhelmed with elation when they killed an enemy soldier. As one US Ranger explained: 'It was not joy that I had killed him but that he hadn't killed me.'

Far left: *French inhabitants and US soldiers rejoice after Cherbourg is won from the Germans.*
Left: *German soldiers surrender to the US military near Toulon, in southern France, following the invasion of the south of the country in August 1944.*

By 15 August 1944 the Germans found southern France was also at risk. 'Operation Dragoon' got underway 10 weeks after D-Day, with the forces of the US 7th Army making landings between Toulon and Cannes and meeting only mild opposition. One of the soldiers to land south of St Tropez was Audie Murphy, later to be a Hollywood hearthrob, who single-handedly wiped out an enemy machine-gun nest.

The advance through France was known as the 'Champagne Campaign'

The US forces drove up France, to link up with their comrades swinging down from the north. Such was the joy of their reception by the French, it soon became known as the 'Champagne Campaign'. Paris was liberated by Free French forces on 25 August.

ARNHEM

By September, Montgomery and American General Omar Bradley had thrust through Belgium and Luxembourg. The fighting remained gruelling with British paratroops experiencing horrific losses when they tried to take Arnhem, Holland, at the end of September.

The successes of the Allies began to take their toll. The front line forces were running out of ammunition and supplies while enemy soldiers were making

Right: Although General de Gaulle was never popular among Allied war leaders, he won the undying adoration of his people for his uncompromising views.

EYE WITNESS

Rudolf Valentin was among the German soldiers who fought at Monte Cassino, and revealed some of his experiences to New Zealand author Alex Borrie. He saw some tough fighting as the Germans tried to recapture Hangman's Hill.

❛Our situation was not an enviable one. Whoever came out of cover during the day became a sure victim for the Indian sharp-shooter. The Gurkhas on Hangman's Hill were in a similar position. They also had to make themselves scarce during the day otherwise they drew German fire.

The set of circumstances meant that almost all attacks were switched to night-time. Just after the onset of darkness, we had to repel the first attack and two others followed. With the beginning of the new day, we had to creep into holes again which we enlarged with the spikes of our jack-knives. We had to survive the armed attacks in these holes.

In the evening the murderous close-combat began again. During this one often had to let the enemy advance until only metres away before one was able to recognise him by the shape of his helmet. In addition to this, hunger and especially thirst were also becoming factors.

At dawn on 19 March the 1st/FJR 4 [a German paratroop unit] came out to us with about 120 men from the monastery with the order to capture Rocca Janula again. After approximately 10 minutes of machine-gun fire and shelling our comrades overwhelmed the Rajputanis at the lower hair-pin curve and stormed the walls.

A terrible hand-to-hand combat flared up there. The Germans were attempting to scale the walls. They succeeded in blasting a hole in the wall. But the enemy from the Essex Battalion fought with the same determination and beat off the attack causing heavy casualties. Courage and the willingness to make sacrifices did not help at all. The castle could no longer be captured. This attack cost the lives of half the comrades, the rest had to retreat.

But the English and the Indians also suffered such heavy casualties that they had to abandon their intentions to capture the monastery in this way. On this day a ceasefire lasting several hours was agreed upon in order to recover the dead and wounded. It was at this point that we exchanged cigarettes with the enemy and helped each other out with bandages. The English even lent us stretchers to transport our wounded to the monastery. At the same time the Gurkhas took their wounded through our positions. A short time later the men who helped each other out in such a comradely fashion were once again the bitterest of enemies. What madness!❜

Right: German soldiers came uncomfortably close to succeeding in their objective of reaching the Belgian port of Antwerp during the Battle of the Bulge.

stronger stands than before. The Allied initiative ground to a halt in December 1944 before going on to make headway in Germany.

The infantrymen were heartily relieved. It had been a long, arduous haul which cost many lives. Combat exhaustion as well as other maladies were striking the servicemen who had survived the fighting. Seemingly ceaseless rain and acres of mud weighed their spirits down.

SLOW ADVANCE

Many soldiers were weary of the inch-by-inch advance they had experienced on the Western front, which resembled the trench warfare known by their fathers two decades earlier. A rash of self-inflicted wounds began bringing waves of soldiers to the sick bays. Anyone suspected of having deliberately injured himself was instantly court martialled.

Their commanders were frustrated in their desire to push relentlessly onwards. Hitler seized the opportunity to strike back.

The fury of the American and British air forces was brought to bear on the Germans

Choosing the same route which had served him so well some four years earlier, he proposed a surprise attack through the Ardennes with the intention of driving a wedge between the Allied forces and capturing

Antwerp, the Belgian port through which vital Allied supplies were being brought.

Luck was with the Germans as the offensive got underway on 16 December. Low cloud kept the Anglo-American reconnaissance aircraft on the ground. The Allied commanders had no idea of what was coming until it arrived.

Field-Marshal von Rundstedt commanded the German forces, comprising ten armoured divisions and 14 other divisions. However, only the 6th SS Panzer Army was up to full strength and adequately equipped. When the weather cleared, the fighting raged on over Christmas and into the New Year, with the Allies gradually gaining the upper hand. The Battle of the Bulge, as it was called, was over by 23 January when the Allies took St Vith, the last remaining German stronghold. Another, less substantial German thrust into northern Alsace which began on 1 January 1945 was also quickly suppressed.

The cost of the two German

assaults was high. Both had weakened the German defences elsewhere, a fact that didn't go unnoticed by Allied commander General Patton. At last the fortified Siegfried line, built to protect Germany, was in danger.

February saw a further big offensive in north west Europe from the Allies. In a series of pushes the Allied armies managed to link up to form a formidable front line.

REMAGEN

They were bucked when a sharp-eyed US sergeant spotted a railway bridge left intact by the retreating Germans, spanning the Rhine at Remagen. The Germans had viewed the Rhine in much the same way as the English saw the Channel, a vital line of defence which would be hard to penetrate. Now troops forged along the bridge while further up- and downstream their comrades made less comfortable crossings on swiftly assembled pontoons. The defences of the Fatherland had been breached.

EYE WITNESS

LeRoy Stein, from Michigan, USA, was 24 when he joined up and was a member of the 87th Division in Patton's 3rd Army in the battle for Normandy.

❝It was very frightening. I was in a mine platoon which was shaky work. We laid mines and booby traps and would take them up if they had no more use. Each one was supposed to be removed. A permanent record was supposed to be kept on the whereabouts of these explosives. But they were not properly taken up. There are still people being killed by them today.❞

Airborne troops helped capture stalwart German towns. By early May, key regions including the Ruhr, Hamburg, Bavaria and Austria were in the hands of the Allies. The German defences were cleverly conceived and included mines and booby traps.

Frequently, the morale of troops was low. In addition to seeing bloody action and burying their friends, the infantry had to endure apparently endless hours of foot-slogging. Their rations were pitiful, consisting mostly of tinned spam, corned beef and soya sausages. Despite the strong cameraderie of men forced to suffer unspeakable hardships, there were numerous instances of insubordination and desertion in the field.

Meanwhile, Russian troops had been pouring into Germany from the east, their target Berlin. Even the most hopeful of German commanders must have realised the end was near when a tidal wave of Russian troops overran the Silesian industrial basin in January. Albert Speer, head of war production, wrote a memo to Hitler, beginning with the words: 'The war is lost.' Speer realised that Germany could not sustain its industry or defence when the region which produced 60 per cent of its coal had been snatched from it. But Hitler refused to listen.

RED FLAG RISES

Russian generals Zhukov and Konev encircled Berlin by 25 April and began another relentless advance towards the very heart of the Reich. Fierce street fighting raged as loyal Nazis battled to stop the Russians closing in on their beloved Führer. Despite their efforts, a Red Flag was raised over the Reichstag on 2 May 1945.

Hitler finally summoned his long-time mistress Eva Braun to be at his side in the middle of April, realising that his days were numbered.

His 56th birthday on 20 April was marked by more catastrophes in the field. Nazis including Goebbels, Göring, Himmler, Ribbentrop and Bormann joined him for the celebrations. They urged him to flee south but Hitler refused to leave Berlin. In fact, he rarely left the 18-room bunker beneath Berlin's Chancellery that had become his home. With him were the commanders who had remained close to him, and his most valued aides.

He slept for no more than three hours at a time, partly as a result of the pounding of the incessant air raids. Incredibly, Hitler still talked of inflicting

Albert Speer, head of war production, wrote a memo to Hitler beginning with the words: 'The war is lost'

defeat on the Allies. The next day he ordered a last-ditch stand against the Russians, bellowing that every last man should be thrown in. When Hitler finally realised there was no hope, he erupted in a volcanic fury, accusing all his closest commanders of cowardice and treachery. For the first time he

Right: US army engineers attempt to put rails across the bridge at Remagen. Four hours after the picture was taken, the bridge collapsed into the Rhine.

Above: Soldiers of the US 9th Army flush out German soldiers in a battle-scarred town over Germany's western border. Meanwhile Russian troops bore down on Berlin from the east.

spoke of killing himself. Still, he refused to abandon the war effort, a stand which cost the lives of countless German soldiers.

Inside the bunker the tension among its occupants reached new heights. Hitler exploded in rage when he heard that his hitherto faithful lieutenants Göring and Himmler were both making advances to the Allies for peace.

On 27 April, Hitler carried out a macabre rehearsal of his suicide and the deaths of the faithful still at his side. However, it wasn't until 29 April that he dictated his will to his secretary. There was no expression of remorse for the misery and death he had caused worldwide, only the same tired tirade against those he held responsible for his misfortunes: 'More than thirty years have now passed since in 1914 I made my modest contribution as a volunteer in the First World War which was forced upon the Reich. In these three decades I have been actuated solely by love and loyalty to my people...

'It is untrue that I, or anyone else in Germany, wanted the war in 1939. It was desired and instigated solely by those international statesmen who were either of Jewish descent or who worked for Jewish interests.'

The last paragraph in Hitler's will read: 'Above all I charge the leaders of the nation and those under them to scrupulous observance of the laws of race and to merciless opposition to the universal poisoner of all peoples, international Jewry.'

HITLER'S END

In the early hours of the same day, Hitler married Eva Braun and had a champagne celebration with Bormann, Goebbels, his secretaries and his cook. Within hours he heard of the death of Mussolini shot with his mistress Clara Petacci and then hung by the ankles in a square in the centre of Milan.

On the afternoon of 30 April, with the Russians just a street away, Hitler said his final farewells, retired to a sitting room with his wife and shot himself. Eva chose to end her life by taking poison.

The instructions he left for the disposal of his body were carried

out, with his remains being burned by petrol fire in the yard of the bunker. His successor as Führer, Grand Admiral Karl Dönitz, Commander in Chief of the German navy, tried negotiating a peace settlement but the Allies wanted unconditional surrender. German resistance capitulated and the surrender was finally signed on 7 May 1945.

BLACK SANDS OF IWO JIMA

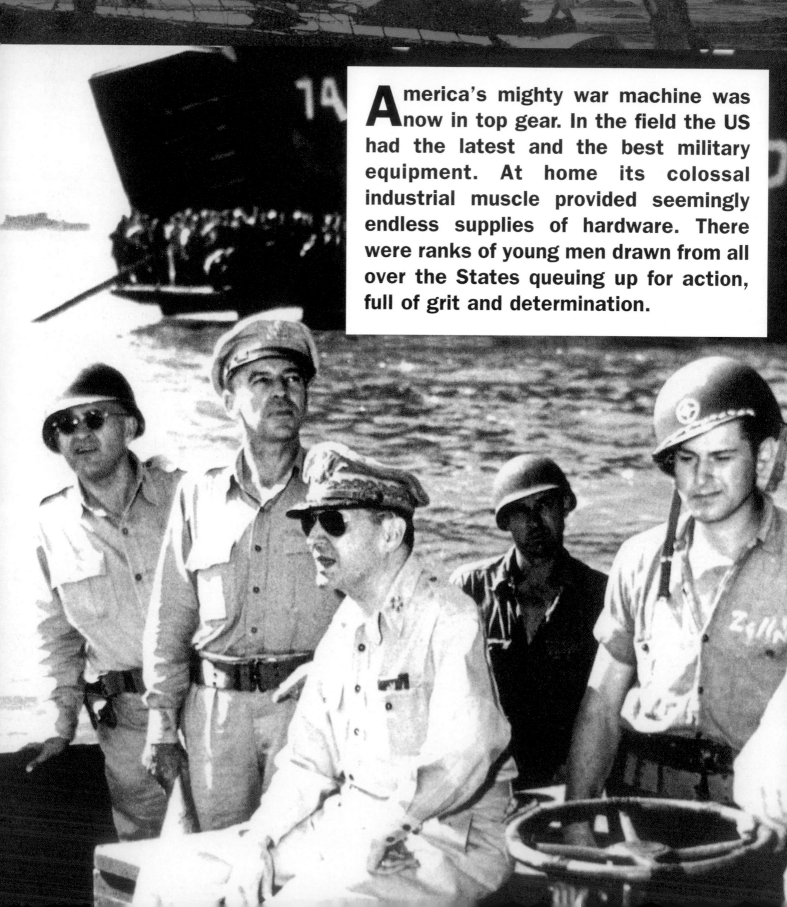

America's mighty war machine was now in top gear. In the field the US had the latest and the best military equipment. At home its colossal industrial muscle provided seemingly endless supplies of hardware. There were ranks of young men drawn from all over the States queuing up for action, full of grit and determination.

In opposition, an over-extended Japan was war-weary. The country's battle losses in ships and planes far outstripped the number of replacements being produced on the home islands. Japan itself was being starved of the materials it desperately needed by the naval blockade imposed by America. Its industry was targeted for devastating air raids. Long-term jungle fighting had taken its toll among the surviving troops, despite their rigorous training.

Against all odds, the Japanese soldiers were determined to hold back the American advance. In-bred in the Emperor's men was an oriental code of honour which dictated that they must fight to the death. In most cases, this is just what they did, costing many Allied lives. The hallmark of the Pacific campaign was pro-longed savage fighting and huge loss of life.

The hallmark of the Pacific campaign was savage fighting and huge loss of life

With a victory established in New Guinea by the start of 1943, Allied Commander of the South West Pacific General Douglas MacArthur was already pondering his route to the Philippines, a campaign dear to his heart. Before he could take it, there

Left: General MacArthur remained determined to push the Japanese out of the Pacific.
Right: An island beach devastated by gunfire becomes a depot for US troops.

Right: Admiral William Halsey, Commander of the 3rd Fleet, sits deep in thought on the bridge of the USS New Jersey *en route for the Philippines.*

was a selection of Japanese strongholds on New Guinea still to be beaten.

Meanwhile, Admiral Halsey, of the South Pacific sector, already had the Russell Islands, Vella Lavella and Bougainville in the Solomon Islands under his belt.

Both MacArthur and Halsey recognised the value of leap-frog-ging many Japanese-held islands and outposts, picking for attack mainly those that were inade-quately defended. The rest were left to 'wither on the vine', increasingly isolated from Japanese lines of communication.

TARAWA

Now nine crucial atolls under Japanese control, collectively known as the Marshall Islands, had to be taken. One of them,

Tarawa, was defended by 5,000 Japanese. When a similar number of US Marines landed on the island on 21 November 1943 they found themselves pinned down on the open beach. Before night had fallen, 500 of the Americans were dead and a further 1,000 wounded. Japanese gun positions were only silenced when their entire crew was killed. Only an additional landing of troops won victory for

the Americans. In all 1,000 Marines died along with virtually all the Japanese.

The Americans learned a valuable lesson. When it came to taking another atoll in the group, Kwajalein, there were no landings until a heavy bombardment neutralised much of the defence.

Fleas, flies, lice and mosquitoes were liable to be carrying appalling disease

Although the American campaign was fast, there was immense hardship for the troops brought about by the conditions. Fleas, flies, lice and mosquitoes plagued them. More than just pests, they were liable to be carrying appalling disease. It wasn't until 1944 that DDT sprays were introduced to combat the insect swarms.

Once an island was taken, it became a top priority to bury the dead on both sides. For the corpses attracted not only flies but also rats, which came in droves.

MARIANAS

Truk, a key naval outpost for the Japanese navy, came under fire on 18 February 1944 in a raid orchestrated by Vice-Admiral Marc Mitscher. There were 30 separate strikes at the base which destroyed 275 aircraft and 39 ships.

Next stop was Saipan in the Mariana Islands, a fearsome task given that 32,000 Japanese soldiers were garrisoned there. Nevertheless, it was a dual disaster for the Japanese. For soon after the American landings on 15 June

EYE WITNESS

Ito Masashi spent 16 years in hiding in the jungle of Guam after it was overrun. He describes his reason for not surrendering in his book *The Emperor's Last Soldiers*.

❝By the start of October the only sound we heard was the shell fire so far off that it sounded like distant thunder. But the fighting continued. The enemy no doubt considered it simply mopping up but for us it was a full-scale and bloody battle.

We had eaten what little there was of our portable battle rations of dried bread and now we lived on what berries and fruits we could find. We kept up a vain defiance with nothing left to help us but our grenades. But now the vital will to fight was absent. Our commanders sent messages advising us to end the senseless resistance, to give up our arms and pack it in. But somehow we didn't. We were afraid to.

Afraid that our useless rifles and guns – marked with the noble crest of the Imperial Chrysanthemum – might fall into enemy hands, we buried them deep in the ground. And we prepared, quite resignedly, for death as the only possible outcome. For us soldiers of Japan, the only thing left to our way of thinking was to deck out our last moment as nobly and bravely as we could.

By now there was no supply base for us to go back to and we didn't know whether there still existed any company or battalion headquarters where we could have got orders. So we formed sad and sorry little squads, hardly alive, now hiding ourselves away in the jungle, now moving aimlessly along the paths and lanes. We had been reduced to the status of a ragged band of stragglers. Even during this period however there were a number of incidents when we tangled with Australian troops backed by tanks or fell foul of a line of pickets. Fortunately, we always managed to get in our grenades and escape. But on every occasion the number of our already small band would dwindle by the odd one or two.❞

came the Battle of the Philippine Sea, in which their Fleet Naval Air Arm was decimated. By July the defenders of Saipan were running short of ammunition. They chose to kill themselves by the score, along with the 22,000 civilians who had been living on the island since before the war, when it was a Japanese dominion. American troops looked on helplessly as women and children joined their menfolk in plunging from high

cliffs to be dashed on the rocks below rather than face the ultimate shame of surrender. Saipan was under US control by 9 July.

The islands of Tinian and Guam were the next to go. Then the Palau group of islands. It didn't take nearly as long to achieve victory here as it had done on Saipan. It frequently included suicidal rushes at secure American positions by shrieking Japanese soldiers, who were duly mowed down in their masses. With fighters refusing to surrender in even the most hopeless of battles, the Americans were forced to use armoured flame-throwers to clear well-protected pockets of resistance.

By October 1944 the Americans were ready to redeem the Philippines. The island of Leyte was their chosen point for invasion, poorly defended by just 16,000 men. While a memorable victory was quickly carved out for the Americans at sea, the land-based struggle for supremacy lasted longer, with the Japanese counter-attacking in December. The losses on both sides were heavy. The Americans mourned 15,500 fighters, while the Japanese suffered the bodyblow of 70,000 deaths. Yet once Leyte was won for the Americans, the rest of the Philippines fell to them with gratifying ease.

At Iwo Jima the US Marines were cut down in droves by the defenders

Now it was time to approach the Japanese home islands. Choosing to by-pass several strongholds, including Formosa, the Americans decided to take the Ryuku Islands, less than 400 miles from Japan itself. A stepping-stone island between the Philippines and the Ryukus was necessary as a rendezvous for American planes. Iwo Jima

Above: US Marines hold their weapons aloft as they wade ashore on the stepping-stone island of Tinian, unsure about what awaits them beyond the beach.

in the Bonin Islands was selected for invasion in February, while an operation to capture Okinawa, the largest of the Ryuku Islands, was time-tabled for April.

At Iwo Jima the US Marines were cut down in droves as they tried to penetrate the complex defensive system constructed by the defenders. Bombardment by battleship prior to the landings had not obliterated the defences as hoped. In fact, the Japanese were so deeply entrenched it had made little noticeable difference.

Amphibious landing transports were beached and blown up and the Marines found themselves without an iota of cover on their route up the beach. There was also little

'FRIENDLY FIRE'

'Friendly fire' took its toll during World War II, particularly during the Normandy campaign.

Bombers had failed to dislodge German gun emplacements before D-Day. This should have acted as a warning against so-called precision bombing. Yet American heavy bombers were called on in July 1944 to target the German lines. Instead, the bombs fell on US troops, killing 25 and wounding 131. The next day, the same mistake was made again, only this time 111 American servicemen were killed and 490 were wounded. Among the dead was US Lieutenant-General Lesley McNair, the highest-ranking Allied officer to be killed in the Normandy campaign.

Three weeks later 'friendly fire' claimed more Allied victims from above. This time 77 Canadians and 72 Polish soldiers died. 'Friendly fire' incidents occurred through poor weather conditions, imprecise briefings, lack of training and sometimes through nervous fingers being on the trigger.

opportunity to remove the wounded from the firing line.

The Japanese commander Lieutenant-General Kurihayashi's order to his men was acidly clear: 'No man must die until he has killed ten of the enemy.' He added that each of his men must think of his defence position as his grave-yard. It was widely considered to be the worst landing the Marines experienced in the war. Iwo Jima finally fell into American hands on 16 March after they had used bulldozers to bury defenders in their bunkers. The tally of dead

Below: Pinned down by mortar fire, marines of the 5th Division inch their way up the slopes of Mount Suribachi, determined to seize Iwo Jima.

among the Americans amounted to 6,821 but yet again there was a far more devastating number for Japan as virtually all the 21,000 troops were killed.

On 1 April the landings by the Marines on Okinawa, as part of 'Operation Iceberg', were in stark contrast to the blood-bathed beaches of Iwo Jima. An estimated 50,000 Americans got ashore barely hearing a shot and for the following five days there was hardly a skirmish. It was a deliberate lull engineered by the Japanese before they unleashed a storm of incredible violence.

The Japanese had drawn up a defence plan code-named 'Ten-Ichigo', which involved

thousands of 'kamikaze' missions. The Japanese commanders were even prepared to sacrifice their prized battleship *Yamato* in a suicidal attack. On 6 April the ship left its base with sufficient fuel for a one-way journey to Okinawa. Its aim was to wreak havoc there among the landing forces.

KAMIKAZE

However, soon picked up on radar, the great warship came under fire from 280 US aircraft until she was finally crippled and sunk on 7 April with her 2,300 crew still aboard.

Meanwhile, swarms of kamikazes were setting about the US Navy as it cruised off Okinawa. On the first day, three destroyers, two ammunition ships and an LST (Landing Ship Tank) were destroyed. It temporarily halted the drive forward, through lack of ammunition. On the next day a battleship, a carrier and two destroyers were hit. Of the 16 destroyers sent forward to give early warning of kamikaze raid, 14 were

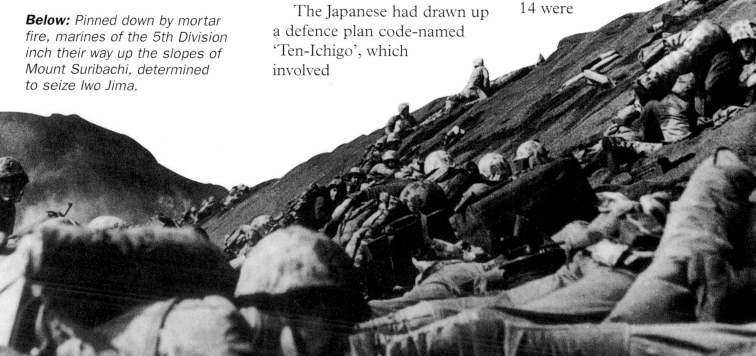

Right: On Okinawa, advancing Americans were forced to use fire power to oust tough Japanese resistance.

of minimal strategic value. The story goes that one destroyer's crew erected a poster complete with arrow bearing the words: 'To Jap Suiciders. Carriers are that way.' And still kamikaze fliers descended on the fleet.

During the battle to secure Okinawa, which raged between April and August, there were an estimated 2,000 kamikaze raids carried out by both army and navy aircraft as well as about 5,000 conventional sorties. In total 20 ships were sunk by kamikazes, against six sunk by other aircraft manoeuvres. Kamikaze planes notched up a further 217 strikes against ships.

Japanese resources were feeling the strain. After two months of sustained kamikaze raids, there were few aircraft left for such missions.

On land the fighting was equally horrific. In one of the early battles, to win the off-island of Ie Shima and its landing strip, more than 4,700 of the 5,000 Japanese defenders died in battle. Towards the end of the eight-day confrontations local women, some with babies strapped to their backs, draped demolition charges around their necks and rushed at American positions.

It took until the last days of June to eradicate the last of the Japanese land-based resistance on Okinawa. American losses amounted to almost 7,000 men as well as numerous ships and 763 planes. The Americans found themselves taking prisoners, some 7,400 in all. 110,000 Japanese died in battle with all the senior officers committing ritual suicide in their offices, and there was carnage among the population. The Japanese stood the loss of 7,800 aircraft.

After two months of sustained kamikaze raids, there were few aircraft left

Hostilites in South East Asia were just as gruesome for the troops involved. Following the Chindit Offensive into Burma the Japanese commander in Burma, General Renya Mutaguchi, decided that attacking the British in India was probably the best form of defence.

On 6 March 1944 the 'U-Go' offensive opened, with three Japanese divisions setting off for Kohima and Imphal, high in the

Left: Billowing smoke marks the path of a kamikaze plane which caused devastation on the USS Bunker Hill, hit off Okinawa on 11 May 1945.

Assam hills. For the first time in the conflict, British troops stood firm against Japanese aggression in defence of India.

KOHIMA

Both Kohima and Imphal were under siege by the first week in April. There followed some of the harshest fighting of the war.

Japanese soldiers were in the majority but the Commonwealth troops were in no mood to be routed this time. The bitterest of the fighting was at Kohima. Japanese soldiers had killed everything in their path until they reached the tennis court of what was once the Deputy Commissioner's bungalow. They dug in on one side while the defenders were holed up just 20 yards away.

Grenades and mortar bombs rained down on Commonwealth forces taking a toll on the troops. However they repelled the frequent Japanese charges with surprising ease. Each one was accompanied by the traditional 'banzai' cry and screaming. The Allies were able to open fire and cut them down. There was little opportunity for the Allies to collect their dead. Bodies lay rotting on the ground, emitting a terrible stench. Sometimes they were buried where they had fallen, in shallow, inadequate graves with arms or knees left exposed. A cloud heavy with the pungent smell of burning flesh hung over the Allied position as the Japanese cremated fallen comrades.

Both sides were exhausted and riddled with disease

Both sides were exhausted and riddled with disease. After 16 days of gruelling fighting the defending regiments were relieved by the 1st Royal Berkshire Regiment.

They left behind 1,419 dead among them 19-year-old Lance

Above: *After a siege by the Japanese, the British 14th Army was finally able to open the Imphal-Kohima road.*

Corporal John Harman who ran up to a Japanese machine gun, shot the crew and hoisted it up on to his shoulders to bring it back behind his own lines.

Further he stormed a bakery held by the Japanese, set it on fire and came back to his dug-out with a wounded Japanese soldier under each arm. It was as he was returning from one of these astonishing feats that he was fatally wounded. He was awarded the Victoria Cross posthumously for his incredible efforts.

Airlifts by the American Air Force and RAF continued to aid the defenders of Kohima and Imphal. The Japanese soldiers had pitiful rations by comparison. It was a staggering 80 days before the Japanese were compelled to withdraw with just a quarter of the original force left on their feet. Over half the casualties were claimed by sickness.

WAR AT SEA

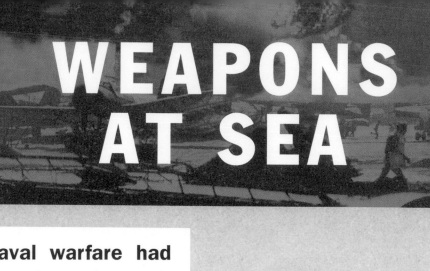

WEAPONS AT SEA

For years naval warfare had remained largely unchanged. It was a case of tactics combining with firepower to achieve the victories sought after by the seafaring nations.

Britain excelled at the art of the sea battle and was proud of her navy traditions. By 1939, however, the rules of the game had changed and, unfortunately, nobody informed the major players.

No longer was it enough to have impressively large ships capable of blasting the enemy vessels out of the water. In fact capital ships were a positive disadvantage as they were large targets which could only move slowly to evade enemy fire. It meant Germany's *Bismarck* and *Tirpitz* ships and Japan's *Yamato* were obsolete when they originally rolled down the slipway in time to see action during World War II. The great hopes that they carried with them were badly misplaced.

The power lay with aircraft and a navy was only as good as its fleet air arm. Britain didn't have a fleet air arm at all as it had been incorporated into the Royal Air Force. Many British naval chiefs refused to believe the age of the big ships had drawn to a close. It took the death of the battleship *Prince of Wales* and battle cruiser *Repulse* off the coast of Malaya in December 1941 at the hands of Japan's skilful fliers to convince them of the fact.

The power lay with aircraft and a navy was only as good as its fleet air arm

Now ships would stay out of reach of enemy guns and send in versatile and effective planes to wreak havoc with opposition navies. As the range of the aircraft increased through the war, the big ships could stay hundreds of miles away from the hub of the fighting.

Britain was, however, better placed regarding the advent of navy planes than Germany. At least the British could call on seven aircraft carriers including the *Ark Royal* and *Illustrious* during the conflict. Hitler, in contrast had only one aircraft carrier in his navy *Graf Zeppelin* which was never completed.

ARMOUR PLATING

The importance of air battles at sea in turn made the bodily defences of each ship key to its survival. Each navy discovered to its cost that only the thickest armour plating was impervious to bombs dropped by planes. Those ships which crumpled easily under fire from above were the first casualties of the conflict.

Left: Mangled wreckage after the surprise Japanese strike at Pearl Harbor, revealing the scale of damage inflicted.
Below: Illustrious *was one of Britain's few aircraft carriers at the outbreak of war.*

At the start of the war Britain had the largest navy in the world – 12 battleships, 3 battle cruisers, 15 heavy and 45 light cruisers, 184 destroyers, 58 submarines and 27 motor torpedo boats. The navy was probably in better shape than the army or the air force but still unprepared for war. At least there was a construction programme that would considerably improve the size of the navy. The largest British ship was *Hood* sunk by *Bismarck* in 1941.

EYE WITNESS

George Miles enlisted in the Australian Army in 1940 when he was 17 years old. He was injured at El Duda in North Africa, and was being ferried to hospital in December 1941 when his ship was blown up in the Mediterranean.

❝There were about 600 people on the Chaktina, mostly wounded although there were some prisoners of war. Only 200 survived, including a German general. Out of 17 members of my battalion, I was among three who lived. We were headed for the 62nd General Hospital in Alexandria. It was night-time when the Italian dive-bombers struck. The sky lit up as if it was day. The ship was blown apart. In the melée you didn't get a chance to worry about anything.

I had a life jacket on. I spent time in a life raft or clinging to the side – it was so crowded that you had to take your turn.

We pushed dying men over the side to let the rest live. It was the following night when we were picked up by a Norwegian corvette.❞

Left: Human torpedoes, nick-named 'pigs', were launched from this tiny hatch on the Italian tanker Olterra.

The largest of the British ships was Hood, sunk by Bismarck in 1941

which consisted of six modern battleships, 19 cruisers, 132 destroyers and torpedo boats and 107 submarines.

In Japan's navy when it entered the war in 1941 the number of aircraft carriers outnumbered the number of battleships by 11 to ten. This accounts for Japan's success on the high seas in the opening months of the war. Also lining up under the emblem of the rising sun were 23 cruisers, 129 destroyers, 67 submarines and 13 gunboats.

Much of the American strength in the area was decimated by the attack on Pearl Harbor. US shipyards laboured to repair the damage wrought by the Japanese planes and refloated many of the sunken vessels. America only had three

On the other hand the German navy was the least favoured branch of Hitler's armed forces. He promised his Admiral Erich Raeder plenty of time to prepare for war in Europe. The conflict arrived about five years too early as far as Raeder was concerned.

He had two battleships *Scharnhorst* and *Gneisenau* in readiness as well as three pocket battleships. In addition there were seven cruisers, 21 destroyers and 12 torpedo boats in the fleet. His strengths lay in U-boats, of which he had 159 and planned many more. He also made good use of auxiliary cruisers or armed raiders as they were better known. Merchant ships in their appearance and war ships in their weaponry, they launched bandit attacks on shipping throughout the world.

Italy had a sizeable navy

operational aircraft carriers in the Pacific, 24 cruisers, nine battleships, 80 destroyers and 56 submarines. The hidden weapon that America possessed was its ability to produce sufficient replacements and reinforcements for its navy throughout the war.

Submarines also came of age during World War II although only Germany and America fully grasped the potential offered by this sleek sinister vessel.

The German U-boats could very well have changed the entire course of World War II if only there had been enough of

The Allies possessed radar which helped them considerably in their war at sea. Pioneering scientist Sir Robert Watson-Watt developed the system and oversaw its use for the benefit of all the British military.

Astonishing advances made in code-breaking offered plenty of new chances to the fleet

Radar detects distant objects by sending out a microwave pulse beam. The reflection of the beam indicates the position of the object.

one-man crew. The bows of the boat were packed with explosives which would fire on impact. It wasn't a suicide vehicle. The courageous pilot escaped by throwing himself backwards with a float before the EMB made contact with its target.

Also among their gadgets was a torpedo submarine measuring about 22ft which was driven by a two-man crew sitting astride the strange weapon. Cast into the water by full-sized submarines the men wearing diving suits guided this timed missile towards its target and attached it to the underside of a

them during the crucial early years. Hitler saw too late the massive opportunity he had passed up by reining in resources due to his navy.

American submarines executed a brilliant strategic move against Japan destroying the vast majority of its merchant shipping and isolating the four home islands from outside trade effectively starving the people and industry of vital goods. Any other country which did not have the shame and dishonour of surrender woven deeply into its culture would have surrendered on the strength of the submarine stranglehold alone.

Its advantage to the Allies was that they would get warning of approaching enemy ships and planes. Bad weather was no longer the cloak to vision it once had been. Action under cover of darkness would now achieve more accurate results.

CODE-BREAKINGS

Also at sea the astonishing advances made in code-breaking offered many new chances to the fleet who were forewarned about enemy movements.

The Italians came up with some ingenious waterborne methods of attack. The first was an Explosive Motor Boat with a

Above: *It took courage and endurance to man the Italian torpedoes which wreaked havoc in the Mediterranean.*

ships hull before making an escape.

The British had their midget submarines, based on an early design, it was 51ft long, eight and a half feet wide and ten feet high. Inside there was enough space for four crew members. a commander, a lieutenant to operate the engine, a navigator and an engineer. The capabilities of the midget submarines were most impressive. They could dive to a depth of 300ft and boasted a speed of four knots.

THE GRAF SPEE AND DUNKIRK

When war was declared, the British people expected an instant torrent of bombs to fall from a sky blackened by enemy aircraft. The wail of the air raid siren sent people scurrying for the bomb shelters clutching their gas masks, fearful of being enveloped in a cloud of poisonous chemicals.

It didn't happen and soon the opening stages of the war were labelled 'the Phoney war' or even 'the Bore War'. The sceptics at home who believed the war would be over once Hitler had his way in Poland had to wait nearly a year to see action over Britain. But at sea it was an entirely different story.

A lone U-boat set the tenor of the sea-farers conflict when the liner *Athenia* sailing out of Glasgow was sunk off Ireland the day after hostilities were officially opened. U-boat captain Fritz-Julius Lemp believed he had an auxiliary cruiser or troopship in his sights. In all, 112 lives were lost including 28 Americans. There was shock at such an atrocity, and it prompted orders to the U-boat commanders, to target only freighters and Navy ships. It was only a matter of months before the tighter rules which governed the U-boats were disregarded once more.

More than 800 sailors died when a U-boat slid into Scapa Flow and destroyed a battleship

The brutal attack on *Athenia* sparked an Allied blockade of Germany in which ships were stopped and searched at the rate of 100 a week. Although the Royal Navy did capture some German ships this way, it caused acrimony between Britain and other neutral countries who resented the intrusive action.

By the end of September 1939, 20 Allied ships had been floored by U-boats, including HMS *Courageous*, lost in the Atlantic with 515 men. Even neutral boats heading to Britain bearing vital supplies were not safe from the prowling German submarines.

MAGNETIC MINES

Britain's mariners fared little better in October. More than 800 sailors died when a U-boat slid into Scapa Flow, the anchorage of the British Fleet 10 miles off the north coast of Scotland, which was thought to be a safe haven, and destroyed a large British battleship. Under the command of Captain Gunther Prien, the submarine manoeuvred through a narrow, unguarded channel leading into the harbour area and dealt a deadly blow to the *Royal Oak*. Claims that the battleship's armour could withstand a torpedo

attack proved to be nothing more than a pipe dream. Just 396 members of the 1200-strong crew survived.

Germany was laying hundreds of mines, with devastating effect.

The Reich had pioneered a deadly magnetic mine which could be dropped by air on to the sea bed, to later rise and attach itself to any passing ship, with deadly consequences. It was far superior to the mines being laid by Britain, designed to defend its shipping.

Fortunately, one of the mystery mines was jettisoned in error on land. Thanks to one courageous naval officer who tackled the explosive, its secret of success became known. The antidote was 'de-gaussing', with an electric cable fitted to ships which neutralised magnetism. The plague of the magnetic mine at least to British ships was quickly overcome.

Above the waves were the determined ships of the Reich's navy equally adept at picking off

Above: *After the Battle of the River Plate the* Graf Spee *limped into Montevideo for repairs. However, it could not escape its predators.*
Left: *U boat Captain Gunther Prien was hailed a hero in his homeland for penetrating Scapa Flow.*

British vessels. Among them was the pocket battleship *Admiral Graf Spee*. By agreement before the war, the Germans were only to build ships up to a certain size. These were tagged pocket battleships, larger than cruisers but smaller and less effective than battleships.

The *Graf Spee* slipped out of port just before war was declared, sidestepped the Royal Navy blockade and headed for the South Atlantic. It was then the pride of the German navy with its high speed and thick protective plating. In the first three months of the war, it had notched up nine British ships, including the liner *Doric Star*.

British commander Commodore H. Harwood guessed that it was only a matter of time before the *Graf Spee* was lured to the River Plate, Uruguay, attracted

Exeter, and two light cruisers, *Ajax* and *Achilles*, one from Britain and one from New Zealand.

CRUISERS DAMAGE

Graf Spee's Captain Hans Langsdorff, believing the heavy cruiser was accompanied only by destroyers, opened fire inflicting serious damage on the *Exeter* and the *Ajax*. The reply from the British· ships crippled his own. With smoke pouring from the German ship, the *Graf Spee* headed for the safety of Montevideo in Uruguay.

Although Uruguay was a neutral country, it supported the Allies. In international law, the *Graf Spee* was only entitled to stay in its capital, Montevideo, for 72 hours and the Uruguayans refused to extend its deadline.

Uruguyan territorial waters, British ships waited for a kill. He believed the mighty *Renown* and *Ark Royal* had joined the pursuit when they were, in fact, hundreds of miles away.

Langsdorff deemed the situation hopeless and asked Berlin for permission to scuttle his ship, rather than have it fall into enemy hands. Consent duly came.

Crowds had gathered on the waterfront eager to witness the great sea battle

On 17 December the *Graf Spee* set off slowly for the middle of the harbour. Crowds had gathered on the waterfront eager to witness the great sea battle that would surely follow. When the majority of the crew had safely disembarked, a huge explosion wrecked her and she sank to the estuary floor.

Langsdorff considered the incident a grave disgrace. Three days afterwards he wrapped himself in the flag of his beloved fatherland and put a bullet through his head.

NEUTRAL NORWAY

Churchill, First Lord of the Admiralty, instantly trumpeted the achievement of his navy even though it was gained by luck and misunderstanding on behalf of the enemy. Yet while Britain celebrated the triumph, it was far from the end of its troubles at sea.

Within a week in January three submarines, HMS *Grenville* and destroyer HMS *Exmouth* were sunk. There was little more by way of encouraging news for

---

EYE WITNESS

Bill Gamble, from Derbyshire, joined up in 1939 when he was 22. The following year, he became one of the thousands of men of the British Expeditionary Force evacuated from Dunkirk.

❛The Germans kept the beach under fire. I had never been under shell fire before. The Luftwaffe planes were strafing the beaches There were rows and rows of fellows waiting to get on a boat. There was no panic because officers were there. They would have shot you if you had panicked.

I have got a vivid memory of the Welsh guards who formed the rear guard action which helped us escape. They were courageous men. I don't think I had properly fired a rifle until then. We didn't have half the equipment we should have had and there had been no training. We were just like civilians in uniform.

I was dead scared. Finally, I got on to a little barge and then on to a destroyer. When the waves came up we had to jump from one to the other. I landed in England on June 2. A few days later that destroyer got blown up. All those brave lads on the ship died.

At least when it came to D-Day, I wasn't bothered about it. By then I was properly trained. I had a job to do and I did it.❜

---

by the British shipping there.

At dawn on 13 December the *Graf Spee* was spotted at the river estuary. Lined up before it were the ships in Harwood's force; the heavy cruiser HMS

It gave Langsdorff time to transfer his injured seamen to a German merchant ship. The most pressing repairs were carried out. But Langsdorff knew that outside the protection of

the British until February when HMS *Cossack* carried out a top secret raid on a German supply ship sheltering in the waters of neutral Norway. Aboard the *Altmark*, concealed in filthy conditions in a hold, were 300 British POW's taken by the *Graf Spee*. Regardless of international regulations which banned such action, the *Altmark* was boarded and the prisoners released. Norway protested about the violation of its neutrality, but the Norwegian authorities had already searched the ship and apparently not found the captives. This persuaded Hitler that Norwegian waters should be under German control if his navy was to get the protection it deserved.

The Royal Navy continued its efforts to contain the U-boat threat and the activities of the German fleet until May 1940 when a task of much greater importance beckoned.

At the start of May, German forces had moved into Belgium. With characteristic speed, the Reich's forces overran Belgium, Holland and northern France. The lightning pace of the attack left everyone gasping for breath, not least the British Expeditionary Force, numbering some 200,000 men, which was sent to France at the outbreak of war to bolster French defences. The British soldiers

The Reich's forces overran Belgium, Holland and northern France

were driven relentlessly back amid some bloody fighting. With them was a section of the French forces, weary and disenchanted with apparently no hope of escape.

Commander of the BEF, General Lord Gort, had quickly realised there was no option but to withdraw his men by sea. The best and shortest route would have been from Calais to Kent, but the French port was almost in the hands of the Germans already. Dunkirk seemed to be the single remaining point from which any kind of meaningful evacuation could take place.

British and French soldiers staggered on to the beach at Dunkirk. All semblance of order was gone after the hasty retreat in which bands of men lost sight of their units. Communication between commanders and their men was cut inland. The soldiers, now acting on initiative, got to Dunkirk as best they could.

The French forces' Commander in Chief, General Gamelin, had been bemused by the German advance. His tanks, evenly spaced down the frontier, were unable to provide a striking action against the rear of the Germans. So while the Panzer armies were tiring and running short of supplies, there was no one to exploit their vulnerability.

Ironically, it was Hitler himself who called a halt to the German march. Concerned that vital tank divisions were at risk if they went into action against the by-now concentrated strength of the Allies on treacherous marshlands and would be unable to complete the invasion of France, Hitler stopped the key Panzer advance. He was made even more anxious by the counter-offensive of sorts that the Allies had managed to stage at Arras.

DUNKIRK

The strategy was perhaps sound. Hitler's decision came on 24 May when a comprehensive rout of the enemy seemed assured. Its unavoidable side effect was to give Allied troops two days' grace without which an evacuation from Dunkirk would surely have been impossible. Historians have subsequently speculated that, had the BEF been lost in northern France, Britain would have sought peace at any price as there would have been no army left to fight with.

As early as 20 May, Admiral Bertram Ramsay, the Flag Officer at Dover, had been gathering a small fleet capable of crossing the English Channel to rescue soldiers. At this stage it was believed just 35,000 men would be saved.

Still more men were straggling on to the beach until the ragged throng numbered 38,000. Many were by now unarmed. There were still rations of sorts, but many soldiers had been without sleep for days. Between periods of calm and order there was panic.

Each hour the shelling grew ever closer. Dunkirk itself was being blown to bits, offering little by way of protection for the British and French forces. There were attacks by the Luftwaffe, too. The low whine of oncoming aircraft followed by the clatter of its guns sent men diving to the ground for cover

'Operation Dynamo', the evacuation at Dunkirk, was officially begun on 26 May 1940

There was a feeling of resentment among many that the Royal Air Force was not doing its bit to aid the plight of the soldiers. In fact, its pilots were going up time and again, helping the rear guard defenders of Dunkirk or hampering the Luftwaffe high above the clouds. But the pilots' role was invisible to the eyes of the stranded soldiers – who were looking for someone to blame for their appalling predicament.

In peacetime Dunkirk had ample harbour facilities from which a major evacuation could have been carried out with ease. Now the town was rubble and the harbour installations in tatters. The only useful jetty left was wooden planking extending a mile into the sea. Yet it was valueless to the big ships for embarkation. Even the mildest wind would have blown the vessel into its concrete foundations causing damage below the waterline. As time went by it became clear that men would have to be taken off the beaches, no matter how cumbersome the task.

Operation Dynamo, the evacuation at Dunkirk, was officially begun shortly before 7pm on 26 May although in fact some support units had already been brought back to Britain. Before midnight fewer than 8,000 men had been brought home.

When the depth of the dilemma facing the bulk of Britain's army became clear, a flotilla of small boats was called upon to assist. Such boats already had to be registered with the government. Now they were recruited for the still-secret operation, with many civilian captains being allowed to stay with their ships.

The British public finally got to hear about 'Operation Dynamo' on 31 May, when about 194,000 British troops had been brought back under the guidance of the Royal Navy. When news about the crisis was broadcast, many more owners of small boats set sail immediately. This was the brave face of Dunkirk that haunts history.

CIVILIAN COURAGE

Their task was no easier than that faced by the Royal Navy. Bombardments by the Luftwaffe continued claiming the lives of servicemen and civilians alike. On 1 June the courage of the civilian boat owners reaped dividends when 64,429 soldiers were rescued. Having ferried their battle-worn cargo to safety, boat owners turned back to face the risks all over again in a bid to haul yet more soldiers to safety. Not least of their worries were the minefields that lay between them and their destination .

By any standards, the rout of the British Army in France by

> ## The courage of the civilian boat owners reaped dividends

Hitler's forces was nothing short of outright defeat. Yet the way in which the cream of the British army slipped through the Führer's grasp and the courage of the evacuation gave an element of heroism to the event, and has ensured it a special place in British military history.

The soldiers who made it back were full of criticism for the army that had sent them to France inadequately armed and supplied. Yet within a few days or weeks, most were posted again, often back to France where remnants of the British contingent were still fighting with the French to keep Hitler out of Paris.

The last Allied boat pulled away from the beaches of Dunkirk on 4 June with the remnants of the 338,000 rescued British and French soldiers aboard. Each man was precious and represented the future fighting force of Britain. Yet behind the retreating force lay its equipment without which no army could fight. Before leaving, the BEF had sabotaged 63,900 vehicles, 289 tanks and 2,472 guns.

EYE WITNESS

Miner Wilf Cowie was 25 when he joined the army and was part of the British Expeditionary Force in France which evacuated from Dunkirk.

'We were in France on the Belgian border for about six months with very little happening, just a bit of bombing and shelling.

When the retreat started, we had to make our way over fields because the Germans were patrolling the roads. The worst thing I ever saw were the refugees streaming out of Belgium pushing prams and carrying beds just machined gunned by German planes. Hundreds of them were killed.

I was one of the last to get out of Dunkirk. It was horrible on the beach. We were lying in bomb craters on the beach, expecting every day to get away. Every day seemed to take forever. Luftwaffe planes were firing at us and then there was the shelling. That was the worst thing of all. The shells screamed as they were going over the top of you and you never knew where they were going to land.

Once I took shelter in a bomb hole with three other lads. I was the only one who came out alive. The others were killed by a machine gun blast from an aeroplane.

There were hundreds of lads killed. We had to go and get the identity discs from the bodies and give them to our superiors. It was a bit upsetting but it was just a job that had to be done. We saw so many young men dead that in the end we didn't worry about it.

I came back in a trawler. It took 36 hours to reach the east coast after the skipper diverted to avoid mines. Several men on the boat died when they were hit by machine gun fire from Luftwaffe planes passing overhead.'

Above: Devastation of the beaches of Dunkirk following the evacuation.

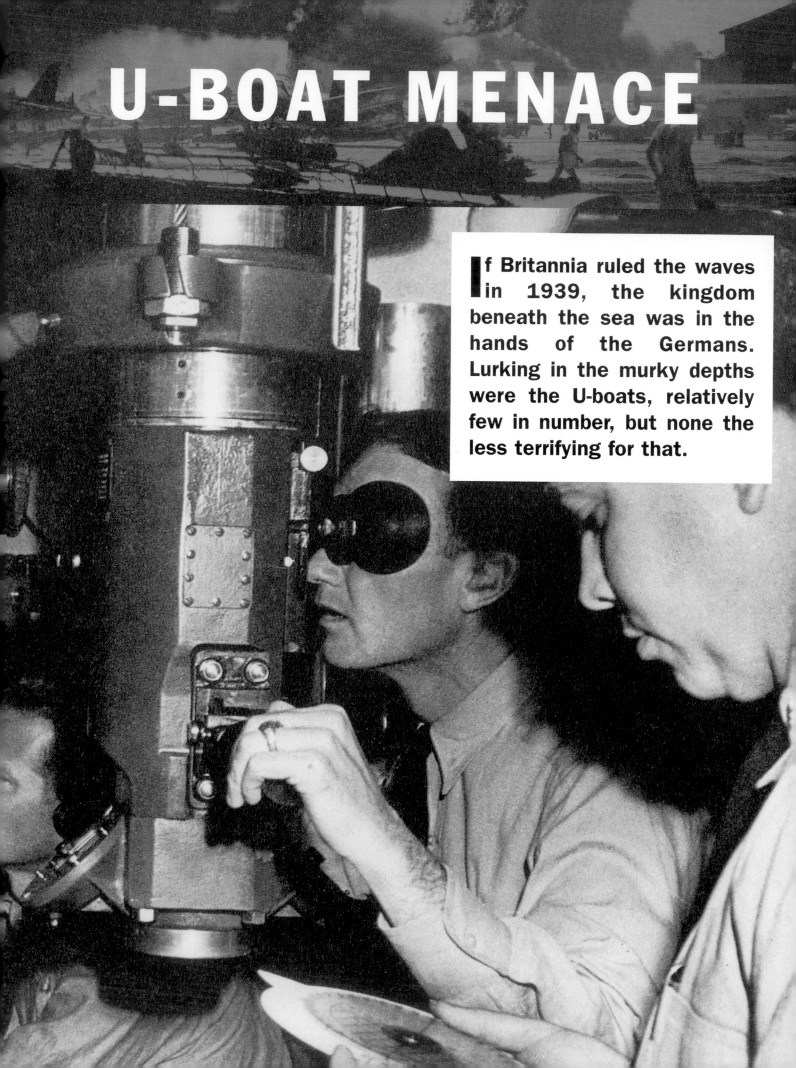

U-BOAT MENACE

If Britannia ruled the waves in 1939, the kingdom beneath the sea was in the hands of the Germans. Lurking in the murky depths were the U-boats, relatively few in number, but none the less terrifying for that.

Just a mention of the name could strike fear into the stout hearts of the English sailors. Winston Churchill confessed later that the U-boat threat in the Battle of the Atlantic was 'the only thing that ever really frightened me during the war'.

For U-boats (Unterseeboot in German) had a habit of creeping up on British shipping and sinking it without warning. At first merchant ships seemed very much like sitting ducks if U-boats were in the area. There appeared to be little opportunity to dilute the threat.

Britain, Canada and America lost thousands of tons of cargo and scores of seamen, to the U-boats. Bitter experience finally taught the Allies effective defences and, later, vital offensive tactics which would ultimately neutralise the stealthy foe.

U-boats soon began to hunt in 'wolf packs', an idea thought

Above: German U-boats came close to their goal of strangling Britain.

Above: Admiral Karl Dönitz knew the potential of his U-boat fleet.
Left: The Allies also had submarines.

up in Germany in the mid-1930s in which a group of submarines orchestrated their attacks on convoys. At first, the concept was thwarted by a lack of boats. Sometimes, in the early stages of the war, there were only a handful of submarines to put to sea, the others being in dock for repairs or in use for training. The lack of air support

By the summer of 1940 there were two 'wolf packs' operating in the Atlantic

from the Luftwaffe to the U-boat service also slightly lessened their menace, since they were compelled to search, sometimes for days, for convoys.

However Raeder, Commander in Chief of the Kriegsmarine was conscious of the golden opportunity that was open to him. While finding it almost impossible to keep more than six U-boats in the sea at a time before February 1941, he devoted much time and energy to rectifying the short-coming. Before the year was out the number of

U-boats in his fleet had been increased tenfold.

By the summer of 1940 there were two wolf packs operating in the Atlantic, preying on the convoys as they supplied troops to Britain from America. Submarine commanders could now pinpoint convoy positions thanks to the German Radio Monitoring Service (B-Dienst). Slung across the Atlantic, the U-boats formed a deadly chain from which the convoys could not escape. The aim was for the boat which first spotted the convoy to shadow it until other submarines could gather for a mass attack. In October, three convoys lost 38 ships to U-boats in the space of just three nights.

U-BOAT TECHNIQUE

The technique used by the U-boats continued to improve. At first, commanders attacked from positions both above and below the waves. Their firepower was far more accurate, however, when the U-boats were on the surface. It became accepted

procedure for the boats to sneak into the centre of a convoy, surface after dark and wreak havoc, disappearing before daybreak when the first of the Allied flight escorts arrived. On the surface, the sleek machines, powered by diesel engines, could outrun larger convoy escort vessels with relative ease.

> ## On the surface, the sleek machines could outrun larger convoy escort vessels

There followed a 'happy time', as it was known among German submariners, in which dozens of merchant ships were sent to the bottom. They were picking off targets with ease and convoy escorts were floundering with exasperation, not knowing how to halt the rising casualty toll. In 1940, U-boats accounted for more than 1,000 ships while just 16 U-boats were knocked out. The following year

Right: Sailors keeping watch from a surfaced submarine got a drenching.

followed a similar pattern with 24 U-boats being sunk.

AMPLE WARNING

Had there been a greater number of U-boats operating at that time, Britain would have been in grave danger of being throttled. Hitler was delighted with the success of the U-boats. Always sceptical of the power of his naval fleet, he became a convert and lavished his favours on the U-boat arm. If he had devoted more resources to them in 1939 instead of waiting until 1941, the outcome of the war might have been very different. By the

Above: One U-boat torpedo was enough to break a ship's back.

time his confidence was raised in the potential of the U-boats, it was just one of many services forced to get in line for the available resources.

As it was, technology came to the rescue for the Allies. Britain finally cracked the German radio code signals. Now operators could give ample warning to the convoys as to the whereabouts of the U-boats. Ships began to successfully bypass the waiting packs which were now forced to

stretch out over huge distances, diminishing their effect.

Although the sinking of the liner *Athenia* at the beginning of the war did serve to tighten up the rules of engagement which governed U-boats, these were soon relaxed, in part because it was difficult for submariners to

Operators could give ample warning as to the whereabouts of the U-boats

abide by such rules without putting themselves into considerable danger. Stipulations like the one laid down in the 1935 London Submarine Agreement that submarines must stop intended victims and order the crew into lifeboats before opening fire were soon forgotten. The hunter quickly became the hunted if he lingered too long trying to establish the identity and purpose of a ship. In the Atlantic neutral, shipping was also at risk from German U-boats. Some vessels flying the flags of unaligned

Below: *In 1942 the remains of a convoy approach beseiged Malta.*

EYE WITNESS

The following personal account of life aboard a patrolling British submarine in the Mediterranean appeared in the *Daily Express* in June 1942.

❝The captain is wearing shorts with a sweater handy in case it is chilly. His favourite dress while submerged in action is a towel wrapped around his loins.

The crew are wearing overalls, shorts, shirts, vests – anything they fancy. There are no badges of rank and it is impossible to tell the captain from the cook.

Life goes on quietly, almost dully, for some days while the submarine continues towards her patrol station. There are only seven gramophone records, some of them scratched and indistinct through constant wear. The captain tells the first lieutenant he will brain the first rating to play *Frankie and Johnnie were lovers* – he swears he has heard it 3,000 times.

At midday the next day the captain is resting in his cabin. The first lieutenant is at the periscope. He swings it, sees smoke on the horizon. Without ceasing to look he says: "Captain, in the control room". The murmur is taken up and goes around the boat. Within a matter of seconds the captain is at the periscope clothed in his towel. He looks and says: "There is smoke on the horizon – a couple of masts."

Then the orders come fast. "Diving stations, full speed ahead together, starboard 25, steer 320." The hum of the motors can be heard through the otherwise silent submarine.

There are three merchant ships escorted by six Italian destroyers. The captain grabs his slipping towel as he snaps the range – 8,000 yards.

Excitement in the submarine is terrific and suppressed. Nobody speaks except the captain. At times the silence is so intense that a movement by a rating sounds like thunder.

As the torpedoes jump from the tubes the submarine shudders a bit. The captain's towel falls off. Nearby ratings chuckle at naked authority.

Stop watches have already started to mark the time the torpedoes take to reach the target. The captain's: "I'll have a cup of tea, please," is hardly necessary. The electric stove was switched on some minutes before. It is a ritual. Everybody in the service knows that you must have a cup of tea before the depth charging begins.

In 55 seconds the explosion which means the target has been hit rocks the submarine. The captain sits on the engine-room artificer's tool box, sipping his tea. Then the first depth charge arrives.

The captain's cup leaps off the tool chest. The submarine vibrates with the clangour of charges exploding nearby.

For two hours the racket of the depth charges goes on. The men behave as if they were on tiptoe. Barely a word is spoken. As the noise of the depth charges dies away the submarine creeps to periscope depth. The captain sees three destroyers picking up survivors from the sunken merchantmen.

One of the ratings off duty has already got hold of the "Jolly Roger" skull and cross bones flag of the submarine service and is preparing to stitch another chevron to the other battle honours. They will fly it when they get back from patrol.❞

countries were hit by accident. Others, suspected of aiding the British, were rammed or torpedoed on purpose.

In November 1939 neutral countries were warned by Germany that their ships could not be guaranteed a safe passage in waters around the British Isles. Meanwhile, secret instructions to U-boat commanders gave them the go-ahead to sink tankers and other key commercial ships approaching Britain unless they were identified as Russian, Japanese, Italian, Spanish, Greek or American. To cover their tracks, the U-boat commanders were told to use only electric torpedoes which did not leave a tell-tale wake in the water. This meant the explosion could be blamed on an engine fault or a mine.

It wasn't only in the Atlantic that the U-boats plied their deadly trade. Six were broken into pieces and transported by road to Linz in Austria where

the water was deep enough for re-assembly and were then launched into the Black Sea. The first to go into action there took to the water on 28 October 1940.

It wasn't only in the Atlantic that the U-boats plied their deadly trade

Operation in the Mediterranean was difficult for the U-boats – which were known by numbers rather than names – as their dark forms could be quickly spotted in the shallow, clear water by aircraft above or nearby ships. Also, the fast flowing eastern currents assisted the U-boats as they sailed into the warm seas but thwarted their exit.

Nevertheless, it was there that the U81 sank HMS *Ark Royal* on 13 November 1941, one of the prestige ships of the Royal Navy.

Above: *Relief as a German U-boat and its crew return safely to port after a long spell on patrol.*

Far easier was the task of the U-boats in the waters off America and Canada. Until Japan's attack on Pearl Harbor and Germany's subsequent declaration of war on America, Hitler had ordered that any ship bearing the stars and stripes standard be allowed freedom of the waters. There had been sinkings of US vessels before December 1941, but presumably these were in error.

When America and Germany were eventually pitted against each other, the U-boats seized the opportunity for yet another 'happy time'. U-boat commander in chief Karl Dönitz, the man who was later to take over from Hitler as Führer of Germany, knew his forces had to pounce before America became wise to the threat.

Five of the largest submarines, called Type IX boats,

EYE WITNESS

Stoker Fernand 'Pedro' Guinard, 69, from Halifax, Nova Scotia, served on several Canadian warships including HMCS *St. Laurent*.

‘My first contact with the enemy came early in the war when we picked up 27 survivors from the German submarine U31. We were four days out of Newfoundland.

A lot of these guys were Czechs and Poles. They told me they'd been offered the chance to fight in the navy or go work in a slave camp. You couldn't really blame them for joining up. I got quite close to them because I had to detail them to hand pump the bilges.

Even that got me into trouble. When we docked and disembarked the POWs, two of the Germans came over to shake hands and say goodbye. That didn't go down well with the officers. I got warned in no uncertain terms not to fraternise with the prisoners.

We only killed one submarine in my first three years of service. But we saw plenty of attacks on our convoys. I remember one time when a wolf pack began torpedoing our boats at sunset. It was so sad to see these ships going down. There were people in the water everywhere but to be honest we didn't give a bag about them. There were guys in a life raft obviously looking for help and we just rode straight through them throwing out depth charges. All we cared about was getting the submarine.

Was I scared? I didn't have much time to be scared. I was part of a team and you just got on with your job.’

were dispatched from the Mediterranean to commence operations in North American coastal waters in 'Operation Paukenschlag'.

EASY TARGETS

Americans living along the eastern seaboard had so far been virtually untouched by the war. There were no blackouts, built-in defences, or restrictions on radio use. Even navigation lights remained helpfully in place. Not only did the U-boats have easy targets but, after the 'kill', the pursuing submarine hunters were inexperienced and ill-prepared. There was little to stop the U-boats getting clean away. In 'Operation Paukenschlag', each boat averaged almost six 'kills' before returning to home waters. Some of the boats sunk were those who had traversed the Atlantic in a convoy to pick up a cargo only to be sunk, as the British saw it, through a reckless lack of defence on behalf of the Americans.

A further wave of 12 smaller boats did their utmost to match the grand total but, thankfully for the Americans, fell short of the target. Within a few months, America began using convoy systems in its home waters and mimicked the successful British methods of hunting U-boats.

The tentacles of the U-boat campaign also spread into the southern oceans. There were plenty of ships carrying essential goods which were poorly equipped to deal with U-boat attack. In addition, it further stretched the Royal Navy ships

Within a few months, America began using convoy systems in its home waters

Below: *Living conditions on a U-boat were cramped and uncomfortable, with restricted fresh food and air.*

charged with hunting for submarines.

Not all of the 1,300 U-boats put to sea by Germany during World War II saw action. Some U-boats were used for training, others for supplying the roving hunters. Still more U-boats

U-boat men got about double the rates of pay awarded to other sailors

were employed carrying goods from the Far East to the Fatherland.

Men who served in the U-boat arm of the Kriegsmarine (German Navy) were considered the elite by their countrymen – although they were loathed and detested by the British. There can be little doubt that they had strong nerves and plenty of courage. Some were volunteers, attracted by the excitement the service

appeared to offer. This was perpetuated by the public accolades which were awarded to U-boat aces like Gunther Prien and Joachim Schepke. U-boat men also got about double the rates of pay awarded to other sailors. Other men who found themselves serving on the U-boats were naval recruits who had been drafted.

Above: A U-boat in harbour is loaded with supplies before embarking on another lengthy ship-bagging voyage.

The day-to-day life for those who had to live on board a U-boat was far from glamorous. Conditions were cramped. There was a curtained-off cabin for the captain but there were not enough beds for every member of the crew. Some men slept in hammocks, while others slept on the floor.

LIFE EXPECTANCY

Until hostilities started with America, the U-boat commanders had little idea of the distances their crafts were able to travel. They were pleasantly surprised to find they could cruise far further than they ever thought possible if they conserved fuel by keeping to reasonable speeds and travelled on the surface.

More supplies were needed on a long voyage. However. They took up valuable living accommodation, leaving the crew of about 50 even fewer comforts.

MASCOTS

Animals featured as mascots to the branches of army, navy and air force throughout the war. On HMS *Duke of York*, the ship's tabby cat was Whiskey who became famous for sleeping soundly through the battle which sunk the *Scharnhorst*. A cat called Susan made herself at home on a Royal Navy tank landing craft and even attended the D-Day invasion. A St Bernard by the name of Bamse was the mascot of the Norwegian fighting ship *Thorod*. He assured himself a place in the heart of his crew by rounding them up from shore leave by visiting their favourite bars and clubs – even boarding a bus to patrol the more far-reaching destinations.

One of the more unusual mascots of the war was a Syrian bear by the name of Voytek, adopted as a cub by the Second Polish Transport Company in Persia. He was thought of as human by his soldier pals who watched distressed as he cried like a child when his carer, Lance Corporal Peter Prendys, disappeared from sight. His love of water led to the shower room having to be locked to prevent him from exhausting the water supply. When he discovered an Arab spy, he was acclaimed a hero and allowed a morning's free play in the bath.

It was as a hero he was greeted in Scotland at the end of the war where he served the army until 1947 when his owner was demobbed. It was then he was handed over to Edinburgh Zoo where he had to get used to a new life behind bars.

Water was rationed and the opportunities for washing were very few. The atmosphere was squalid, sweaty and unpleasant.

Early models were very spartan. There was inadequate heating aboard. So men soaked from taking their turn on the watch when the boat was on the surface found themselves unable to dry their sodden clothes. Men wore layers of jumpers and still felt chilled.

Above: A U-boat is armed with a giant torpedo before a trip.
Left: Sailors stood little chance when a U-boat was blown up.

When the most primitive U-boats were forced to submerge, the men had to wear breathing masks to prevent poisoning by carbon dioxide. Later, more sophisticated air purifiers were built into the wall of the ships, so masks became obsolete.

Voyages lasted for months at a time and there was little chance

The greatest shadow over a U-boat crewman was his brief life expectancy

to breath fresh air. U-boat men operating in the darkened Arctic region during the winter months were known to queue up patiently for a glimpse of sunlight.

Perhaps the greatest shadow over the life of a U-boat crewman, though, was his brief life expectancy.

During the first two years of war, their existence was perilous

Left: *Depth charges were one antidote to roaming U-boats.*

became more impotent which prompted the desperate Dönitz, by now Admiral of the entire Kriegsmarine, to order a kamikaze-style attack by them following D-Day.

RECKLESS ATTACK

On 11 June 1944 he issued an order which read: 'The Invasion Fleet is to be attacked with complete recklessness. Every enemy vessel that aids the landing, even if it puts no more than half a hundred men or a tank ashore, is a target calling for all-out effort from the U-boat.

'It is to be attacked even at the risk of losing one's boat. When it is necessary to get to grips with the enemy landing fleet, there is no question of any regard to danger through shallow water or possible minefields.'

Even with the benefit of hindsight it is difficult to discern whether the U-boat captains, carried out assaults and were

due entirely to the shortcomings in their torpedo systems. Then, when they bore the brunt of Allied air and sea power, U-boats became an endangered species. Apart from torpedoes and mines, the only weapon the

German sailors grew into the habit of calling their craft 'iron coffins'

U-boats could use against their enemies was an undersized machine gun. German sailors grew into the habit of calling their craft 'iron coffins'.

After attacking, there are examples of U-boat captains displaying concern for their victims, passing on food and water and radioing their position so help could be sent. Survivors were never allowed on board, however.

Equally, there were stories of men from sunken ships being machine-gunned to death by callous U-boat captains as they lay helpless in the water. While that may have occurred, there is the strong possibility such stories were used for propaganda

purposes by a Ministry of Information which depicted U-boat captains as callous, dedicated Nazis.

The most successful U-boat was U48, which came into service in April 1939 and sank a record 59 ships before being sunk itself in October 1943. Many of the submarines sunk five or fewer ships, many making no hits at all before they were sent to the ocean bed.

The U-boat force gradually

ORAN DILEMMA

In one of the most controversial moves of the war, Churchill turned British guns against former ally France a little more than a week after the French armistice with Germany was signed.

A British squadron led by Vice Admiral James Somerville encircled the pride of the French fleet harboured in the Algerian port of Oran on 3 July 1940 as part of 'Operation Catapult' and issued an ultimatum to the ships sheltering there to sail for Britain or America. When the order was refused, the mighty force of British ships including the ill-fated battle cruiser *Hood* opened fire.

Prestige ships, among them the *Provence*, *Bretagne* and *Dunkerque* were sunk or badly damaged and 1,300 French sailors were killed. The aim was to prevent the ships falling into German hands but it caused a major outcry in France and among French-speaking nations around the world.

Churchill said he regretted the loss of life but insisted the action was necessary. 'I leave the judgement of our actions with confidence to Parliament. I leave it to the nation and I leave it to the United States. I leave it to the world and to history.'

The French ships in British ports were confiscated with barely one shot being fired.

defeated or if indeed the U-boat force was already so depleted and poorly supplied that they were unable to take any meaningful action. Certainly, there is little evidence of U-boat activity in the Channel following D-Day.

Despite the Allied successes in combatting the U-boat menace, the Nazi hierarchy continued to pin great hopes on the success of a renewed campaign. Hitler, keeping faith with the U-boat service, was convinced the newest model designed by Germany was a war-winner. In his diaries, dated 6 March 1945, his aide Goebbels reflected those optimistic opinions. With the Allies crossing the borders of Germany into the Fatherland, he wrote: 'There is considerable hope for us here. Our U-boats

Above: *U-boat construction sites became priority targets for Allied air forces.*

must get to work hard; above all it may be anticipated that as the new type gets into action, far greater results should be achieved than with our old U-boats...' Later, on 28 March, barely a month before the collapse of Hitler's Germany, he noted the Allied bombing campaign against the new submarines in dock at Bremen and penned with satisfaction: 'Clearly the revival of our U-boat war has made a great impression on the war.'

Below: *Another convoy ship falls victim to U-boats, Hitler's underused war weapon.*

BATTLE OF THE ATLANTIC

During World War II, German U-boats almost succeeded in severing the supply routes from America and Canada to Britain. Without shiploads of goods, including fuel, from overseas the prospects for Britain were dim.

Unable to support herself, Britain had for years relied on trade to keep her people fed, clothed and employed. If those vital links were cut during conflict, Britain would have been forced to capitulate or see her population starve. Now in World War II the grim scenario was being played out once more. U-boats, in tandem with the German Navy or Kriegsmarine, were set to exploit the Achilles heel of the British Empire. They nearly succeeded.

Both Britain and Germany's navies had been unprepared for war. Navy chief Erich Raeder had far fewer U-boats at his disposal than he would have liked. In addition, the submarine construction programme was almost at a halt. Hitler had little faith in his navy and earmarked only limited resources for it.

Meanwhile, Britain had a mighty fleet of Royal Navy vessels and numerous merchant ships. But the Admiralty appeared to have devoted little time or effort in the years between the wars in looking at ways to counter the U-boat threat. It still believed in the outdated notion that wars could be won with offensive action by battleships.

Putting their lives on the line alongside sailors in the Royal Navy were volunteer merchant seamen. It was their job to ferry the all-important supplies to Britain, mostly from America and Canada across the Atlantic. Instantly, they became targets for the roaming U-boats. Their pay was £9 a month with an additional two shillings and sixpence in danger money.

The major threat in the Atlantic was always from U-boats

Immediately, the convoy system when merchant ships banded together and travelled under armed escort was in use once again, as it had been with marked success in World War I. There were some drawbacks, however, which made shortages more acute on the homefront. For example, it took valuable time for a convoy to be assembled and some ships were compelled to travel by a longer route than they otherwise would have done. Speedier ships were impeded by

Left: *Freezing weather in the Atlantic had the crew thawing out anchor chains.*
Below: *U-boats on far-flung missions were dependent on supply ships.*

the pace of slower vessels. Also, dockyards became hopelessly congested when a glut of ships arrived all at once.

ESCORT SHIPS

Nevertheless, the accompanying Royal Navy ships at least offered some protection to the merchant fleet. At first, however, the short range of the accompanying ships meant that escorts could only be offered for some 200 miles out of Britain. The convoy was then on its own until it met with a reciprocal Canadian escort a few hundred miles from the other side. It offered a mid-Atlantic gap which was ideal for hunter U-boats.

Even the proximity of the armed destroyers at the outset and close of the voyages proved little deterrent to the U-boats in the opening years of World War II. The major threat in the Atlantic was always from U-boats and sometimes from merchant ships fitted out with weaponry, known as armed raiders.

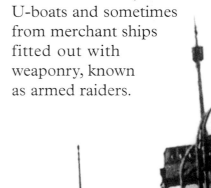

Hitler was unwilling to risk his capital ships in the open sea after the *Bismarck* disaster. Lacking any aircraft carriers, the Germans were unable to launch air bombardments out of range of their airfields.

By the close of 1940, more than 4,700,000 tons of British shipping was lost

If they operated at night, the U-boats often went unnoticed by the escort ships even on the surface. Low in the water and much smaller than a surface ship, the most vigilant watch could be forgiven for letting the streamlined craft slip by.

The only technology available to counter the threat from U-boats was Asdic, a sonar device which sent out underwater impulses that could, by the sound of the echoes, indicate the presence of solid objects. Not only was it almost useless at speed or against surface objects, but early models were also unable to produce an accurate range and operators were very inexperienced.

In a bid to flush out U-boats during the early months of the war, Royal Navy warships attempted sweeps of convoy routes. The U-boats would simply dive and wait for the danger to pass. Even if their presence was detected, there was every chance the depth charge dropped by a pursuing vessel would fall short of its intended mark.

As the war progressed, Germany eased the way for its U-boat captains in their task of sinking trans-Atlantic shipping by providing new ports from which they could operate. The fall of Norway and France offered plenty of fresh and friendly harbours for repairs and restocking. In port, the U-boats were housed in specially built bunkers with two metre thick walls. That meant that although the docks came under heavy fire during Allied bombing raids the U-boats remained safe. It wasn't until 1944 that the Allies found sufficient fire power to shatter these solid defences.

By the close of 1940, more than 4,700,000 tons of British shipping had been lost in the form of 1,281 vessels, about one fifth of the pre-war merchant fleet.

EYE WITNESS

Dennis Bell, 67, of Waterlooville, Hampshire, was one of the youngest seamen to sail with the D-Day invasion fleet. At 16 he was a galley boy in the merchant navy, serving aboard the converted troop ship *Liberation of Europe*. His pay was £2 per week, including £1 3s 4d 'war risk money'.

❛ I spent the early months of 1944 chugging along the south coast to drop off soldiers for secret beach-storming exercises. Looking back, I was incredibly naïve about the whole business of war. I was only a kid and I knew nothing. I used to think I'd be all right because I was wearing my lifejacket.

By D-Day I'd already had a taste of the Atlantic War. At 15 I was galley boy aboard a crude carrier called the *Robert F. Hind*, bringing oil from the States to Britain and North Africa. Nobody would ever tell me what was going on – they would just shout at me to get back to the galley and work.

I soon cottoned on to the fact that none of the escort ships wanted to come too close to us. Obviously a tanker was a nice juicy target for the U-boats and if we'd gone up in flames we'd have lit up the sky. ❜

Left: Crewmen on board an escort warship observe the progress of a southbound convoy.

Above: Always alert, seamen knew the threat of attack was never far away. *Right:* Germany housed her precious U-boats in sturdy concrete bunkers.

In May 1941, the first convoy to receive protection for the entirety of its voyage set sail. It was an important first step towards victory in the Battle of the Atlantic.

Soon after came the introduction of radar, still far from foolproof but a huge boon to the navy ships charged with

Now, at last, aircraft could be brought to bear against the undersea menace

spotting predators. Radar also aided Coastal Command aircraft as to the whereabouts of U-boats. Now, at last, aircraft could be brought to bear against the undersea menace and the planes posted to coastal duties appeared to be reaping a reward. Britain's Admiralty, without a fleet air arm, was constantly battling to keep those few planes in place when many in the RAF and the war office thought they would be better employed bombing land-based targets in Europe. It took several years for the Germans in command to become fully aware of the danger posed by radar to its U-boats.

Also, the British cashed in on a fatal flaw of the wolf pack system used by U-boats, in which a handful of craft operated together during a convoy attack. To alert nearby boats to the presence of a convoy, the German commanders had to use their radios. The prospect of the British being able to track the signals was dismissed out of hand by the Germans for months. But that is just what did happen when the High Frequency Direction Finder was pioneered, affectionately known as 'Huff-duff'. When the U-boat position was fixed by

the radio operators, it gave Royal Navy vessels far greater scope in their attack.

Convoy defences were reorganised so that extra escort boats could loiter over submerged submarines for up to two days, waiting for the craft to surface for air. Then it was an

1941 proved to be a key year for the Allies in their fight against the U-boats

easy target. Other vessels manoeuvred themselves around the precious convoy ships to fill the gap left by the lingering vessel for fear that another U-boat would make merry in the unexpected opening.

In the British armoury, too, was the increasing ability of the decoders to pinpoint the position of U-boats. At the start of the war, the translation of the messages sent between the German admiralty and its ships was slow and provided only retrospective information. With practice, the 'tapping' system speeded up, providing accurate and detailed assistance for convoys and British ships on the whereabouts of the enemy. While the German commanders suspected a breach in security, they never identified where the leak was.

So 1941 proved to be a key year for the Allies in their fight against the U-boats. Although 432 ships were sunk, the total was less than in the previous year. The

Above: *A US destroyer pulls alongside HMS Norfolk to refuel mid-voyage.*

U-boat arm lost 35 of its craft.

When the U-boats turned their attentions to the pickings off America in early 1942, the pressure on the Atlantic convoys eased. But when the U-boats returned to Atlantic waters, it was with a vengeance.

AIRCRAFT ATTACKS

At last U-boat manufacture was approaching the levels hoped for by Dönitz. Every month, 20 new U-boats left the ship yards. The boost for the Kriegsmarine was bad news for British sailors in the Atlantic who found themselves once more at the heart of a fierce battle for survival.

EYE WITNESS

Forbes Brown, from Victoria, British Columbia, joined the Royal Canadian Navy in 1941, training as an Asdic operator.

❛Being a Canadian ship, we didn't drink much tea. When we were docked in Londonderry, my pal Bob took me to see 'Black Dan'. He sold 'Black Dan' an enormous box of tea for £1. Bob took the money and later that night tied the box of tea to a rope and lowered it down the side of the ship to the dockside where Dan was waiting.

When I next went ashore, Bob asked me to find 'Black Dan' and offer him a bag of sugar for £1. When Dan came to collect the sugar he tasted it before handing over the money to Bob and making off.

Two nights later I was on gang plank duty when Bob was brought back with a great gash in his head. He had concussion and was severely bruised up. I went to see him later on.

He confessed there was only a fraction of sugar in the bag he had sold 'Black Dan'. The rest was salt, dirt cheap even then. I never went back to see 'Black Dan' again after that and neither did Bob.❜

Although the extended air patrols aided the safety of the ships and significantly improved the rate at which U-boats were knocked out, it was still a fearful fight to the death. U-boats began to attack once more during daylight hours, a sign of their boosted confidence.

During the two months of August and September U-boats – helped by the German advances in cracking British codes – found 21 convoys and sank 43 ships. By the end of 1942, Allied tonnage totalling 7,500,000 had been sunk, more than the combined totals for the three previous years of war.

Allied aircraft stepped up the number of attacks against

Above: When a convoy put to sea, the Atlantic throbbed with activity.

Below: A cargo ship is lost amid smoke following an air attack.

U-boats during 1943 after the long-awaited allocation of more long-range aircraft. Between March 1943 and the end of the

Between March 1943 and the end of the war, air attack accounted for 290 U-boats

war, air attack accounted for 290 U-boats alone. A surface U-boat could offer little by way of defence to an aircraft as its guns were so small as to be useless.

Suddenly, the campaign against U-boats was accelerating. That spring eight U-boats were lost in the battle to protect one convoy. During May alone 41 U-boats were sent to the bottom of the ocean, causing a concerned Dönitz to pull the ranks of remaining U-boats out of

The importance of the Battle of the Atlantic suddenly loomed large for Hitler

the Atlantic for a few months. Still, he failed to question the security of his cipher system.

The importance of the Battle of the Atlantic suddenly loomed large for Hitler, who had previously been wholly absorbed in his bid to conquer Russia.

In January 1943 Admiral Raeder was replaced as the Commander in Chief of the

EYE WITNESS

Swedish-born Nels Olson, 72, from Chicago, USA, was a gunner in the US Navy Armed Guard, responsible for manning 5-inch guns on Atlantic convoy merchant ships.

'There were 1800 of us in the Armed Guard and they split us up to around 25 per ship. I signed up in December 1942 and was assigned to the Alcobanner, built during World War I. Later I moved on to Liberty ships. The US built 2,700 of these during the war and it was just as well because the Germans sank so many. I guess we lost nearly 800 in the first eight months.

The Armed Guard took heavier losses than any other US naval unit. Merchant ships were a prime target because there was so little with which to defend them. We knew it was bad when we volunteered. They only took volunteers. No one was ordered to do it.

When the German submarines got in among a convoy it was a terrible sight. They always attacked at night and there was always pandemonium. I remember watching an oil tanker explode. It lit up the skies for miles around. And we had no target to fire back at.'

Kriegsmarine by Dönitz. Hitler saw Dönitz with new eyes after the impressive successes of the U-boat war. Now Dönitz found it impossible to achieve similar standards.

U-boat production was still

relatively healthy, despite an increasing shortage of manpower in the dockyards. However, the lack of crews was becoming a dilemma for Dönitz who was compelled to send barely trained men into action despite the fact he believed the success of the U-boats lay at least in part with a rigorous training for the men aboard.

LIBERTY SHIPS

The Allies, meanwhile, had the bonus of Liberty ships – US built craft which went to replace the mercantile fleet decimated by U-boat action. By July 1943,

Left: Young, fit men were always needed for the fight against the U-boats.

"SUB SPOTTED – LET 'EM HAVE IT!"

LEND A HAND – Enlist in your Navy today

the number of new ships coming out of the American yards was greater in total than the amount being lost.

With losses being so severe, the pack formation was abandoned in the autumn of 1943 and U-boats returned to the Atlantic hunting alone, cutting their effectiveness

In looking at the Battle of the Atlantic, it is vital to remember the contribution made by Britain's own submarines. During the war they sank 15 U-boats. Only three British submarines were sent to the bottom by U-boats. Submarines were never sighted by their own kind until they were at very close range. For a successful attack to be pressed home, the two could be no more than half a mile apart. The first U-boat fell victim to HMS *Salmon* as early as December 1939.

COST OF CONFLICT

In the last four months of 1943, the U-boats succeeded in sinking 67 ships at a cost of 64 U-boats.

Above: *A convoy reaches port, thanks this time to the Royal Canadian Navy.*

Clearly, the Battle of the Atlantic was lost by the Germans although it would be months before shipping in the Atlantic was completely safe from U-boat attack.

At the end of the war, it became clear that the conflicts at sea – chiefly the Battle of the Atlantic – had been costly for both sides. During the war, the Allies lost 5,150 merchant ships, 2,828 of them to U-boats. The number of merchant seamen whose lives were lost amounted to 50,000. The U-boat tally also included 148 Allied warships.

As for the U-boat arm, 785 of its 1,131 strong fleet were lost, costing the lives of at least 27,491 crew and officers. Approximately 5,000 were taken prisoners of war.

EYE WITNESS

J. H. Blonk, from Eindhoven, Holland, was blinded in one eye in 1941 when he was serving as an engineer on the cargo ship *de Friesland* which was hit off the English coast.

❝We knew that if we were hit, we were on our own – the other ships would not and were not allowed to turn back otherwise they would be easy targets. The ship sank so fast that we didn't even manage to get a float from the deck.

I can still remember how the wireless operator who I shared a cabin with was standing beside me. Then the water came and I never saw him again, I just felt his hand on my leg.

I was in the water for four hours. I held on to a panel from the deck that had gone overboard. An English communications officer was holding on to the other side. After an hour or so he said to me: "I think I'm going to let myself go, I'm so tired, I can't hang on any more."

I begged him to keep going. After he went, I lost all conception of time and that is the greatest danger for a drowning man – he thinks he is bobbing around for hours when in reality it is a much shorter time.

After four hours a trawler returned from the convoy to see if there were any survivors. Thirteen members of a 27-man crew were saved.❞

MATAPAN

J ostling for position in the Mediterranean, the tussle between the Italian and British navies was set to be of epic proportions. In the event, the British navy pulled off a tactical master-stroke which decided the debate before Italy celebrated its first anniversary at war.

Britain had its own Mediterranean fleet. Key bases for Britain were Gibraltar, at the teeth of the Mediterranean, the hard-pressed island of Malta and Alexandria, the Egyptian port operating under Admiral Sir Andrew Cunningham, from which supplies were being shipped to Greece.

Italy had well-established ports of its home territory opening into the Mediterranean and the Aegean as well as control of Albania and Libya, on the northern coast of Africa.

When war broke out, the British had a grasp of Italian naval codes and gathered enough information to sink nine Italian submarines before the end of June 1940. But a fortuitous switch in cipher systems by the Italians in July prevented the British from cracking the codes again.

The Italian air force wasted no time in bombing the British big ships when they were at sea. Italian intelligence about British

The Italian air force wasted no time in bombing the British big ships

sea traffic was good. It enabled her captains to circumnavigate all convoys to Libya around the British forces.

Against this background, Cunningham was determined to punish his Italian enemies and put to sea 16 times between June and October 1940. Yet he only managed to track Mussolini's ships three times.

So it was a priceless morale booster for the British when, on 11 November 1940, the Fleet Air Arm attacked Taranto, an Italian port. In port were six Italian battleships. A dozen Swordfish aircraft from the aircraft carrier *Illustrious* took off at dusk and flew 170 miles to attack the Italian navy vessels, struggling to gain height with their heavy load of explosives.

They notched up two strikes against the battleships *Cavour* and *Littorio*. A second wave of Swordfish arrived less than an hour afterwards, directed to their target by the blaze now roaring at the base. Together, they damaged the battleship *Duilio*. At a cost of two aircraft, the Italian fleet was deprived of three valuable battleships – *Cavour* permanently; *Littorio* and *Duilio* until the late spring of 1941.

At the turn of the year, Fliegerkorps X, the Luftwaffe's anti-shipping force, transferred 200 of its aircraft to Sicily. By 10 January 1941 bombers from the precision corps bombed *Illustrious* and also struck *Warspite*, although neither ship was terminally damaged.

It demonstrated, however, the need for air superiority if the Allies were to control the Mediterranean. Unfortunately, there was a shortage of Allied aircraft in the area, worsened when the *Illustrious* was hit again while in dock at Malta. Air attacks against Malta were so heavy and so frequent that it proved impossible to carry out adequate repairs to the much-needed aircraft carrier there. Consequently she had to be withdrawn from the Mediterranean.

ITALIAN THREAT

The British resolve to eradicate the Italian naval threat hardened and its objective was carried out in spectacular fashion, off Cape Matapan, in Greece. On 27 March 1941, a British plane

Below: *Italian cruisers* Flume, Gorizia *and* Pola *undergoing manoeuvres.*
Left: *HMS* Revenge *sets sail from Malta in 1939, before the siege.*

spotted a large gathering of Italian ships. The squadron comprised eight cruisers, the prestige battleship *Vittorio Veneto* and a host of destroyers. *Vittorio Veneto* was the pride of the Italian fleet. Her sister ship *Littorio* had been holed by the British at Taranto. Now she was poised with her support vessels to blow convoys destined for Greece out of the water.

Cunningham was instantly informed at his base in Alexandria. To back the aircraft

Below: The big guns of the Vittorio Veneto *unleash their fire power.*

DAKAR DEBACLE

Among the military calamities faced by Britain in the first half of the war was the debacle of Dakar. British ships sailed to the colony of French West Africa with the aim of landing Free French Forces who would take control from the Vichy regime.

❛As they anchored off the main port of Dakar on 23 September 1940, General de Gaulle broadcast a series of messages to the colony's governor stating his intention to land troops. All of the messages were ignored. Five messengers sent ashore with similar news were likewise rebuffed.

De Gaulle began threatening to use force. In reply, the coastal guns and ships at anchor in the port let off a barrage at the British ships, preventing the planned landing. The next day the exchange of fire continued with the British battleship *Barham* being struck. Twenty four hours later the battle ship *Resolution* was hit, this time sustaining more serious damage.

At this the British commanders and de Gaulle realised that their carefully laid plans to steal a march on Vichy France was quite literally being shot to pieces. Consequently, the ships pulled out of the engagement and returned humiliated to Freetown, the capital of Sierra Leone. Apart from the damage to its ships, the British also had to endure a reprisal air raid by the leaders of Vichy France directed against Gibraltar.❜

sighting there were messages passed through the Italian secret service cipher which had been broken by the Allies. He grouped together three battleships, the aircraft carrier *Formidable*, four cruisers and as many destroyers as he could muster. If trouble was coming, the Royal Navy together with its Australian contingent were prepared.

Admiral Cunningham then

made a move to protect the secrecy of the British activities which has since gone down as wartime folklore. A very keen golfer, he played regularly in the same club in Alexandria as the Japanese consul who reported every move made by the British Mediterranean Fleet to its enemies. Not only did Cunningham take his clubs to play golf that afternoon but

ostentatiously carried a suitcase, clearly bound for a night ashore. Having duped the tell-tale consul, he abandoned the case and slipped back aboard the battleship *Warspite* in time for an evening departure. Fortunately, the British ships did not pull out until after the Italians had carried out aerial reconnaissance of Alexandria harbour which revealed all were still at anchor. Italian Admiral Iachino believed the British posed no danger.

The British launched waves of aircraft to pester the Italians

The two forces first clashed in the morning of 28 March. After 40 minutes of exchanging shells, neither side had scored a hit and the action was broken off. The British launched waves of aircraft to pester the Italians who were themselves left virtually unprotected by their own air forces – which were stationed within easy range.

Above: Vittorio Veneto *was the jewel in the Italian navy crown.*

Vittorio Veneto was hit by one torpedo but still managed to escape the ravages of the air bombardment. However the cruiser *Pola* was stopped in her tracks by British firepower. Iachino, who was without the benefit of radar and apparently oblivious to the presence of British big ships, ordered two other cruisers to assist her. That night all three were attacked at short range. Two were quickly sunk without firing a shot. *Pola* and two other vessels were also sent to the bottom.

TIMED EXPLOSIVES

The British ships in the vicinity picked up 900 survivors before being scared off by the arrival of Luftwaffe planes. A further 270 men were plucked from the sea in the subsequent days but still the Italian casualties amounted to a devastating 2,400. The Battle of Matapan had been the biggest naval engagement of the war so far and dealt a serious blow to the Italian navy.

Vittorio Veneto was not to escape for long. A British submarine torpedoed her again in December 1941.

Despite the inferiority of Allied air cover, the Royal Navy continued to carry out admirable harrassing manoeuvres against the Italians and the Germans in the Mediterranean. Most notable were the contributions made by the cruisers *Aurora* and *Penelope* operating out of Malta who targeted convoys destined for Libya with immense success. Hitler and Mussolini were counting the cost of the contribution to the North African campaign made by the small island.

But the British didn't have it all their own way. When U-boats arrived in the Mediterranean, the fleet was deprived of the aircraft carrier *Ark Royal* which was sunk in November 1941, as well as the battleship *Barham* and two cruisers.

In the naval armoury were minute submarines, nick-named 'pigs' by their crew who were clad in frogmen's suits and sat astride the 22ft long craft. The 'pigs' were carried close to their position by regular submarines. Then it was the job of the crew to go in close to the target and attach timed explosives.

The Italians had made two abortive attempts using 'pigs' against the British during August and September 1940. This time there were to be no mistakes.

The Battle of Matapan dealt a serious blow to the Italian navy

After dark on 18 December an Italian submarine picked its way quietly and cautiously through mined seas to the approach of Alexandria harbour. There it off-loaded three 'pigs' and six crew, with a noiseless ripple on the water.

Beneath the waterline of the Royal Navy battleship *Queen*

Elizabeth, one team placed an explosive charge. Unseen, the two divers went ashore and posed as French sailors until they were seized by Egyptian police some time afterwards.

The second Italian team struggled to affix explosives to the side of a tanker. They were cold and stricken with sickness after spending too long underwater. But they didn't emerge from the water until their task had been completed. Egyptians arrested them as they attempted

Below: Vittorio Veneto *smokes after attack by British Albacore planes.*

to pass the first control post of the harbour.

The men were still there when an explosion sent the ship lurching to portside

One member of the third team passed out but bobbed back to the surface and clutched a buoy until his partner finished the job in hand. The latter was having problems of his own, meanwhile, with a torn diving suit exposing him to lethal cold. Then the 'pig' plunged to the sea bed. Despite the growing

Above: *Probably the last photo taken of the Italian big ships before Matapan.*

effects of exposure, he dived to retrieve it, manhandled it 60 feet back to the base of his target, the *Valiant,* and set the detonator.

He and his partner, now recovered, were picked up out of the water by a British motorboat and interrogated aboard *Valiant.* When they refused to speak about their operation, they were sent into the bowels of the ship close to where the charge was planted. The men were still there when an explosion sent the ship lurching to portside. They

MALTESE CROSS

Malta was awarded the George Cross in April 1942 after four months of continuous bombardment by the Axis air forces. As the Royal Navy battled to get convoys containing vital supplies through to the island, they were hampered by U-boats and airborne attacks which wrecked merchant shipping. It wasn't until August 1942 that a convoy arrived intact. With the volley of bombs coming from the sky the people of Malta and the beleaguered defending forces were subject to the most appalling privations. Yet Malta was a key point in the Allied defences. Had it fallen into the hands of Germany, Rommel would probably have won the battle for North Africa and the outcome of the war might have been different.

witnesed the effects of the blasts on the *Queen Elizabeth* and the tanker.

The Italian navy with Luftwaffe assistance continued to blockade Malta, the island which held the key to victory in North Africa. In December 1941 the Germans flew 169 bombing raids over Malta. In January 1942 the number rose to 262. The devastation took effect and Axis convoys began seeping through again as Allied ships were put out of action, deprived themselves of fresh supplies. Nevertheless, Churchill was determined to keep Malta in Allied hands at all costs.

DAILY BOMBINGS

It wasn't until March 1942 that a British convoy managed to slip through the Italian net bringing in vital supplies. Attempts to get supplies to the island in June failed. Yet still the vicious air bombardment continued. Much of the island was laid waste by the daily bombings as Hitler and Mussolini plotted an invasion.

The Allies planned a convoy of unprecedented size and strength in 'Operation Pedestal'. Setting off from Gibraltar were three aircraft carriers, two battleships, seven cruisers, 34 destroyers and eight submarines. The US carrier *Wasp* was also in evidence to bring new air forces to the island. The convoy departed on 10 August 1942 and came under repeated air attack. Both the Luftwaffe and Italy's Regia Aeronautica launched endless attacks with dive bombers, torpedo

Churchill was determined to keep Malta in Allied hands at all costs

bombers and fighter aircraft.

In the four day battle which pursued the convoy, the carrier *Eagle* was lost when it was sunk by U73, the cruisers *Cairo* and *Manchester* and the destroyer *Foresight*. Many of the surviving escort ships were damaged. The Italian navy, denied air cover by its own airforce. refused to join the offensive and fell victim to a British submarine as it made its way back to port.

CRITICAL LOSSES

Although the losses were critical, Malta was saved. Supplies that did filter through, amounting to some 30,000 tons, allowed the islanders and its battered forces to rebuild. It continued as a vital Allied base and deprived the Axis powers of a toehold which would have given them access to North Africa and the Middle East.

Woollen skull cap covered with a fine mesh camouflage net

Mouthpiece and airtube

Rubber tunic, water tight at the wrists, neck and waist

Underwater breathing equipment and oxygen bottle

Rubber trousers

Frogmen feet

SINKING THE BISMARCK

Majestic and mighty, the brand new battleship which sailed under the swastika for the first time in May 1941 drew gasps of admiration from friend and foe alike.

The *Bismarck* cut an awesome sight as it sped through the waves. More than 800 feet long and almost 120 feet wide, it was heavy with armour plating and bristled with giant guns yet was still sleek and fast. Who could blame the proud Germans for believing it was unsinkable?

It was down to the Royal Navy to send the great ship to the ocean floor and it was an urgent task which they were eager to undertake. A powerful battleship like the *Bismarck* posed an enormous threat to the convoys bringing essential food and materials from across the Atlantic. Without this lifeline from America and Canada, Britain would have quickly been strangled.

Left: *Deck of the mighty* Bismarck.
Below: *The battleship* Bismarck *undergoing sea trials.*

On *Bismarck*'s maiden voyage it confronted HMS *Hood*, elegant queen of the Royal Navy and sank it with the loss of almost all the crew. It was a devastating blow to navy pride and one which had to be avenged. The humblest sailor and the most powerful admiral in the British fleet felt to a man that *Bismarck*'s maiden voyage must also be its last.

Bismarck was built in Hamburg long before the opening salvoes of World War II were fired. The vessel was launched amid great pomp and ceremony on 14 February 1939. Nazi top brass, including navy chief Raeder, Göring, Goebbels and Hess, joined Hitler on a lofty podium when the great hull rumbled down the slipway. There to christen the ship was Dorothea von Loewenfeld, granddaughter of the celebrated German Chancellor Bismarck

after whom the ship was named.

After World War I, the German navy had been stripped of virtually all its assets and the Treaty of Versailles had strictly forbidden the creation of military muscle like the *Bismarck*. Hitler had been rebuilding the fleet and *Bismarck* was the largest addition to date. It was officially listed at 35,000 tons, some 7,000 tons lighter than it actually was.

A powerful battleship like the Bismarck posed an enormous threat to the convoys

When war came, *Bismarck* stayed in dock while having chunky plating affixed to its sides and decks, the 22 sealed chambers beneath its waterline made watertight and the latest technology installed on the bridge. It was being fitted out for

conflict to become, as Germany's Admiral Tirpitz put it, 'an unsinkable gun platform'.

Its first taste of sea salt came when it left Hamburg on 15 September 1940 for trials in the shelter of Kiel Bay. There were teething troubles and *Bismarck* had to slink back to Hamburg for modifications. It wasn't until the following May that the ship was ready to set forth.

AIRCRAFT COVER

Hitler arrived at Gotenhafen (now Gdynia) for an inspection of his seaborne gem on 5 May, where *Bismarck* was patiently waiting to embark on its first trip. He was, it appears, kept unaware that its sailing date was imminent. The Führer was wary of losing his prize vessel and admiralty chiefs feared he would scupper their chances of getting underway at last.

Grand Admiral Erich Raeder believed it was vital to get *Bismarck* to sea. Germany now had the advantage of Atlantic

---

EYE WITNESS

Frank Hewlett joined the Royal Marines in 1939 when he was 20 years old.

❛I was on HMS *Aurora*, an escort to the *Hood*. We followed her a day after she left Scapa Flow. When *Hood* was sunk we were 40 miles away. We saw a big flash on the horizon. When we heard the news, nobody believed it.

Then the *Prince of Wales* came within our sights. She was damaged and we escorted her back to Iceland. There was an unexploded shell inside her bows. If it had gone off it would have destroyed the ship. When the shell was removed, it was full of sand. It must have been sabotaged in Germany.

Afterwards, we went to Newfoundland and sank the supply ship *Max Albrecht*, sister ship to the *Altmark*. She went down with a U-boat still attached to her.❜

In one sense, the Bismarck was out of date even before setting sail

---

ports in occupied France to provide bolt holes for its ships. There was now extended aircraft cover from the Luftwaffe operating out of France and the lighter nights would significantly reduce the cover which was needed to spirit the ship into the Atlantic through the British sea blockade. There was also the increasing threat of America joining the war on the side of the Allies. The United States' naval power would dwarf that of Nazi Germany.

Fleet commander Gunther Lutjens was as confident in the strength of his new ship as the rest of Germany. But he had one nagging doubt that was shared by many senior officers in the Germany navy. It was the wisdom of going to sea without round-the-clock aircraft cover. In one sense, the Bismarck was out of date even before setting sail. The sun was rising on the

Below: HMS Hood, *like the* Bismarck, *was thought by admirals to be invincible.*

fleet air arms which could offer much more by way of flexibility and accuracy. While both Japan and America were gearing up their navies for the new age, Germany and Britain were lagging behind, both caught unawares by the outbreak of war.

Lutjens was a veteran of the sea assaults in World War I, he had already earned the distinction of a Knight's Cross during World War II through his courage in the Norwegian campaign of 1940.

> ## It was only a matter of time before sighting of this monster was confirmed to London

Loyal to his country, 51-year-old Lutjens was not a Nazi and refused to offer the party salute. Instead he preferred the time honoured navy salute and wore the old fashioned insignia of the Kaiser's navy instead of a swastika.

On 19 May the *Bismarck* sailed under cover of darkness to begin 'Operation Rheinubung'. In the company of the 17,000-ton heavy cruiser *Prinz Eugen*, itself a formidable ship, the *Bismarck* purred off into the Baltic to be joined by other German vessels for its historic voyage. Its aim was to sink the battleships protecting convoys while the smaller *Prinz Eugen* picked off the merchantmen.

VULNERABILITY

Slipping down the Danish waterways and shadowing the Swedish coastline, it was only a matter of time before the sighting was confirmed to London. Sir John Tovey, Commander in Chief of the Home Fleet, went into action. At the pinnacle of his plan would be HMS *Hood*, 20 years old but still an inspiring sight. It was a match for the *Bismarck* in size and gunnery but its weakness lay in the thin armour plating which covered its body and decks. It was this vulnerability that *Bismarck* exploited to the full.

On 22 May, just a day after news of the *Bismarck* arrived in London, *Hood*, the *Prince of Wales* and six other vessels set off from Scapa Flow. The following day, two of the fleet, the *Norfolk* and the *Suffolk*, encountered the *Bismarck* in the Denmark Strait, between Iceland and Greenland. As they dashed for cover in the icy fog, the *Bismarck* registered their presence and fired off a warning shot.

DEADLY BLOW

The mood was tense among officers and men on the *Hood* and the *Prince of Wales* as the hunt for their fearsome quarry continued. All th crew were poised to strike but lost their chance when their ships slipped past the giant battleship in the darkness as it skirted the Greenland ice pack.

Bismarck continued altering it course, not greatly but enough to put the ships commanded by Vice Admiral Lancelot Holland in a quandary. The initial plan had been to creep up on the *Bismarck* under cover of darkness in a short range strike. Now the *Hood* was forced to make a broad sweep at the

Above: *Following his encounter with* Hood, *Admiral Lutjens bolted for France.*

HUNTING THE BISMARCK

On 19 May the *Bismarck* sailed under cover of darkness to begin Operation Rheinubung. In the company of the heavy cruiser *Prinz Eugen*, *Bismarck* headed through the Skagerrak to the Norwegian coast. Passing so close to the Danish and Swedish coasts, it was only a matter of time before the two warships were sighted by British agents, and the news transmitted to London. Sir John Tovey was ordered to get the *Bismarck*.

On 22 May, just a day after news of the *Bismarck* arrived in London, the largest ship in the Royal Navy, HMS *Hood*, and the brand-new battleship HMS *Prince of Wales* set off from Scapa Flow in the Orkneys, accompanied by six other vessels.

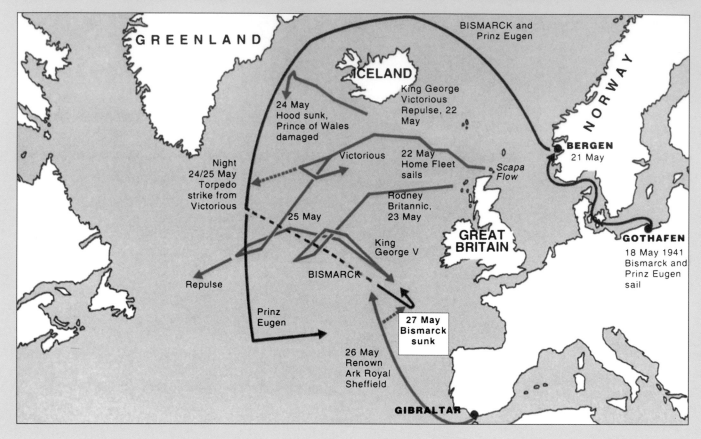

enemy and would be exposed to the brunt of its firepower.

When they sighted *Bismarck*, the *Hood* and *Prince of Wales*, travelling in close formation, were about 17 miles distant. At Admiral Holland's command, both ships began a charge at the enemy.

Lutjens was under orders to engage only the escorts of convoys. He wasn't looking for a duel and had hoped to avoid one. But now he had no choice. When the *Hood* and *Prince of Wales* closed the gap to 13 miles, they fired. Seconds later, the *Bismarck* and the *Prinz Eugen*

replied in kind. And while the British ships failed to find their targets, the Germans had them well and truly in range.

The initial plan had been to creep up on the Bismarck under cover of darkness

The second salvo from *Prinz Eugen*'s guns struck the *Hood*, igniting anti-aircraft ammunition. Another hit and then a third slaughtered many of the gun crews taking shelter. Still the guns from both sides continued firing

It was during a manouevre by the *Hood* trying for a better angle that the deadly blow was delivered by the *Bismarck*. A shell plunged down into the heart of the ship, penetrating the deck with apparent ease. Somewhere in the bowels, it silently sparked an ammunition store, maybe two. The effect was catastrophic. Observers from both sides were astonished to see a massive plume of fire and smoke burst from the middle, of the ship when there had been no explosion. The *Hood*, the most prestigious ship in old England, folded in two and

Above: Prinz Eugen *was released from escort duty to escape the Royal Navy.*

plunged to the bottom of the sea.

With it went the vast majority of the 1,400 crew, trapped in the wreckage. It was several hours before a British cruiser

The Hood folded in two and plunged to the bottom of the sea

came hunting for survivors. It found only three, cold and near death, clinging to small rafts in the middle of an oil slick.

The *Prince of Wales* was soon reeling from the effect of shells. It had been hit seven times, lost two officers and 11 men and was plagued with difficulties in its gunnery, making its own attack ineffective. Moments after its stunned crew saw the *Hood* ditching into the sea, it was decided to withdraw. The show-down had lasted just 21 minutes.

Britain was devastated by the loss of the *Hood* and its men. After the shock, the public were baying for revenge – or feared the *Bismarck* really was indestructible. There was no time for sentimentality among the naval officers now in hot

pursuit of the *Bismarck*.

The battleship *Prince of Wales*, plus the cruisers *Norfolk* and *Suffolk* shadowed the *Bismarck* as it moved south. Admiral Tovey, aboard *King George V*, was in command of *Victorious, Repulse*, four cruisers and nine destroyers hoping to intercept *Bismarck* from the south.

Visibility was poor, however, and the radar used by *Suffolk* to track its movements was patchy. *Bismarck* had, in fact, not escaped unscathed. It was holed twice by British shells which forced it to reduce speed and lost the vessel valuable fuel.

BISMARCK HURT

Lutjens felt he had no choice but to head for France for repairs. He released the *Prinz Eugen* to make a clean getaway, firing lazily at the *Prince of Wales* by way of distraction. Then he set a course which he hoped would take him to friendly France or within the torpedo range of a protective U-boat.

It was with some degree of surprise that he and his crew looked up to the skies some hours later and saw a group of circus-style planes buzzing

towards them. These were the Swordfish planes which had set off from the *Victorious* in order to wreak havoc on the *Bismarck*. With their single propellers and stacked wings they look like something from a different age. Nevertheless, the torpedo they carried beneath their fuselage was powerful enough to reckon with. The pilots of the Swordfish planes flew in low despite the barrage of anti-aircraft fire.

Below: *Hitler failed to share the nation's pride in the navy.*

EYE WITNESS

Able Seaman Robert Kilburn was one of the three who survived the sinking of the *Hood*.

❛ I was a member of the anti-aircraft gun crew but, of course, we weren't needed. There were only two other people with me at the time. The others were in a shelter deck – a shell had gone in there and killed all of them, about 200 men – but I didn't know that at the time. One of the shells hit one of the ready-fuse lockers for the four inch guns and there was a fire on board the upper deck and the ammunition was exploding. We were laid on the deck and then there was this terrific explosion. It was most peculiar, the dead silence that followed it – I don't know if we were deaf.

One of the other men was dead and the other one had his sides cut open and all his innards were tumbling out. I went to the ship's side to be sick. I noticed that the ship was rolling over and the bows were coming out of the water so I started taking off my tin hat, gas mask, anti-flash gear, overcoat, oilskin, so that I would have a chance to swim. With the ship rolling over, I just went into the water and the water came up to me.

I was terrified. I had a small rubber life belt on which you blew up – it was partially blown up. I started swimming away from the ship. The ship rolled over and the yard arms which had been broken during the action hit me across the legs and the wireless aerials tangled around my legs, pulling me down with the ship. I cut my seaboots off with the knife and shot up, like a cork out of a bottle. I must have been about 10ft down by then. The ship was around 10 yards away from me with her bows straight up in the air – and she just sank. ❜

In 1989 a team led by Dr Robert Ballard located the crusted hulk of the *Bismarck* (above) nestling on the ocean floor. Dr Ballard, the man who found and photographed the wreck of the *Titanic*, was aboard the *Star Hercules* when he discovered the *Bismarck* three miles beneath the ocean during a 10-day expedition. Among the photographs he took with a remote controlled underwater camera were those of discarded boots, the teak deck which was still intact and a 14-inch gun with a sea anenome bursting from its barrel.

Lutjens review his course. With masterly intuition he turned suddenly westwards and, in doing so, shook off the Royal Navy shadow. It took 31 hours for the British to locate the *Bismarck* again.

By now most of the British ships in reach had been called in to help. Yet due to a series of mishaps and misunderstandings, they were unable to find the roaming battleship, having

On 26 May intrepid Swordfish planes found Bismarck again and attacked

turned in the wrong direction. In addition, many were running short of fuel and had to splinter from the body of the fleet to find more. Navy top brass was becoming increasingly nervous. Unaware that the *Bismarck* had been wounded, they knew its path must be taking it towards the 11 Allied convoys presently crossing the Atlantic.

On 26 May intrepid Swordfish, this time from the *Ark Royal*, found *Bismarck* again and attacked. Two torpedoes struck the big ship, wrecking the steering gear and ruining a propeller. It meant that *Bismarck* not only had to slow down further but also became locked on to a course which brought it directly into the path of the opposition, thanks to the jammed rudder.

The following day *Bismarck* came within range of the battleships *Rodney* and *King George V*. They weren't alone and soon the *Bismarck* was surrounded by British ships firing when they could. *Bismarck* took punch

Just one torpedo hit the mark. Yet all the eight attacking Swordfish planes survived the hair-raising attack and landed safely back on *Victorious* in the dark with next to no fuel.

The damage sustained by *Bismarck* was enough to make

Above: *The* Prince of Wales *was one of many ships to hunt the* Bismarck.

after punch, losing men and guns with the merciless onslaught. Fires raged fore and aft while ammunition exploded all around. Yet still it stayed afloat.

Afterwards, British sailors admitted they felt little joy seeing the enemy ship battered so badly. However, they had no option but to continue the barrage while the *Bismarck* still fired back.

HITLER'S OUTRAGE

When streams of German sailors plunged into the sea, the shelling stopped. Admiral Tovey was mindful of their safety as well as that of his own men. Fuel and ammunition were running desperately low in his fleet. It would not be long before the lurking U-boats would turn up looking for easy pickings.

Satisfied the *Bismarck* would no longer menace the shipping lanes of the Atlantic, he gave orders for the British ships to withdraw. The only ship left with torpedoes, the *Dorsetshire*, remained to finish off the job.

Controversy raged afterwards whether it was a British torpedo or a German sailor who sank the *Bismarck* by opening the sea-cocks.

At first the *Dorsetshire* and the destroyer *Maori* hauled up survivors. But their goodwill came to an abrupt end following the reported sighting of a U-boat. The ships pulled away from the bobbing survivors, leaving them to suffer a lingering death in the waves. Two other vessels rescued a handful of survivors between them.

Only 115 of the crew escaped with their lives out of a total of 2,206.

When news of the sinking reached Hitler he was outraged. Never mind that a fleet of five battleships, three battle cruisers, two aircraft carriers, 13 cruisers, 33 destroyers and eight submarines had been involved in the execution. He bitterly regretted ever putting his classic ship to sea.

Below: *How the incredible story of pursuit was told to the British public.*

ARCTIC CONVOYS

Manning a ship on one of the treacherous Arctic convoys was perhaps the bleakest role in the whole war. For on these storm-lashed northern routes the weather collaborated with the enemy to make each day more miserable than the last.

Arctic convoys began after Soviet Russia was invaded by Germany and became an eminent ally of Great Britain. It wasn't a matter of survival to Britain as in the case of the Atlantic convoys.

Here was an exercise designed to appease Russia's leader Stalin. To exploit the opportunities for trade between the two countries, ships had to travel in the vicinity of the north pole where, for winter weeks on end, the sun never rose.

Hidden dangers under the waves included icebergs as well as U-boats. In the air the threat lay in frostbite alongside the dive-bombing planes of the Luftwaffe. The iron-grey steel hulls belonging to the powerful surface ships of the German navy were often masked by soupy fogs or dense blizzards.

REGULAR LOSSES

The sailors aboard knew they were being hunted. The buzz of a German reconnaissance plane overhead was a sure indication that an attack was being

prepared. Sometimes, not often enough, the convoy skirted the edge of the polar ice and slid through the ocean without being noticed. Sole reward for the hapless mariners was the chance of arriving in one piece at their destination.

Ships carrying the precious cargoes travelled under protection of British and American warships in convoys, usually between Scotland or Iceland and Murmansk, Russia. These northern waters were particularly risky. After Germany invaded

Above: A U-boat crew operating in northern waters survey their iced-up weapons.

Norway, it meant there were ports and airfields accessible to German forces within easy range. Hitler was also dedicated to victory over Russia. The

Hidden underwater dangers included icebergs and U-boats

sea battles to stop the convoys getting through to Stalin assumed greater importance given the personal interest of the Führer.

In reply the Allies did have the benefit of technology. Their grasp of the German naval secret codes was now accomplished. Yet despite re-routing to evade the attentions of the Arctic U-boats, convoys were still suffering regular losses. Virtually every convoy which

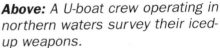

Far left: A British convoy leaves the warmth of British waters for Russia.
Left: Two Valentine tanks included in the aid sent to Russia.

set sail between March and June 1942 was attacked, either by U-boat or by the Luftwaffe. In all, 21 ships were lost in addition to the cruisers *Edinburgh* and *Trinidad*. Those losses were balanced against the safe arrival of 124 ships.

Now it seemed Germany was ready to pitch its prestige big ships into the fray. Britain's Admiralty was nervous.

Virtually every convoy which set sail between March and June 1944 was attacked

Knowing that ships like the *Admiral Hipper* and *Admiral Scheer* were in northern waters, made the prospects for any future convoys seem gloomy. Also there was *Lutzow* formerly known as *Deutschland*. (Hitler changed the name because the sinking of a ship called 'Germany' would cause depression at home and would be the butt

EYE WITNESS

Forbes Brown, from Victoria, British Columbia, joined the Royal Canadian Navy in 1941 and trained as an Asdic operator.

❛My first trip was in a corvette, HMCS *Algoma*, across the North Atlantic as a convoy escort. With Asdic we transmitted a sound beam and it reflected back if there was a submarine under the water. I could hardly believe it when I picked up a contact. Action stations were sounded. It was about 600 yards ahead. About 40 depth charges were dropped.

Following the last one there was a tremendous explosion underwater. It blew out all the safety valves on the engine and there were blue flames shooting off the deck. We suspected the last charge hit a torpedo head. Still there were plenty of other U-boats about. We started off with 62 ships in the convoy and ended up with 41. It was hairy. After that trip we were supplied with sheepskins so we suspected we were going north. As usual, it was a foul up. We were off to the Mediterranean.❜

of jokes among his enemies.) Worst of all was the presence of the huge battleship *Tirpitz*, sister ship of the *Bismarck* and the pride of the German fleet, with awesome firepower and astonishing capabilities.

Code-crackers revealed the large boats were preparing to depart and do battle. Convoy PQ17, sailing out of Iceland's capital, Reykjavik, on 27 June, comprised 33 ships and a tanker with an escort of six destroyers, four corvettes, two submarines and two anti-aircraft ships.

Left: *Some of the British and US ships involved in safeguarding the Arctic convoy routes.*

In London, it was clear that the enemy could pounce at any time. At sea, the convoy captains were equally expectant, wondering where and when the ferocious strike would come. Each bank of fog came as a welcome relief as the convoy made its way steadily northwards.

Information now coming out of the cipher service indicated the big ships were setting out from their base. It was enough for Sir Dudley Pound, First Lord of the Admiralty, to order the convoy ships to scatter for their

the convoy. The information from the secret message service had been misconstrued – with devastating results. As ordered, the convoy scattered. Armed ships pulled away from the merchant ships to search for the

Watch officers scanned the horizon, expecting to see the massive vessel looming

Below: Scharnhorst *was the scourge of convoys in northern waters.*

The *Tirpitz* did sail on 5 July but was recalled following the success the attack had already achieved. Neither did the big ships take part in action against the subsequent convoy, PQ18. Hitler once again erred on the side of caution rather than risk another humiliating loss at sea to parallel the *Bismarck*. Before reaching safety, PQ18 lost ten ships to aircraft and three to U-boats. The escort ships which this time stayed close to their charges, claimed a number of planes with anti-aircraft fire and

best protection. Little did he know that Hitler himself had intervened in the operation. He barred the use of valuable, prestige ships like the *Tirpitz* unless complete safety could be guaranteed. That meant British and American aircraft carriers were safely out of range.

Tirpitz was not heading for

Tirpitz and its team. The watch officers scanned the horizon, expecting to see the massive vessel looming. Nothing appeared. Now their nagging anxieties lay with the fate of the ships they had left behind. Twenty of Convoy PQ17's vessels were lost when the U-boats and the Luftwaffe seized the golden opportunity.

Allied fighter aircraft while one U-boat was sunk.

When the might of the German navy next put to sea it was at the end of the year following some intensive exercises. Their target was a 14-ship convoy, JW51B, which set out from Scotland destined for Kola on 22 December. It was

the second leg of a convoy, the first of which had crossed the sea without being spotted. A flotilla of destroyers joined up with the convoy on Christmas Day. Sailing to meet them were

The weather was poor, hampering visibility and identification of ships

the cruisers which had accompanied the first part of the convoy.

This time, the code-breakers let down the protection ships by failing to translate a vital enemy message in good time. *Admiral Hipper* and the pocket battleship *Lützow*, in the company of six destroyers, put to sea on 30 December. The British had no idea of the threat in the absence of deciphered enemy messages.

The weather was poor, hampering visibility and therefore the identification of ships whose shadows suddenly appeared in the mist. The first the Allied destroyers knew of the imminent danger was when the destroyer *Obdurate* was fired on by one of the German destroyers.

While the convoy pulled back under the cover of a smoke screen, the destroyers set about repelling the advance. Four times the *Hipper* tried to break through to fire on the convoy and on each occasion the destroyers pushed it back. The only damage *Admiral Hipper* did was on the last attack when an eight inch shell ploughed into the *Onslow*. One other destroyer, *Achates*, was sunk along with the minesweeper *Bramble* before the Battle of the Barents Sea was over.

GERMAN DEFEAT

Hipper was forced to retire into a snow storm when it was hit three times. *Lützow*, although in a prime position to attack the convoy, kept its guns silent. A German destroyer which suddenly emerged from a snowstorm close to the *Sheffield*, by now pursuing *Hipper*, was soon sunk. The convoy continued on its way.

A squally, inconclusive battle, it was nevertheless a humiliating defeat for the German navy. One of its prestige ships was forced to pull away with substantial damage while the aim of the attack, the sinking of the convoy, was frustrated.

Hitler was furious at the debacle. On New Year's Day 1943 he threatened to decommission the German fleet completely and break up the big ships for scrap. Grand Admiral Raeder, he claimed, lacked the pioneering spirit of adventure that was necessary to win wars. Raeder responded immediately, by asking to be relieved of his command.

DARING PLAN

In his place came Admiral Karl Dönitz, hitherto commander of the U-boat service. Hitler much preferred Dönitz to his predecessor and, in turn, Dönitz was able to convince the Führer of the need to maintain the surface

Below: An X-craft, like those used against Tirpitz, *with its commander on deck.*

fleet. Nevertheless, he too was unable to find further successes, despite his efforts.

The British Admiralty chiefs appeared to have a greater faith in the destructive power of the German fleet than Hitler himself. In northern waters, they remained wary of the threat posed by *Tirpitz*, *Lützow* and *Scharnhorst*. Indeed, Arctic convoys were even cancelled on the basis that the big three might sail.

By September 1943 a daring plan was drawn up to rid the convoys of the naval menace once and for all. The aim was for that four-man midget submarines each armed with two one-ton charges to creep into the Norwegian anchorage at Altenfjord and place crippling explosives on the undersides of *Scharnhorst*, *Lützow* and *Tirpitz*. In utmost secrecy, the mission began with full-sized submarines towing the midgets to the mouth of the fiord.

Unluckily, *Scharnhorst* was at

sea for trials when the six midget submarines went into action. The tiny undersea craft assigned to blow up *Lützow* was lost as it made its way there. Another lost its tow and was forced to jettison the charges. A third caught fire and had to turn back. The success of submarines X5, X6 and X7 more than made up for the disappointing performances of the other three.

Hitler threatened to decommission the German fleet completely

When one of the midgets was spotted the alarm was raised. One was forced to surrender. The other sank with the loss of two lives and the third was sunk, although it is not known when and how. But all this unfolded after at least three of the charges had been laid. Although held captive on the ship itself, the seamen who surrendered refused to reveal the whereabouts of

the explosives. Finally, the Germans got their answer when the mighty *Tirpitz* was lifted five feet out of the water. It would take seven months to fully complete the repairs. The two surviving submarine commanders, Lieutenants Donald Cameron and Godfrey Place, were rewarded after the war with the VC.

POOR WEATHER

Lützow abandoned the hunt for the Arctic convoys soon afterwards, returning to occupied Poland for operations in the Baltic. That left the last remaining danger – *Scharnhorst* – in Norwegian waters, fully equipped and ready for action. It was only a matter of time before she would venture forth to take on a convoy and this troubled the British commanders whose job it was to protect the merchant ships.

Scharnhorst *had no idea it was heading towards the Royal Navy's big cruisers*

On Christmas Day 1943 the order to sail finally came through for the expectant *Scharnhorst* crew, eager as they were to salvage the good name of the German navy. The ship emerged from its protective fjord in the company of five destroyers that evening in search of convoy JW55B.

Poor weather once again played its part, this time to the advantage of the Allies.

Scharnhorst hived away from its destroyer escorts. Lacking the superior intelligence assistance open to the Allies, it had no idea it was heading towards some of the Royal Navy's big cruisers in the region.

First to fire on the German was HMS *Belfast* who picked up the enemy by radar. *Norfolk* then joined the battle by opening fire and scoring a hit. The British ships broke off their action, not wanting to scare *Scharnhorst* back into port.

Next to spy it was *Sheffield* some two hours later. In the spat that followed it was *Norfolk*'s turn to sustain damage. Yet the British cruisers did a brilliant job. They drove the unsuspecting *Scharnhorst* into the arms of Admiral Fraser on the *Duke of York*. At a range of 1,200 yards, the *Duke of York* opened fire with its devastating 14-inch guns. This time *Scharnhorst* fled to the east, making good ground against its pursuers. But critical damage

forced the German ship to steady its speed. It gave British destroyers ample opportunity to unleash some torpedoes finally sinking the *Scharnhorst* at 7.45pm. Just 36 survivors were saved from a crew of 2,000.

Although *Tirpitz* rarely saw action, its presence alone was sufficient cause to divert air and naval craft from other duties. It would be aircraft that finally delivered the death-blows to this massive battlewagon.

TIRPITZ SUNK

The first sortie against Tirpitz began from Scapa Flow on 30 March 1944 with the *Duke of York*, *Belfast*, *Anson* and the aircraft carrier *Victorious* in 'Operation Tungsten'. On 3 April, 42 Barracuda aircraft loaded with powerful, armour-piercing bombs set off after their quarry, which was in Norway's Altenfjord, preparing to go to sea.

LEND-LEASE

Still hoping to keep his country out of war, President Roosevelt steered the Lend-Lease Act through Congress in March 1941. It gave the President powers to send military and material aid to countries at war with Germany and Italy with the sole provision being that they repay the loans at the end of the war. Although it was opposed fiercely by some factions, the Act had the beneficial effect of boosting the American defence industry even before the country went to war with Japan.

Above: *Wintry seas kept British sailors perpetually wet.*
Left: *Proud gunners on HMS* Duke of York *posed for the camera in front of their guns after sinking the German battlecruiser* Scharnhorst.

The action devastated the upper decks of *Tirpitz* and killed 122 men. Yet the super-ship stayed afloat, to the dismay of the Allies.

Several other bids to sink the ship by Fleet Air Arm aircraft were thwarted by poor weather. Aircraft were being lost in these vain attempts, forcing the Admiralty to think again. They called in the assistance of Bomber Command which had vast 'Tallboy' bombs.

Taking off from a Russian base on 15 September 1944, a cloud of Lancaster bombers rained 16 such bombs on the *Tirpitz*, causing extensive damage.

This time it would take nine months to make the repairs.

If the crippled *Tirpitz* had not moved to Tromsö that October, the Allies might have been satisfied. Germany wanted it as a floating gun platform to defend an expected invasion in the region by the Allies. Yet the Admiralty was disturbed by the ship's sudden activity and feared new attacks at sea.

On 29 October, 32 Lancaster bombers in 'Operation Obviate' caused considerable devastation. However, it wasn't until 'Operation Catechism' got underway involving the men and Lancaster aircraft of 617 Squadron – 'the Dambusters' – on 12 November 1944 that *Tirpitz* finally rolled over and died. About 1,000 crewmen were lost, trapped inside the great ship as it turned turtle.

CORAL SEA AND MIDWAY

Pearl Harbor may have been the most spectacular action that was undertaken by the Japanese navy but it certainly wasn't the last.

Here was the world's third most powerful navy staffed by efficient, skilled commanders and loyal sailors. It was their brief to roam the seas around Japan's newly acquired territories, protecting land-based flanks by fending off attacks from air and sea.

The Japanese navy played a major role in the domino fall of Asian and Pacific lands and islands, including that of Thailand, Hong Kong, the Philippines and Burma. Indeed, the noose put around Singapore by the Japanese navy during February 1942 ensured that none of the defending British or Australian troops could escape by sea and all those who survived the fighting were consequently taken prisoner.

When the Japanese cast their eyes in the direction of Java, the jewel they wanted in their crown, an allied naval force squared up to the challenge. Under Dutch officer Admiral Karel Doorman, a fleet of heavy and light cruisers and destroyers gathered from the British, American, Australian and Dutch navies determined to keep the Japanese out of the oil-rich colony.

BATTLE OF JAVA

The Battle of the Java Sea began on 27 February and was one of the largest naval confrontations the world had seen since World War I. Both sides seemed equally matched when they began a mutual bombardment with guns. But the Japanese wreaked havoc when they edged closer to the Allied fleet and opened up with torpedoes.

Hostilities ceased while the Allied ships refuelled only to resume within hours beneath the moonlight. Doorman was delighted when he once again encountered the Japanese and sought to end their plans to invade Java once and for all. Little did he realise that he was being snapped up in a tactical pincer. When more torpedoes blasted his force in a surprise

The Japanese wreaked havoc when they edged closer to the Allied fleet

Left: Crews from USS Lexington go into action in the Coral Sea in May 1942.
Below: Carrying the wounded off USS Marblehead in Netherlands East docks after the Battle of Java in February 1942.

from the carriers *Yorktown* and *Lexington* to attack two ports on Papua New Guinea which had just been overrun by the Japanese. Again, the results were negligible.

America determinedly began to gather its strength. US troops were sent to Darwin in Australia

The US felt confident enough only to take pot shots at the Japanese

and were by February under the command of General Douglas MacArthur. In fact, almost four times as many troops were sent from America to the Pacific at the time than took the shorter hop across the Atlantic to reinforce the Allied armies aiming to defeat Hitler.

Australian divisions, too, were recalled from the Middle East to help defend their homeland.

The tide of the Japanese successes was set to ebb as early as May 1942 with two historic seaborne clashes between Japan and America, one in the Coral Sea and the other around the island of Midway.

attack from a second angle there was chaos. In just seven hours, five Allied warships were sunk, while only one Japanese destroyer sustained damage. Doorman himself was lost when his cruiser *De Ruyter* went down.

BATTLE OF MIDWAY

So far the Emperor's fleet remained virtually unscathed by the ravages of war. During all its activities in the sea-borne invasions of Pacific and South East Asian islands only a total of four destroyers had been put out of action. Meanwhile, only four US destroyers had escaped to Australia from the treacherous waters around the Dutch East Indies. It seemed as if the

Japanese navy was invincible.

At the time the US felt confident enough only to take pot shots at the Japanese. The first skirmish took place in January when two US task forces bombed Japanese bases on the Marshalls and Gilberts. It was a tame event but nevertheless proved a small boost for American morale, being the first strike back at the enemy.

In March US planes took off

Above, right, far right: The triumphant Doolittle raid on Tokyo. A B-25 comes under starter's orders on its way to Japan. Doolittle is pictured later by his crashed aircraft in China.

BATTLE OF MIDWAY

Japan wanted a base within striking range of Hawaii. It also wanted the US fleet destroyed. Yamamoto hatched a plan to secure the base and lure the US Navy to its downfall in the process. He launched a diversionary attack on the Aleutians while he struck at Midway Island. Unfortunately for him the Americans knew he was coming and had put to sea. The first wave of Japanese bombers caught many US aircraft on the ground at Midway. Nevertheless, enough got airborne to make a second Japanese strike necessary. It was while the Japanese were rearming that US *Admiral Spruance* struck. Aircraft from *Yorktown* and *Enterprise* destroyed four Japanese carriers; on the US side, *Yorktown* was sunk.

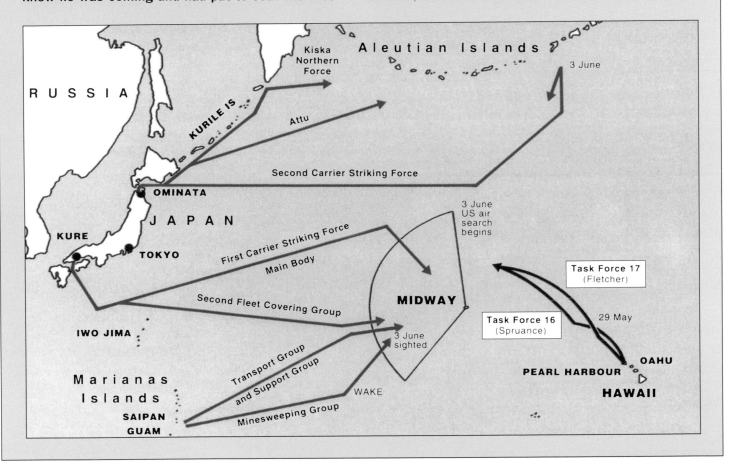

The Battle of the Coral Sea was not notable for its end result as the outcome was so murky it was difficult to distinguish a winner. Japan certainly wasn't defeated but its navy was for the first time halted. However, it was the first ever confrontation at sea to take place with the enemy ships placed hundreds of miles apart.

The firepower was carried to the opposition entirely by the planes stationed on the mighty carriers ranged against each other, capable of causing wholesale devastation.

Meanwhile, the Battle of Midway proved to be a turning point in the fortunes of war and gave America the opportunity once more to assert naval superiority.

By May, Japan had control of New Britain, parts of Papua New Guinea and the majority of the Solomon Islands. It formed the outer edge of a

The island of Midway was a glaring hole in Japan's line of defence

Pacific empire which was fanning out towards Australia. The country's remaining aim was to secure the line of defence by conquering the remainder of Papua New Guinea.

Japanese priorities changed, however, with the most effective nuisance raid mounted by the Americans to date. It came with Lieutenant Colonel J. Doolittle's bombing raid over Tokyo in April mounted through an open

EYE WITNESS

Normand N. Silver, from Montreal, was a stoker first class. A member of the Royal Canadian Navy Volunteer Reserve, he served aboard aircraft carriers HMS *Thames* and HMCS *Punchuard* and also the minesweeper HMCS *Quatisino*.

❛I volunteered principally because I thought it was my duty. We all guessed that if Hitler wasn't stopped, then in 1945 or 1950 he might send his armies across to Canada.

The main action I saw was around the coast of Alaska in Quatisino. The Americans had a lot of their ships berthed up there and they didn't want another Pearl Harbor on their hands. Our job was to seek and destroy any Japanese subs that wanted to try their luck. This meant we were on round the clock patrol.

We were credited with killing one sub, but you could never be certain. In the engine room you didn't get to see much anyway.

It's hard to explain the pressure when you're fighting submarines. If you are a nervous person then you are in real trouble. You have to expect an attack every minute of every hour of every day. You don't know where the attack will come from and you don't know how long it will be before the next. You don't sleep much and you don't relax. I think that is the story of most men's war.❜

door from Midway. The island of Midway was held by a small garrison of American marines and was a glaring hole in Japan's line of defence. Although the damage caused during the 16-plane raid was light, it gave the Japanese hierarchy a shake up and compelled them to look again at domestic security.

FIRST BLOOD

Admiral Yamamoto confident in the continuing might of his navy, was appalled at the Tokyo air raid. He felt sure the best way ahead was to knock the heart out of the American navy once again. To do it he wanted to put Midway Island under threat.

Yamamoto knew America valued the island because of its proximity to Pearl Harbor and would defend it in force with its navy, so he planned to lure the remaining big ships into action and then destroy them.

Below: *The last gasp of the Japanese carrier* Shoho.

Above: USS Lexington *sustains critical damage at the Battle of the Coral Sea.*

Meanwhile, the Japanese navy would also support a new thrust into Papua New Guinea where vital new forward bases could be installed.

Intelligence experts quickly grasped details of the preparations which would lead to the attack on Port Moresby, Papua New Guinea, after successfully decoding Japanese communications. Tempted by the presence of some of Japan's finest ships, America's Admiral Chester Nimitz hastily drew together as many ships as he could for a surprise rendezvous with the Japanese in the Coral Sea.

Australian cruisers which had gone ahead to secure a vital seaway for the heavier ships came under attack from Japanese planes but miracu-lously escaped damage. So first blood in the four day battle went to the Americans when a wave of planes located the light carrier *Shoho* and blasted it out of the water. It left the Japanese in a quandary as they had no idea where the attacking aircraft had come from.

The US tally included three direct hits on the aircraft carrier Shokaku

As night fell, Japanese planes were launched to locate their hidden enemy but, hampered by low cloud, were forced to ditch their bombs and head back to base. En route, they happened across the USS *Yorktown* which sent up aircraft for a confrontation. In total 17 Japanese planes were lost that night against only three American casualties. In fact, for a while both sides suffered from the main disadvantage that this new, long-distance warfare offered. Neither could locate the enemy ships.

TACTICAL VICTORY

The next day both sides sent waves of aircraft in pursuit of the other. The US tally included three direct hits on the aircraft carrier *Shokaku* which was forced to limp back to its home port for major repairs.

Meanwhile, the Japanese struck the carriers *Yorktown*

and *Lexington*. The *Yorktown* escaped with comparatively minor damage while the *Lexington* was crippled by three bombs and two torpedoes. It was to sink days later following an internal explosion. Both admirals decided against continuing the battle and pulled away from their respective battle lines.

The Lexington was to sink days later following an internal explosion

Japan appeared to have inflicted the most damage on the opposition. In reality, the tactical victory belonged to the Americans. The Japanese had been contained and were forced to call off their strike at Port Moresby due to the large losses of essential aircraft.

EYE WITNESS

Mitsuo Fuchida, who led the air strike against Pearl Harbor, was aboard the aircraft carrier *Akagi* during the Battle of Midway.

❝For Japan, the Battle of Midway was indeed a tragic defeat. The Japanese Combined Fleet, placing its faith in "quality rather than quantity" had long trained and prepared to defeat a numerically superior enemy. Yet at Midway a stronger Japanese force went down to defeat before a weaker enemy.

Not only were our participating surface forces far superior in number to those of the enemy but the initiative was in our hands. Nor were we inferior qualitatively in the crucial element of air strength which played a major role throughout the Pacific War. In spite of this we suffered a decisive defeat such as the modern Japanese navy had never before experienced.

With Midway as the turning point, the fortunes of war appeared definitely to shift from our own to the Allied side. The defeat taught us many lessons and impelled our navy, for the first time since the outbreak of war, to indulge in critical self examination.

The Japanese public, of course, was not told the truth about the battle. Instead, Imperial General Headquarters announcements tried to make it appear that both sides had suffered equal losses. The United States, however, promptly announced to the whole world the damage inflicted on the Japanese accurately naming the ships damaged and sunk. Thus it was clear that our efforts to conceal the truth were aimed at maintaining morale at home rather than keeping valuable knowledge from the enemy.

I myself had a rather painful taste of the extreme measures taken to preserve secrecy. During the battle I had been wounded on board *Akagi* and then transferred to hospital ship *Hikawa Maru* which brought me to Yokosuka Naval Base. I was not moved ashore until after dark when the streets of the base were deserted. Then I was taken to the hospital on a covered stretcher and carried in through the rear entrance. My room was placed in complete isolation. No nurses or corpsmen were allowed entry and I could not communicate with the outside.

In such a manner were those wounded at Midway cut off from the rest of the world. It was really confinement in the guise of medical treatment and I sometimes had the feeling of being a prisoner of war.❞

Above: Shokaku, *pulled back to Japan following the Coral Sea battle.*

The Japanese High Command decided to abandon that first objective in favour of the capture of Midway, a far more ambitious undertaking. While the commanders had sought outright victory in the Coral Sea, they were convinced by their own glowing track record that the US navy could still be annihilated.

Once again intelligence reports gave the United States fair warning of the Japanese plans which they had tagged Operation MI. And again Admiral Nimitz called in as much support as he could from ships and submarines in the region. Aircraft carriers *Enterprise* and *Hornet* were

Japanese commanders were convinced that the US Navy could be annihilated

summoned along with the damaged *Yorktown* which had been hurriedly repaired so it could rejoin the action. They sailed with six cruisers, 14 destroyers and 19 submarines to the north of Midway to await the attackers. On the island itself the garrison had been strengthened and increased numbers of aircraft brought in.

The Japanese strike force, including half the navy's aircraft carriers, came from several directions, one arm to land troops, another to tackle the American naval presence.

SUNRISE RAID

At dawn on 4 June, bombers took off from Japanese aircraft carriers and blasted the land-based defenders of Midway. Aircraft from the island attempting to deflect the invaders suffered huge losses and made little impact. It seemed the Japanese navy was to escape once more intact.

But before a second wave of bombers could be launched, Japan's Vice-Admiral Chuichi Nagumo was told of the presence of enemy ships signalled from the first attack by their planes. Instead of the continuing bombardment of the already shattered small island, he decided to swing north and pursue the US Navy prey.

By now torpedo bombers from all the aircraft carriers had been launched and began a comprehensive strike lasting 55 minutes on three of Japan's aircraft carriers. Japanese pilots supported by anti-aircraft fire defended the ships fiercely. Of the 41 US planes which set out

Of the 41 US planes which set out on that mission, only six returned

on that mission, only six returned. It seemed victory was in the grasp of the Japanese. Yet they barely had time to congratulate themselves on their luck and judgement when the subsequent wave of dive-bombers sent by the Americans arrived on the scene.

As the Japanese sailors and airmen struggled to rearm in the disarray, bombs rained down on

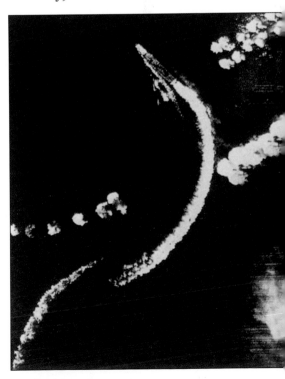

Above: Akagi, *another Japanese navy gem, weaves its way out of fire at Midway.*

them and exploded on the decks which were crowded with aircraft. Afterwards, Japanese sailors told how the raid took them by surprise – which is why the prized planes were on deck. It took a matter of minutes to

It took a matter of minutes to reduce the carriers to smoking crates

reduce the carriers to smoking crates. Two of the Japanese carriers, the *Kaga* and *Soryu*, sank within hours. The *Akagi* drifted on hopelessly and helplessly until a Japanese submarine punctured it for the last time the following day.

Half an hour afterwards, bombers from an unscarred Japanese carrier, the *Hiryu*, went

Below: *The giant USS* Yorktown *lists helplessly following Midway.*

looking for revenge. Their target was the *Yorktown* on which the battle commander Rear Admiral Frank Fletcher was based. A volley of hits during two onslaughts finally put paid to the veteran carrier which was abandoned by its crew later the same day. A Japanese submarine sent its skeleton to the bottom two days later.

It was not the end of the bloody battle, however. At 5pm, less than 12 hours after the conflict began, USS *Enterprise* – nicknamed the 'Big E' – launched bombers in pursuit of the *Hiryu*. They caught up with their target and sparked a catastrophic blaze on board. The *Hiryu*, Japan's fourth and final aircraft carrier in the offensive, was finally laid to rest by a Japanese cruiser.

Admiral Yamamoto continued his assault on Midway from the heavy cruisers that remained.

But when two of them collided trying to evade an American submarine, he was finally convinced of its folly.

HUGE VICTORY

The American navy's Rear-Admiral Raymond Spruance risked one final foray against the Japanese, holing one of the already damaged cruisers and sinking the other. Even then Admiral Yamamoto was ready to spring a trap on the American fleet by luring them into combat with a light force and then pounce with much bigger guns.

Admiral Spruance was not to be drawn. Content with his enormous victory, he headed for home, leaving *Yamamoto* helpless in his wake. A Japanese submarine managed to claim one destroyer before Spruance pulled out of the region.

The decisive result was

Left: Admiral Raymond Spruance.

trumpeted around the Allied world. From Pearl Harbor Admiral Nimitz announced: '. . . the enemy's damage is very heavy indeed, involving several ships in each of the carrier, battleship, cruiser and transport classes. This damage is far out of proportion to that which we have received.

'The brunt of the defence to date has fallen upon our aviation personnel, in which the Army, Navy and Marine Corps are all represented. They have added another shining page to their record of achievements.'

From a position of seemingly indomitable strength, the Japanese navy had within a few short days been for the first time mauled and gored. The defeat was so terrible that it was cloaked in secrecy in Japan for the duration of the war. While scores of heroic US pilots lost their lives in the battle, they inflicted devastation on their hitherto unbroken enemy and it was their courage alone that turned the tables. Four aircraft carriers, together with more than 300 aircraft and the cream of the Japanese naval pilots were

The steamroller successes of the Japanese forces had been stopped

at the bottom of the ocean. The steamroller successes of the Japanese forces had been stopped, Midway was saved and further plans by the Japanese to occupy other Pacific islands were shelved.

Below: Admiral Nimitz considers his next move from the bridge of a destroyer.

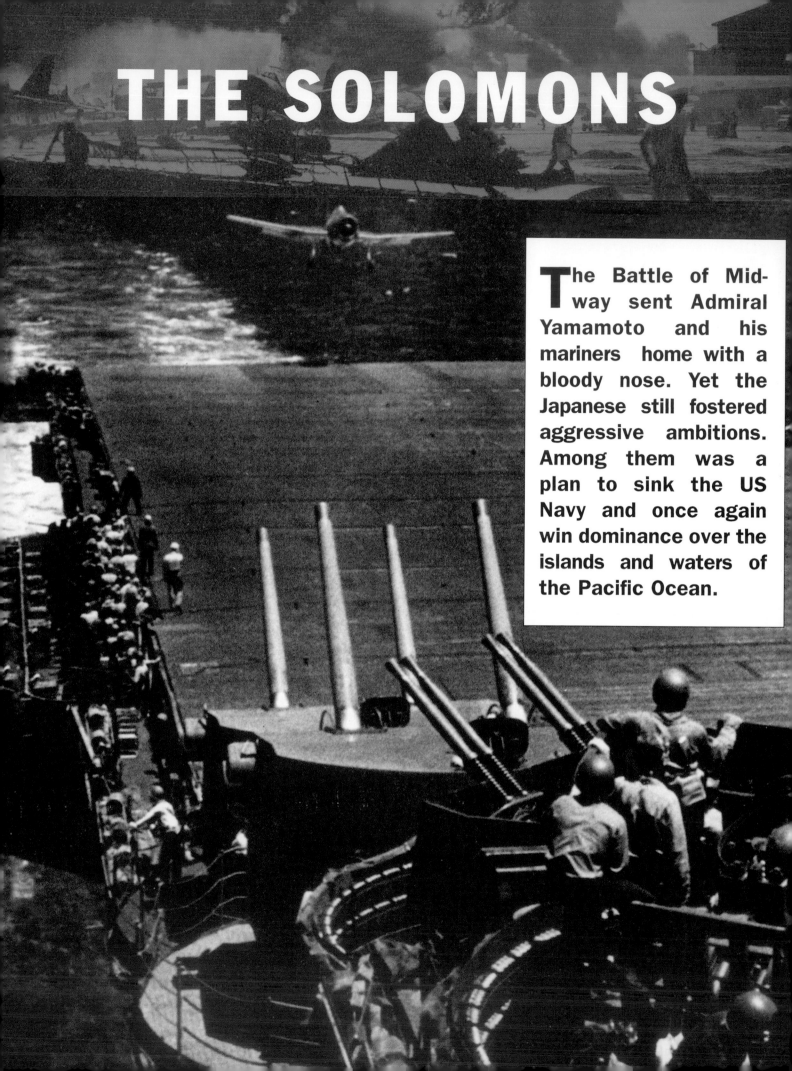

THE SOLOMONS

The Battle of Midway sent Admiral Yamamoto and his mariners home with a bloody nose. Yet the Japanese still fostered aggressive ambitions. Among them was a plan to sink the US Navy and once again win dominance over the islands and waters of the Pacific Ocean.

By May 1942 Japanese forces occupied Tulagi, one of the Solomon Islands. The Americans were keen to keep this Pacific route open as it represented a vital line of communication with Australia. So American military planners devised a plan, 'Operation Watchtower', to rout the Japanese from the region.

Initially, US and Australian troops were to liberate Tulagi and a few other selected islands. Then their aim was to free the rest of the occupied Solomon Islands and Papua in New Guinea. The final phase of the operation would be the capture of the Bismarck Archipelago; New Britain and New Ireland.

The Americans busied themselves gathering their forces, including three aircraft carriers, a battleship, 14 cruisers and plenty of destroyers. After setting off from Wellington, New Zealand, on 22 July, there were four days of practice runs on a remote Pacific Island before the operation got underway.

Meanwhile, the Japanese were also making plans. They had high hopes of capturing Port Moresby in Papua, their target before the Battle of the Coral Sea. Instead of using a waterborne force this time, they would go overland. A fleet comprising five heavy and three light cruisers, five submarines and a number of destroyers was based at Rabaul on New Britain and the Japanese further tried to strengthen their position by

Above: A Marine's eye-view of a Pacific landing operation, this one at Tulagi. **Left:** A Grumann Hellcat fighter returns to USS in the Pacific. **Below:** US Marines practise for their invasion of the Solomon Islands.

building new airfields right across the occupied territories.

The islands they were fighting over offered little more than strategic value to either side. The Solomon Islands had been a British Protectorate although two of the major islands fell

On 7 August, 11,000 US Marines landed on the Solomons without meeting opposition

under the domain of Australia. They stretch for some 600 miles encircling a waterway called The Slot.

It was a fighting man's nightmare. The climate was damp and humid encouraging thick jungle and forest to cling to the sides of the mountains throughout the centre of the isles alongside smokey volcanoes. On the coastal plains there were, apart from coconut plantations, acres of dense, spikey grass, sharp as a knife.

On the morning of 7 August, 11,000 US Marines landed on Guadalcanal in the Solomons without meeting any opposition. Within 24 hours they had taken the airstrip as their own.

The three battalions that landed on Tulagi were not so fortunate. The Marines encountered fierce resistance from the 1,500 Japanese defenders of the island. It cost the Marines 108 of their men before the island was theirs, in addition to many more wounded.

JAPAN ENRAGED

It was the work of a few days to win the islands. Ahead lay a bloody six months as they battled to keep them out of the hands of the Japanese.

The Japanese were surprised and enraged when they found out that one of their new prizes had been overrun. First response by Imperial General Headquarters was to send a convoy of 500 troops to reinforce

Below: The first wave of Marines find their feet on the Solomons.

the islands. However, a US submarine put paid to the plan with a single torpedo. Those troops that survived were forced to turn back to New Britain.

However, their next strike was markedly more successful. Armed with reconnaissance information about the size and strength of the enemy forces, Admiral Mikawa and a rogue squadron slipped in to The Slot unnoticed by the watching Allied ships on 8 August, their silhouettes blotted out by bad weather.

SAVO ISLAND

Aided by flares dropped from his carrier planes, Admiral Mikawa gleefully caught sight of the Royal Australian Navy cruiser *Canberra* and the US Navy cruiser *Chicago*, patrolling The Slot. Both Allied ships were unaware their lines had been penetrated by enemy vessels. It meant the Japanese squadron was able to open up at point-blank range with shells and torpedoes.

Canberra came off worse.

Right: Japanese air power prior to the 'Marianas Turkey Shoot'.

The damage that the ship sustained was so bad it had to be abandoned. *Chicago* escaped with just one hit from a torpedo. But before its gunners could fire back, the Japanese squadron was heading north, straight towards another Allied patrol. Three more American cruisers were set alight and sank. The Japanese squadron pulled out at speed, completely unscathed. Even though they had left the transports delivering to Guadalcanal untouched, victory in the Battle of Savo Island was theirs for the cost of 38 men, while more than 1,000 American and Australian sailors perished.

Eleven days later a sizeable force of Japanese soldiers charged with winning back Guadalcanal set off from Rabaul under the protection of two aircraft carriers, a light carrier, two battleships, five cruisers and 17 destroyers.

Allied ships were unaware their lines had been penetrated by enemy vessels

Ready to meet them this time was an Allied task force of three aircraft carriers and a battleship. Japan's Admiral Kondo sent his light aircraft carrier ahead as a decoy. It drew the fire of the American fleet air arm and sank on the afternoon of 24 August.

When the wave of Japanese aircraft arrived, there was a reception committee of US fighters to meet them. Although the Japanese lost a number of planes, the Battle of the Eastern Solomons was inconclusive. Both navies withdrew that night. It was the land-based bombers who later attacked the Japanese transports that forced them away from their destination.

The sorties were nicknamed the 'Tokyo Express' by the watching Marines

The Japanese navy ships sped down The Slot regularly, both to fire on the American positions and to land troops and supplies. The sorties were nicknamed the 'Tokyo Express' by the watching Marines.

At the end of August the US aircraft carrier *Saratoga* was torpedoed by a submarine and was forced back to Pearl Harbor for repairs. The US naval strength in the area, already inferior to Japan's, continued to take a battering from both submarines and aircraft attacks.

America had to wait six weeks before replying in kind. A squadron escorting some American transporters happened on a Japanese naval force which was preparing to fire on a US-controlled airstrip. In the confrontation that followed one Japanese cruiser and two destroyers were sunk for the cost of one American destroyer.

A major Japanese effort to recapture Guadalcanal was knocked back to the end of October but still the Japanese would not give up. At the ensuing Battle of Santa Cruz, the outnumbered Americans lost seventy aircraft compared to an estimated 100 downed from the Japanese ranks. All Japan's ships stayed afloat although five sustained damage.

SAVAGE ACTION

It wasn't until the three-day naval battle of Guadalcanal that the American Navy found the outright victory which had eluded it so far. It began with a savage encounter between a small American escort force against a powerful Japanese squadron. Although the US contingent was cut through during the battle, which lasted just 24 minutes, it saved the Guadalcanal airstrip from bombardment and it bought valuable time for the pursuing US task force.

Two days afterwards, the Americans unleashed their firepower at the Japanese with another close range bloody battle at sea. A Japanese battleship was so badly damaged she had to be scuttled. One Japanese and three American destroyers were sunk. The key to the American success was the attack the following day on the transports bringing an attacking Japanese force to Guadalcanal. Three-fifths of the landing troops were annihilated. The rest were rendered an ineffective fighting force, trapped

as they were without supplies.

The final conflict in seas surrounding the Solomons was the Battle of Tassaronga, which turned out to be equally damaging to both Japan and America. The losses suffered by the Japanese navy were sufficient to persuade its leaders not to venture again into such fateful waters.

Japanese destroyers went to the Solomons just once more, to help in the evacuation of

tally of damage to the Japanese was a destroyer which sank and damage to seven cruisers and three more destroyers. In later air battles an estimated two-thirds of the Japanese carrier aircraft were gunned down, the cream of its pilots lost forever. It finally squeezed the Japanese navy out of Rabaul once and for all.

US SUPERIORITY

At home Japan tried to nurture a new generation of navy pilots to

by Admiral Spruance. At last the Americans had found an antidote to Japan's Zero fighter. The new US Hellcat was faster and more powerful.

It was known among Americans as 'The Great Marianas Turkey Shoot' after waves of Japanese planes were bagged and brought down. In total the Japanese lost 223 aircraft. Only 17 aircraft returned from an attacking force of 69 in the first wave of aircraft.

EYE WITNESS

Swedish-born Nels Olson, 72, from Chicago, USA, was a gunner in the US Navy Armed Guard, who later served in the Pacific at the time of the Japanese surrender.

'My war ended in the Pacific. I arrived on the island of Okinawa two or three weeks after the Japanese surrender. All the guys wore guns when they went ashore but there were no problems. The Japanese bowed to us whenever they saw us. It was like they went out of their way to show they did not want to fight.

For a country that caused us such problems I was amazed at how primitive some of the people were. I once had to supervise the unloading of coal from a cargo ship. They did it by sending men on board with two buckets strapped to their shoulders. It was amazing to watch.'

troops from Guadalcanal in January 1943.

With every month that passed the Americans managed to reinforce their navy and its vital fleet air arm. There was little the Japanese could do to replace its lost ships, planes or pilots.

The Japanese Navy took its next severe pounding in port at Rabaul in October 1943. Aircraft from the growing number of American carriers in the region launched two raids. The

replace those it had lost in the Solomons and soon afterwards. Their destination was the Marianas, a series of islands being heavily reinforced by the Japanese to fend off US invasion.

But the students were ill-equipped to deal with intense warfare and they were lost in their droves. In the two-day Battle of the Philippine Sea in June 1944 the Japanese navy received yet another drubbing from Task Force 58 commanded

In the next wave the Japanese lost 98 out of its force of 130 planes and in the disastrous fourth wave, just nine survived out of 82. The Americans were down by just 29 aircraft. In addition, three Japanese aircraft carriers were sunk.

The Americans outnumbered the Japanese in all classes of ship. None of the four Japanese aircraft carriers had planes aboard and all were listing from battle damage.

AMPHIBIOUS WARFARE

When British, Australian and New Zealand troops tried to land at Gallipoli during World War I, the sea ran with their blood.

Bullets from defending Turkish guns rained down on unfortunate troops as soon as they emerged from boats just short of the shore line. It remains one of the most appalling military disasters in history in which there were more than a quarter of a million casualties on the Allied side alone.

Winston Churchill, then First Lord of the Admiralty and a keen exponent of the plan, resigned over the Gallipoli debacle and it blighted his career for years afterwards.

The adventure achieved little, but served to illustrate the gap in military manoeuvres which reduced soldiers, trying to take a fortified coast, to cannon fodder.

The lesson was not lost on Major Earl Ellis in the United

Left: The Americans led the field in the development of amphibious techniques.
Below: LVTs and LCWs approach the island of Aguni Shima in the Pacific.

States. He realised the importance of safe transport of troops from ship to shore during invasion. His aim was to give American Marines the best chance of survival. As early as 1921 he had written a 50,000-word plan which was intended as a blueprint for a Marine advance in the Pacific. He argued that men should be specifically trained to overcome the hazards of amphibious warfare and that the Marines were the best task force to undergo that instruction.

LANDING VEHICLES

Ellis wrote: 'It is not enough that the troops be skilled infantry men and jungle men or artillery men of high morale. They must be skilled water men and jungle men who know it can be done – marines with marine training.'

By 1933 the Fleet Marine Force came into being to oversee the challenge of amphibious landings. There followed a series

of experiments with tracked landing vehicles which could travel in the sea, offering protection to soldiers on leaving landing boats. It wasn't until the war years, however, that an effective ship-to-shore craft was constructed, the LVT or Landing Vehicle, Tracked. Even then, due to its mechanical

'It wasn't until the war that an effective ship-to-shore craft was constructed

shortcomings, the amtrac was mainly used to travel up beaches rather than on to them.

Boatbuilder Andrew Higgins, from New Orleans, then came to the notice of the US Marines after he built a shallow craft vessel for crossing the Mississippi River. It beached with ease and could be pulled back into the water at speed. Here was a craft far superior to anything else the marines had found to date.

Bizarrely, the US Navy's Bureau of Ships was reluctant to adopt a design from someone outside the service. Continuing its costly probes into making landing craft for years afterwards, it still failed to come up with an adequate rival to Higgins' model. The fiasco was roundly condemned by a Senate Committee during the war.

EYE WITNESS

Gordon Kendall, from Portsmouth, UK, served with 4 Commando.

❝British commandos were assigned to set out guns on either side of the Dieppe basin ready for a seaborne Canadian invasion force. Around 150 of us went ashore before dawn, did the job and got out.

The Canadians didn't arrive until much later. That was a mistake because they were absolutely chopped to pieces. We reckoned that of the 3,000 who went ashore, 900 died on the beach and more than a thousand were taken prisoner.

The irony is that they should never even have been there. The British Northumberland Division had been training for this operation but the Canadians were restless and took it over. It seems some of their commanding officers were hungry for action after hanging around in the UK for so long.❞

Below: US troops emerge from the bowels of USS LSM-168 in March 1945.

That original Higgins design finally became the father of the LCP(L)s, Landing Craft Personnel (Large) used by both Britain and the Americans during World War II. Work continued throughout the war to perfect landing craft of differing capabilities; some were armed, some were ocean-going; some were tracked. They proved a formidable amphibious force.

MARINE TRAINING

The Japanese were also testing the possibilities of amphibious landing craft. The Japanese army built an early version of LSDs (Landing Ships, Dock) for their operations in China during the 1930s called Shinshu Maru. Inside its cavernous interior the vessel could house a number of landing craft which rolled up a ramp and out of the ship's open doors.

In order to land troops, they had a 46ft landing craft which they modified to bear arms for the men of the Special Naval Landing Force, the equivalent of the marines.

In Britain, only a fleeting interest was expressed in the dilemma. Recovering from its battering in World War I, the service chiefs in the main neglected to look ahead and plan for another war. It wasn't until 1937 that Admiral Sir

> **In Britain, service chiefs neglected to look ahead and plan for another war**

Reginald Ernest-Ernle-Plunkett-Drax suggested that several brigades of Royal Marines should be trained especially for amphibious landings. The eventual outcome was the establishment of the Inter-Service Training

168

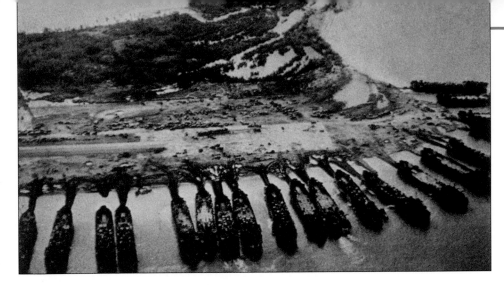

Above: An armada of LSTs offload onto a recently captured beach.

and Development Centre based near Portsmouth, in southern England, which involved all the defence forces and developed a policy for amphibious operations.

Staff in the unit addressed the problems of specialised landing craft, navy gunfire support, floating piers to aid the disembarkation of tanks and trucks and an array of workable tactics.

TANK SHIPMENT

The ranks of the Royal Marines, standing at just 12,000 when war broke out, were substantially boosted. Their role of manning guns aboard Royal Navy ships and guarding navy shore-based establishments was expanded to man commando raiding parties.

Following the evacuation of British troops from Dunkirk in 1940, the need for armoured ocean-going craft able to carry men and machines into shallow water was once again highlighted. While there was relief at the number of soldiers who got out

Right: Motorised equipment from an LST rolls on to a 'rhino' to reach the sand.

of France, they barely managed to bring back a gun between them. The army lost every tank and major piece of artillery it had committed to France. If a suitable transport craft had been available, at least some of it might have been saved.

Until his men and tanks could be transported across the Channel, there would be no opportunity for Churchill to make up the ground he had lost in France. Tanks were a primary tool of war and shipment of them in any amphibious assault was vital.

A British prototype Landing Ship, Tank (LST) came into

being in October 1940. It was further improved when tankers made in Britain especially to traverse a troublesome sand bank in South America were converted to carry tanks. These were fitted to carry 20 tanks or 33 trucks but were unable to come close into shore.

The army lost every single tank and major piece of artillery it had committed to France

A new design was created to overcome the problem. The problems posed in getting the ships produced in Britain's shipyards was overcome when America agreed to take on the contract. Shipyards across the States became involved in producing LSTs, launching the first of the new design on 7 September 1942. Before the war was over, 1,050 more came out of US yards to see action in amphibious landings across the world. They would join the Landing

Ships, Infantry (LSI) and Landing Ships, Dock (LSD) already in service. The seeds of a successful amphibious landing force had been sown, but there was a long way to go before it would threaten the Reich.

DIEPPE LANDINGS

The Allied landings in Dieppe in August 1942 ended in almost complete disaster. The Allies referred to it as a raid while Hitler insisted it was a fully-fledged invasion.

The Allied force consisted of 5,000 Canadians, 1,057 British, 50 Americans and a few Free French soldiers. They ran into difficulty when the landing craft were swept along the beach. Armed German trawlers happened on the scene and began shooting at a British section.

The Germans greeted the arrival of 27 light tanks with a hail of gunfire. All were destroyed while the landing forces suffered appalling casualties. It was just 9am when the troops were pulled out. More than 1,500 prisoners were taken and most of the equipment was left scattered on the beach.

The Germans greeted the arrival of 27 light tanks with a hail of gunfire

A clutch of Allied boats was sunk and almost 100 of the aircraft dispatched to provide aerial cover were shot down. It was the largest in a succession of raids.

The Dieppe incident led Prime Minister Churchill and other British commanders to doubt the sense of making another attempt against well-fortified German positions.

Valuable lessons were learned from the raids in time to execute the biggest amphibious landing ever, on D-Day.

EYE WITNESS

Henry 'Marty' Martin, from Chicopee, Massachusetts, USA, stormed Omaha beach in a DD (Duplex Drive amphibious tank). He landed in the first wave aboard LCT 586.

'My job was to drop the ramp. These men trained to get out in 30 seconds but we didn't have time to check that they all got out safely. We did four drops that day.

For our first we laid off 200 yards because it was so rough. The next one, though, we went right on to the beach. We were carrying three tanks and they had to get in close.

I watched the first tank take off to the right. He made it, but the second took a direct hit as he tried to follow. The third stayed closer to the shore and looked to be OK.

As they left a US officer came up to me literally holding the insides of his stomach in his hands. He was one of the underwater demolition experts who had gone in in advance of the landings. Those guys didn't have very good luck. I think nine in every ten were killed.

He told me we were the first ship to come right on to the beach. We got him back to the hospital ship but I never knew how he made out.

Sometimes historical accounts fail to mention the disputes and the arguments that took place. There was one officer who had it in for me. After D-Day I got a ten-day leave to Kilmarnock in Scotland and the thought of going back to work for this guy meant I decided to unofficially extend that leave for another ten days.

I served 30 days in the brig at Plymouth for that. But I reckoned that just because a man's an officer doesn't mean he can't be an asshole as well!'

Below: A few moment's relaxation by an empty landing craft for weary troops.

EYE WITNESS

Ernie Marshall joined the Royal Navy at the end of 1942 aged 18. After three months training he joined a combined operations unit and was stationed on LCT554.

❛When I saw it my heart dropped. It looked pretty rough. The living quarters and the engine room were at the back while the tanks were in the front. There were 12 of us aboard. I was a stoker in the engine room. I just learnt as I went, I had no training whatsoever. Eventually we sailed to North Africa. It seemed like the whole of the Atlantic was coming up at us. Then we had to slide down these huge waves. I stayed in the engine room.

We worked every port up to Tripoli. Once we carried German prisoners of war. Then we joined the landings at Sicily. We beached at 4am when it was very quiet. Next morning the Germans really came at us. We stayed there ferrying supplies for a couple of months until we went up to Anzio. We were stuck there for three months surrounded by Germans. The beachhead was about five miles inland. Once the Germans broke through and got to within two miles of the beach. Eventually, they were pushed back again.

The long range guns were more frightening than anything. Shells just landed without warning. One morning a plane attacked us. Shrapnel from one of its bombs came right through the stern, across the mess deck, through the next steel bulk head and into the engine room. Everywhere was filled with smoke and sparks. One bloke had an injured shoulder but the rest of us survived.

That afternoon we were alongside a boat unloading supplies when a bomb from a plane went straight into the hold. We managed to get ashore. Survivors got thrown into the water and were shouting to us for help. We fished a lot out of the water but we couldn't stop because the ship was burning so fiercely. That was the worst day of the war for me.

It was two and a half years before I got home. On the whole I enjoyed the experience. The rest of the crew became like family. The captain never gave us any trouble and we had some good times. I had never travelled before so to see Arabs in their African villages was really something.❜

In the rough seas off the Normandy coast, British soldiers were instructed to carry not only their 20lb packs but also bicycles for use in France. On arrival, they were told to ditch the cycles in order to fight for their lives – and never saw the cycles again.

No amount of improvements in the technique of amphibious landings could save the infantry from being held in cramped vessels for hours, sometimes days, on end before the final moment of invasion came. The food was generally poor and home comforts were lacking. Only the lucky ones got to sleep in hammocks.

Before attacking Guam in July 1944, the US 3rd Marine Division spent weeks suffering like this at sea. The Channel weather on D-Day was awful.

Below: Australian troops boarding a beach landing ship after successful operations at Lae, New Guinea.

Specially trained civilian aircraft recognition teams from the Royal Observer Corps put to sea with the troops on 6 June 1944. This was to cut the rate of Allied aircraft shot down by jittery comrades on the ground.

The design of specialised landing craft was improved. They kept their speed and low silhouettes but were enlarged to carry more men. The armament they carried was also beefed up to provide greater support for the men they off-loaded.

The beaches of Normandy, unlike that of Dieppe, were away from major towns where the German defences were strongest.

JAPAN'S LAST GASP

When America's war horse was harnessed, it galloped through the Pacific at a thundering pace. Advances made in 1944 by the combined efforts of the Army, Navy and Marine Corps mimicked those of the Japanese three years before.

By now the US strength at sea was awesome. Since the outbreak of the war with Japan a further 21 aircraft carriers had come into service capable of holding a total of about 3,000 planes.

That was in addition to a splendid array of new battleships, transports, cruisers, destroyers and landing craft newly arrived and ready for action.

On the other hand, the Japanese had suffered severe losses at sea and were continuing to do so. Apart from naval conflicts, the Japanese ships had to contend with the numerous American submarines now patrolling the Pacific in force.

Japan, so dependent on the resources it imported from overseas, was unable to replenish the fleet, with much of its merchant fleet being sunk bringing home vital war production materials. By 1944 two thirds of the tanker fleet bringing oil to Japan from the South Pacific fields had been wrecked by the Allies. While 40 per cent of the oil produced in those fields reached Japan in 1942, only 13.5 per cent was unloaded at Japanese ports in 1944 due to the efficiency of the submarines and fleet ships. Oil reserves were dwindling fast, threatening to grind the war effort to a halt. Hopelessly outnumbered, it seemed on paper that Japan's navy was all but finished.

When it became clear that the US was preparing to attack the Philippines in the autumn of 1944, however, Japan drew

In the autumn of 1944 Japan drew up plans for one final sea battle

up the plans for one final sea battle which could have tipped the balance in its favour. It was a simple manoeuvre by what remained of the Japanese navy

Left: All eyes turn skywards when a Kamikaze aircraft is spotted in the vicinity.
Below: Vice Admiral Jisaburo Ozawa was defeated by superior US tactics.
Bottom: The scale of the US seapower is illustrated in this picture of Task Force 58 in the Pacific.

Above: *Vice-Admiral William Halsey looks out to sea and draws up a winning strategy for the American fleet.*

but might have been enough to defend the Philippines. And it was a gamble worth risking for the Japanese. If the Americans had installed themselves on the Philippines, it would have meant the end of oil supplies

The arrival of Admiral Ozawa and his decoy carriers went unnoticed

from the Dutch East Indies, now more crucial than ever before to the teetering Japanese.

After the war, Japan's Admiral S. Toyoda explained his country's actions: 'If the worst should happen there was a chance that we would lose the entire fleet; but felt that chance had to be taken . . . should we lose in the Philippine operations, the shipping lane to the south would be

completely cut off so that the fleet if it should come back to Japanese waters, could not obtain its fuel supply. There would be no sense in saving the fleet at the expense of the loss of the Philippines.'

In essence, Japan's ploy was to use what was left of the carrier fleet as a decoy to lure the main thrust of the American navy away from the Philippines. Once the large ships were out of the way, a two-pronged attack from the sea was planned on Leyte, the small island in the centre of the Philippines on which the Americans had already began an assault.

AMERICAN ATTACK

The operation began badly for the Japanese. One arm of the fleet earmarked to blast Leyte was itself fired on by American submarines on 23 October, well before it reached its destination. Three cruisers were damaged.

There was a two-fold result to this action. The strength of this attacking arm was depleted and all the American shipping for miles around became focused on this single Japanese force. Despite frantic efforts to announce his presence by uncoded radio messages, the arrival of Admiral Ozawa and his decoy carriers went unnoticed by the Americans.

Now American battleships joined the attack on the hapless Japanese detachment whose brief had been to slip unobtrusively into the Philippine Sea. Japanese land-based bombers and

also from distant carriers rained bombs on the American fleet, crippling the carrier *Princeton*.

There was a high price for this success, however. The relentless onslaught by the American fighter planes finally sank the majestic *Musashi*, one of the biggest battleships in the world. It had been struck by 19 torpedoes and 17 bombs. Japanese commander Admiral Kurita finally broke off from the action and appeared to retreat.

BATTLE OF LEYTE

The absence of Japan's aircraft carriers was spotted by the sharp-witted Vice-Admiral William 'Bull' Halsey, who was in control of the American fleet. When he sent out reconnaissance planes to assess the movements of the Japanese fleet, Ozawa was finally detected. It seemed a golden opportunity to Halsey who gathered up his entire force to pursue the prized

Left: The carrier USS Princeton *is hosed after taking a direct hit from a bomber during the Battle of Leyte.*

Above: Devastation among Japanese shipping in the run-up to the invasion of the Philippine island of Leyte.

carrier, Japan's last surviving ship of the type in action.

Almost as soon as American backs were turned, Kurita reversed his course and began steaming towards his initial target once more, Leyte.

American sea defences were badly lacking after Halsey set off with his full complement of ships. Mostly it comprised a small force protecting the landing beaches at Leyte, just six escort carriers and five destroyers. In charge, Vice-Admiral T.C. Kinkaid sent a series of urgent messages to Halsey, asking him to return at once. Halsey, however, was determined to snare the carrier once and for all. He refused to turn around until he delivered some decisive damage to the carrier force. Only time would tell if his instincts were the right ones.

Meanwhile, the destroyers were defending the vulnerable section of the US fleet as best they could. One escort carrier and three destroyers were lost, however, in its retreat.

Now Kurita was steaming towards the Leyte Gulf where a collection of US transports and men lay wide open to attack. Then he hesitated. As Kinkaid watched and waited with bated breath, Kurita finally pulled his forces to the north, away from the beach targets.

Thanks to confusion among the intercepted radio messages aboard Kurita's ship, he believed Halsey and his powerful ships were only 70 miles away when in fact there were hundreds of miles between them. He was also gravely concerned about the risk of attack by air when he himself had no air cover.

SITTING DUCKS

While the survivors of Kurita's force escaped, the fate of the carriers gave credence to Halsey's actions. All four – *Chitose*, *Zuikaku*, *Zuiho* and *Chiyoda* – were sunk, completing the effective destruction of the Japanese navy. With the long-range power of aircraft, Japan's remaining battleships were no more than sitting ducks to the enemy. There was little more

Yasuo Kuwahara was a skilled Japanese pilot who was in a Kamikaze squadron in the final year of the war.

❛ It was New Year's Day 1945 at Hiro Air Base in western Honshu. Captain Yoshiro Tsubaki, commander of the Fourth Fighter Squadron, has just called a special meeting. A silence settled over us.

After a long while, he spoke sonorously: "The time has at last arrived. We are faced with a great decision."

Again he pauses but I feel the fear, greater than I have yet known. Death is there with us, enfolding each man, lingering, growing stronger. And the words from our captain flow strangely.

"Any of you unwilling to give your lives as divine sons of the great Nippon empire will not be required to do so'. Those incapable of accepting this honour will raise their hands – now!"

Once more silence and death are almost palpable. Hesitantly, timidly, one hand goes up, then another and another ... six in all. I can choose to live or die. But somehow ... Of course, I want to live. But my hands – they remain at my sides trembling. I want to raise them but I can't. Am I a coward? I cannot do it.

"Ah so," Captain Tsubaki fixes those who have responded in his stare. "It is good to know exactly where we stand." They are summoned before us. "Here gentlemen," he points to the ashen faces, "are six men who have openly admitted their disloyalty. Since they are completely devoid of honour without spirit – it is our duty to provide them with some. These men shall be Hiro's first attack group."

The breath, held so long within me, struggled out. I want to draw in more air, to expel it with relief, but something clenches inside, Six men from my squadron have just been picked for death. Hiro's first human bombs. ❜

Above: *A Japanese destroyer is smashed in two at Ormoc, Leyte, by a US B-25.*

they could contribute to Japan's war effort.

From first to last, the three-day Battle of Leyte Gulf was the largest in history. In total, 282 ships were engaged along with hundreds of aircraft. It took the title of largest battle from the World War I Battle of Jutland when 250 British and German ships had met in combat, with only five seaplanes.

Those who felt disgraced would commit 'hari kiri'

At the end of it, the Japanese had lost not only four carriers but also three battleships, six heavy cruisers, three light cruisers and eight destroyers. The triumph clearly belonged to the Americans whose casualties amounted to just one light carrier, two escort carriers and three destroyers.

Had the Japanese Admiral Kurita been different on the day and had he chosen to bombard the American beach positions, history might have had a different story to tell.

SUICIDE SQUADS

The Battle of Leyte Gulf is not only remembered as being the biggest naval battle ever. It was also the first to see the co-ordinated use of kamikazes – Japanese suicide squads.

Among the Japanese there was a strict code of honour, instilled in them for centuries, that death was better than dishonour or defeat. The first form of ritual suicide in Japan, called 'seppuku', was reserved by law for the samurai and was considered a privilege. Suicides could equally be carried out as a mark of respect.

Centuries later, those who felt disgraced in some way would commit 'hari kiri', literally translated to 'a cut to the stomach'. The aim for the person was to disembowel themselves by using a ceremonial sword, an agonising process. As the years wore on, many made a symbolic cut in the stomach before turning a gun on themselves.

Surrender was abhorred by the Japanese, particularly among the troops, which explains the antipathy they displayed towards their own prisoners of war. Many Japanese servicemen

Allied soldier stopped to help a wounded or dying Japanese victim, the latter would devote his last burst of energy to pulling the pin from his final grenade, killing both men outright.

DESPERATE ACTS

Others would strap explosives to their bodies and hurl themselves at tanks or enemy positions to cause as much devastation as

possible. Until now, these acts were committed very much on an individual basis. But by 1944, staring into the jaws of defeat, the Japanese commanders decided to orchestrate suicide missions to cause the maximum hardship and loss of life to their enemies. Behind the enterprise was Vice-Admiral Takijiro Onishi who himself committed 'hari kiri' at the end of the war.

Japanese commanders orchestrated suicide missions to cause maximum loss of life

Kamikaze pilots in small planes would target the deck of an enemy ship. While bombs dropped from planes often missed their target, the kamikazes' aim was very accurate. British ships with often more deck armoury than their American counterparts were better defended against such attacks.

There were plans for suicide

Above: USS St Lô *takes a direct hit from a kamikaze.*
Right: USS Suwanee *gets running repairs after sustaining damage from a kamikaze.*

readily chose suicide rather than shame. High ranking officers also used to inspire courage and commitment among their men by killing themselves.

This made the Japanese difficult enemies in the field. They were reluctant to be rescued if their missions went awry. At sea, Allied sailors watched as the survivors of a wrecked ship tried to drown themselves or cut their own throats if they were armed. For if any unfortunate

motorboats to target major ships. Beneath the waves there were one-man midget submarines which would set themselves on a collision course with a much larger vessel. These were difficult tactics to counter.

Stepping forward for these 'special' one-way missions were upright, traditional, fervent and deeply patriotic young men who

Those without the necessary iron nerve were just as likely to plunge themselves and their aircraft into the sea instead of a ship, representing a waste of valuable resources. In a panic, many chose the first ships they saw to descend on. These were generally strategically less important than others in the fleet, once again wasting man and

Lieutenant-General Torashiro Kawabe explained the reasoning behind kamikaze attacks. 'We believed that our spiritual convictions and moral strength could balance your material and

Those without the necessary iron nerve were just as likely to plunge into the sea

scientific advantages. We did not consider our attacks to be 'suicide'. The pilot looked upon himself as a human bomb which would destroy a certain part of the enemy fleet ... he died happy in the conviction that his death was a step towards the final victory.'

At the Battle of Leyte Gulf, six aircraft took off from Cebu in the Philippines on 25 October 1944. Two hours later when they arrived at Leyte the planes deliberately rammed the US carriers *Santee* and *Suwanee*, causing extensive damage. The next day one American ship, *St Lô*, was sunk by use of kamikaze.

BEST DEFENCE

In the next three months, 22 Allied naval vessels were sunk by kamikaze pilots against 12 holed in conventional air attack. A further 110 kamikaze strikes damaged shipping.

They were a hazard which was to plague the Americans, Australians and British for the rest of the war. The best defence against kamikaze was interception by fighter planes or a volley of anti-aircraft fire, but it was not always successful. One Japanese pilot could still destroy many lives.

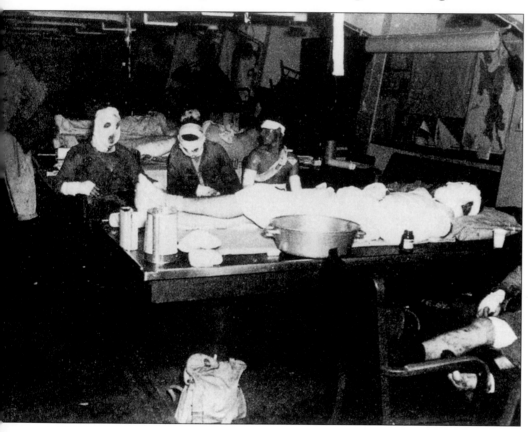

Above: *Wardroom of the carrier USS* Suwanee *becomes an emergency sick bay after the kamikaze attack during the Battle of Leyte Gulf.*

thought little of laying down their lives for their country. Despite the glory heaped on such pilots in domestic propaganda, the volunteers for the kamikaze ('divine wind') squads were drying up. The Japanese commanders had no choice but to brand units as kamikaze squads whether the men were willing to die or not.

machine. Others would fly off in search of a specified target and return claiming the ship they were after could not be found. There were many accidents as the fuel-starved Japanese economised on oil and stoked up the kamikaze aircraft with 50 per cent alcohol. If the aircraft engine failed, it was impossible to restart.

Commanders had no idea about the kamikaze success rate as there was no one left to report a result.

Following the war, Japan's

BATTLE FOR THE SKIES

BATTLE OF BRITAIN

When France was overrun, Führer Adolf Hitler cast his eyes across the English Channel and set his sights on Britain.

Although he never had an appetite for war with the island, he now saw it as the next jewel in his crown. He believed its government and people would choose to make peace after the unstoppable power of the Reich had been so amply illustrated in France.

He was, of course, wrong. A peace offer made to Britain in July 1940 was rebuffed – even though the remnants of its army, hounded out of Europe via Dunkirk, were in disarray. Hitler made up his mind to invade and began gathering the necessary invasion forces in the newly acquired Channel ports of Holland, Belgium and France.

Göring pledged to the Führer that the Royal Air Force would be banished forever

Yet while the Germans were veterans of waging attacking wars on land, they had never tackled the sea before. Nor was Germany a great seafaring nation. Hitler believed the arrangements for taking war across the water could be made in a matter of weeks. Given that 'Operation Overlord', carried out from Britain in 1944 to free France, took upwards of a year to plan, he was very shortsighted.

It was clear even to Hitler that an invasion could not go

Left: Spitfires proved the saviours of Britain.
Top right: Göring believed the Luftwaffe aircraft could finish the RAF.
Right: Air crews were scrambled at a moment's notice when attacks came.

ahead until his air force had charge of the skies. It was one of the few issues that united his warring chiefs of staff, too.

'The British Air Force must be eliminated to such an extent that it will be incapable of putting up any substantial opposition to the invading troops,' Hitler announced to his generals. Göring, the supremo of German air power, was all ears. He pledged to the Führer that the Royal Air Force would be banished forever.

IN EASY REACH

On paper, Göring had good reason to be confident. The Luftwaffe had a three-to-one numerical superiority against the RAF. German pilots were experienced, having flown missions throughout the Spanish Civil War. Now they were based in airfields in France, the Low Countries and Norway, within easy reach of Britain.

Göring believed his men would smash the Royal Air Force.

'Operation Sealion', Hitler's planned offensive against Britain which would bear him triumphantly to London, was set for 15 September 1940. The German navy chief Admiral Raeder had convinced Hitler his forces could not be prepared any sooner. Nor could it happen much later than that for fear of the invasion force falling foul of autumn storms.

Timing was crucial – but this did not unduly concern the Luftwaffe chief. When operations began against Britain in July,

Top: *Formations of Messerschmitt 110s became a familiar sight in the skies.*
Above: *Britain and the Commonwealth countries were recruiting air crews.*

Göring was sure he had time enough to fulfil his part of the bargain. Privately, he thought four days would be sufficient to virtually destroy his opposition. Events proved his optimism to be wildly misplaced.

For its part, Britain waited in anticipation during the summer of 1940 for the start of a battle for its very existence. Air reconnaissance teams spotted the gathering German forces. Hitler's intentions were clear.

Many of the men plucked from the beach at Dunkirk were redeployed on coastal defences. The Royal Navy played its part by attacking the collection of landing craft gathering at the occupied ports. Airmen joined the action and laid still more mines in the Channel to hamper a seaborne force destined for Britain.

There was a new evacuation among the children of London and the south east. As tension and expectation mounted on the home front, production doubled during June in factories working round-the-clock in a bid to help Britain's defenders meet the foe on equal terms. Lord Beaverbrook, Minister of Aircraft Production, appealed to the public to donate its metal scrap to build fighters. The result was mountains of old iron which could not be transformed into Spitfires or Hurricanes. But in terms of a morale-boosting exercise, it was a runaway success.

CONVOYS ATTACKED

As the German victory parades and celebrations died down in France there came the opening salvos of the Battle of Britain. They were quite tame by comparison with what was to come, a bid to 'soften up' Britain.

Lord Beaverbrook appealed to the public to donate its metal scrap to build fighters

---

The targets were Britain's lifeline convoys as they reached home waters and the coastal ports, most notably Portsmouth and Dover. Both sides suffered losses in the air, with the English pilots, ground controllers and radar operators learning some valuable lessons.

Germany began with about 2,600 aircraft ready for action. They were in the main Messerschmitt fighters and Dornier, Heinkel, and Junkers bombers. Well organised into groups – Luftflotte 2 flew from Belgium, Luftflotte 3 from northern France, and Luftflotte 5 was based in either Norway or Denmark.

FIGHTER COMMAND

Lining up against them were fewer than 700 operational aircraft for the Royal Air Force. There were the legendary Spitfires and Hurricanes and some outdated Bleinheim bombers.

Britain's aerial defences were divided into four groups. Fighter

In the middle of August Göring opened phase two of the Battle of Britain

some 217 planes. The losses by Fighter Command were fewer than 100 but its outlook was bleaker than that of the enemy. British aircraft reserves were tiny. Yet it was the loss of experienced pilots either by death or injury that began to concern Air Chief Marshal Sir Hugh Dowding most. Despite the acute pressure of his position, Dowding, a master tactician, did a first-class job of keeping the marauding German planes at bay during those hectic months of summer and autumn 1940.

Above: Göring and his staff officers survey England across the Channel, convinced the island would easily fall.

Command 10 Group covered south west England, Fighter Command 11 Group oversaw the south east including London, Fighter Command 12 Group patrolled the airspace over the Midlands, while Fighter Command 13 Group was based in northern England and Scotland.

Britain was not standing entirely alone, as the line-up for the ensuing battle proved. Although more than 2,500 of the men who took part were British, there were also 147 Poles, 101 New Zealanders, 94 Canadians, 87 Czechs, 29 Belgians, 22 South Africans, 22 Australians, 14 Free French, ten Irish, seven Americans, two Rhodesians, one Jamaican and a Palestinian.

Now Germany was down by

Yet Churchill unceremoniously replaced him once the threat of 'Operation Sealion' had passed.

In the middle of August, Göring opened phase two of the Battle of Britain. His target now was RAF Fighter Command itself. Daily attacks were made on the airfields of southern England. Unlike the unfortunate air forces of crushed Allies Poland and France, the British planes were not caught on the ground. Britain's radar system,

to waste vital manpower and resources, ground control never scrambled pilots until the last moment when they were sure a raid was imminent. It gave them little time to plan the most effective attack.

Both sides fell victim to erroneous propaganda. The RAF airmen were buoyed to hear that German air force losses were running at three or four times their own. In fact, vastly inflated German casualty figures were

Left: *Air crews at Biggin Hill, Kent, enjoy a few moments' respite.*
Below: *Pilots and crews always appeared relaxed.*

the most advanced in the world, gave early warning after seeing incoming formations of enemy bombers. There was just enough time to scramble the pilots and bring the valuable men and planes into the air.

Smoke from planes embroiled in dog-fights was scrawled across the sky

For now the heroes of the battle were the ground crews. It was their job to patch up not only the planes which were battered during aerial spats but also the hangars and runways damaged by bombs, to keep the Royal Air Force working.

Göring earmarked 13 August as 'Eagle Day' when a preponderance of German planes would swarm over the British skies and finally subjugate the stubborn RAF. Despite wave upon wave of Luftwaffe planes, his plan failed. Smoke from planes embroiled in dog-fights

was scrawled across the sky. The British fighters held their own.

NIMBLE SPITFIRES

German bombers were at a disadvantage against the nimble Spitfires. Laden with bombs, they were no match for the British planes. But the RAF fighters were struggling to achieve the best height and position to carry out attacks on the German formations as they crossed into Britain. Not wishing

broadcast, some of which were not rectified until after the war. Göring, meanwhile, was happily convinced during the early stages of the Battle of Britain that many airfields were out of action and scores of British planes were destroyed, estimates which were grossly exaggerated.

On 15 August nearly 1,800 sorties were flown by the German airmen, attacking targets from Newcastle to Hampshire. Britain was forewarned by radar,

BATTLE OF BRITAIN

In the Battle of Britain, RAF Fighter Command was divided into groups distributed throughout the country. The south west of England was the responsibility of 10 Group, London and the south east was covered by 11 Group, the Midlands region was patrolled by 12 Group, northern England and Scotland was the beat of 13 Group. Against these forces were three Luftwaffe formations – Luftflotte 2, Luftflotte 3 and Luftflotte 5.

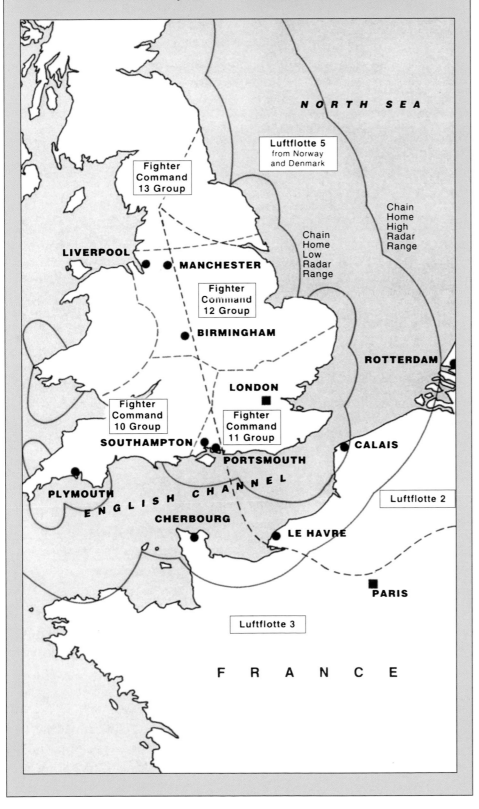

and each flight was attacked from the ground and the air and there were 75 German losses against Britain's 34.

The following day 1,700 sorties were made over Britain, with Göring confident the RAF would be left in tatters. Yet on that day, the German pilots found themselves confronted with healthy numbers of British planes and pilots.

Göring was left fuming at the apparent inability of his men to finish off the RAF. In addition, he was counting the cost of 363 lost aircraft and crew.

Of course, the incessant demands on each and every British squadron were causing immense difficulties by mid-

Above: *A Heinkel 111 over the Thames, taken from another German plane.*

August. Britain had lost 181 fighters in the air and 30 more on the ground. Only 170 replacement aircraft had thus far been manufactured, while just 63 new pilots had been brought up to replace the 154

Left: Temple Underground station doubled as an air-raid shelter during the Blitz.

lost in battle. The raiders had succeeded in knocking out a radar station at Ventnor on the Isle of Wight, which was a serious blow, although their main aim of wrecking airfields had been frustrated. How long could the casual, seemingly cheery young men in silk scarves and leather jackets who laid their lives on the line several times a day without an outward trace of anxiety hold out?

Dowding, by skilful management, contained the mounting problems. Yet he was wearied by the effort and certain in the knowledge that Fighter Command could not cope with many more all-out raids. Another change in German tack saved the force from certain defeat.

Stage three of the Battle of Britain was sparked in part by accident. On 23 August a German pilot ditched his bombs over London, not to cause mayhem in the capital but rather to speed his flight home. Churchill was outraged. In retaliation, he ordered the bombing of the German capital, Berlin.

Now it was Hitler's turn to be furious. He pledged in turn to annihilate London, abandoning his deeply held wish to occupy the city unscarred by bomb damage. With the German campaign to obliterate the RAF clearly failing, he thought it was time for a new and different tactic. The wholesale bombing of London would not only hit at the heart of the British government but would demoralise its people. 'Sealion', he believed, would still go ahead as planned. The gloves were now off. It was the start of an arduous period of bombing raids which would test the

Below: The unmistakeable shape of St Paul's Cathedral stands firm among the bomb damage in the City of London.

strength of the RAF and also the people of Britain to the very limit.

Now the German forces were throwing their entire weight at Britain. With their losses amounting to 60 planes on 15 September, the decision to undertake mostly night bombing raids was made.

Searchlights in London were unable to track the fast-moving attackers. Night fighters in the RAF squadrons badly needed airborne interception radar to hit back, which took valuable time to provide. The demands on the men of the RAF, already weary from their exertions, were enormous, and their ability to strike back under cover of darkness was limited. They were sleeping for just a few hours in every 24 before being scrambled once more. The casualties among them continued to mount and, for the first time, their losses exceeded those of the enemy.

It took hours, some times days, to find bodies trapped in their wrecked homes

On the ground, the conditions for residents of London and, eventually, other main British cities were appalling.

The London docks were among the first targets in a daring daylight attack on 7 September. Residents watched in horror as scores of German bombers sparked a ferocious blaze. It took just an hour for the Luftwaffe to drop 300 tons of high explosives and countless numbers of incendiaries.

EYE WITNESS

Fred Graves, of Swindon, Wiltshire, served in the RAF ground crews which worked on Hurricanes and Spitfires during the Battle of Britain. Later in the war he serviced Lancasters of Bomber Command and was based near Newmarket.

❛ I remember the Battle of Britain as a non-stop series of dog-fights in the skies above us. Our pilots knew they had a very low life expectancy. I lost an awful lot of friends.

I was particularly impressed by the Polish airmen serving with us. Every time there was a scramble alert they would race out, usually still in their shirt sleeves, jump into a plane and take off. They were very highly motivated to hit back at Germany.

Airmen rarely if ever showed they were scared. Even the Lancaster bomber crews assigned to missions over the Ruhr somehow coped with the pressure. You could detect a reluctance among them – simply because the Ruhr industrial region was so heavily defended – but they did their duty.

I think teamwork helped beat the fear. Bomber air crews were teams. If one of them wasn't fit or well then the whole crew was grounded until he was. They also had to have faith in their aircraft and in us as ground crew. We were the last friendly faces they saw before they flew east.

Looking back it is a miracle some of these men ever made it home. Their aircraft were so shot up they were almost unrecognisable. ❜

At night the raging fires burned like beacons, guiding Luftwaffe pilots to their target.

Soon London Underground stations became shelters for frightened city folk despite an immediate ban on such a use. People slept end to end in close proximity to friends, neighbours and complete strangers. Those lucky enough to have gardens and shelters in their gardens became accustomed to retiring to them in time for tea and staying put until daybreak. It was soon clear that the option of sheltering under a sturdy wooden table was dangerous as homes were reduced to rubble by the bombs.

It took hours to find bodies trapped in their wrecked homes. If bombs had failed to explode, there was still danger for the residents of London after the planes were long gone.

Fire-watchers, full-time fire-fighters and auxiliaries, air raid wardens and the Home Guard did their best to combat the terrible ravages of the raids.

Above: *Coventry was blitzed in a raid code-named 'Moonlight Sonata'. The raid claimed 568 lives.*

Despite all this, the mood in London was far from one of defeatism. The spin-off planned by Hitler of grinding the British public into the ground with the incessant bombing raids was failing miserably. In the tube stations there was impromptu entertainment from singers and musicians. Cups of tea were passed around and soon people learned to pay little heed to the sound of pounding bombs above.

BUSINESS AS USUAL

Instead of people weeping and wailing on the streets when the harsh light of day revealed the full extent of the night raids, there was a camaraderie which no one could have foreseen. Business went on as usual in daylight hours, despite broken windows, fractured gas and water pipes. The spirit of the people of London was ultimately symbolised in the great cathedral of St Pauls, which stood intact overlooking the battered city

while smoke from incendiary fires plumed around its dome.

If anyone was demoralised by the successive and apparently fruitless attacks it was the German pilots who were patently failing in their task of bringing Britain to its knees.

The attacks came in earnest from 15 September as Göring tried to ground the British air force in time for 'Sealion'. That day a record 56 Luftwaffe planes were brought down. Hitler twice postponed making a final decision on whether or not to go ahead before making his decision day 17 September. As the day dawned, London was smoking. But the Luftwaffe had paid a heavy price for the privilege of setting alight this historic capital, and the planes of the Royal Air Force were not only still challenging their fighters but also found time to bombard

FINEST HOUR

'Never in the field of human conflict was so much owed by so many to so few.'

(Winston Churchill after the Battle of Britain.)

the Channel ports where the German invasion fleet was based.

Hitler had no option but to call off 'Sealion' indefinitely. The Battle of Britain was won and the little island was safe from invasion. That meant renewed hope for occupied Europe, for without Britain from which to mount an attack on Hitler's Nazi empire there would have been barely a flicker of opportunity for liberation. Churchill's words of praise and thanks for the gallant RAF, spoken back in August, echoed through the free world. 'Never in the field of human conflict was so much owed by so many to so few.'

Yet the ordeal went on for both the men of the RAF and the people of Britain. Luftwaffe attacks continued unabated. London was attacked for 76 nights in succession and enjoyed little more than a few hours of eerie peace until the middle of 1941.

Anti-aircraft guns boomed in answer to the rain of bombs. There was little chance of them hitting their target. Only 75 aircraft were brought down by anti-aircraft shells – when the

RUDOLPH HESS

The Führer flew into a three-day rage when his deputy, Rudolph Walter Richard Hess, flew to Britain to make peace. A full day after the flight from Germany in a Messerschmitt 110 fighter aircraft, German radio explained away the demoralising desertion by claiming Hess was suffering from hallucinations.

British intelligence chiefs, meanwhile, were similarly at a loss to know what to make of the ace pilot who had been a loyal member of the Nazi party since 1920. On 10 May 1941, when he came down to earth at the end of a parachute and suffered a broken ankle, he claimed he had an important message for the Duke of Hamilton. This message was, apparently, a peace formula which would end the conflict between Britain and Germany.

High-ranking British officers and Churchill himself would not hear of making peace by the back door. Nevertheless, they were reluctant to trumpet the capture of such a key Nazi. Were they being duped by Hitler? Was there a further dimension to this unexpected prize which had fallen into their laps?

Even today, no one can tell whether Hess was demented at the scale of the bloodshed and hatched his plan to end the war accordingly; whether he discussed the plan with Hitler who wished to secure peace with Britain before invading Russia; or whether it was in fact the real Hess who carried out the madcap caper. Years later there were claims that the man held by the Allies was in fact an imposter, dispatched by Himmler or Göring after the murder of Hess.

What remains certain is that the man who fell to earth that night in 1941 was tried as a war criminal at Nuremberg, sentenced to life imprisonment and incarcerated at Spandau prison in Germany for 46 years until his death, apparently by suicide.

civilians were foremost among the casualties.

In Coventry, 568 people were killed on 14 November 1940 when German bombers opened their doors and let 450 tons of bombs drop on the city and destroyed its historic cathedral. Birmingham, Cardiff, Exeter, Manchester, Southampton, Liverpool, Norwich, Swansea, Plymouth, Ipswich, Bath, Sheffield, Sunderland, Hull, Canterbury and Middlesborough all received a battering.

BITTER TRUTH

Thousands of people were made homeless by these air raids. During the worst of them which occurred in December 1940 and May 1941 in London, the firefighters ran out of water as they fought hundreds of blazes and were left with little option but to let them rage on. On 10 May 1941 550 German bombers unleashed 700 tons of high explosives and thousands of incendiaries, killing 1,436 people and destroying 700 acres of city. Just 14 of the attackers were brought down.

From August 1940 to May 1941, 44,000 civilians died and 103,000 were injured. The destruction and misery was merely a camouflage for Hitler's real intentions, to expand eastwards across the Russian borders, to Moscow and beyond. Only when Luftwaffe planes were pulled out of France to concentrate on the Russian front did the attacks on Britain subside.

Luftwaffe flew about 12,000 sorties over Britain. Post-war investigation proved that for every bomber shot down by an anti-aircraft gun in September 1940 the gun had to expend an enormous 20,000 rounds. By February 1941 the figure was down to 3,000. The knowledge that something was being done

was at least a small comfort to the population.

Göring also turned his attention to other British cities. Perhaps his intention was to eliminate great industrial centres and not simply to mete out punishment to British civilians. In fact, the lack of accuracy among bombers, ensured that

Left: As dawn breaks, the destruction of the previous night's raid on London's docklands is revealed.

AIR BATTLE – BALKANS

Both Axis and Allied powers saw benefit in opening a battle-front in the Balkans.

For Hitler, there was a chance of mopping up a potentially troublesome southern flank before mounting 'Operation Barbarossa', the invasion of Russia.

Churchill and his top brass saw a successful campaign in Greece or Yugoslavia offering a possible back-door entry into Germany when no access seemed available at the front.

In the event, the short and bloody campaign in the region left both sides as losers when it illustrated both the advantages – and drawbacks – of an airborne campaign.

Mussolini had opened hostilities when he invaded Greece on 28 October 1940. It was an impetuous decision which he lived to regret. Not only did it infuriate his ally Hitler, who had fostered an amenable relationship with Greece's ruler General Metaxas and considered the country in the bag. But it served to further humiliate Mussolini and his troops in addition to their inept showing in North and East Africa.

For the Greeks, although poorly equipped for modern warfare, were imbued with fighting spirit and managed to see off the Italians, pushing them back behind their lines in occupied Albania.

Britain was determined to stand by pledges of aid made to Greece – even though it had been unable to honour promises made to Romania, which was occupied by German troops at the start of October 1940.

ALLIES IN GREECE

Hitler had no option but to intervene in the action. However, for a few months he bided his time.

Having dispatched several thousand men, the British were keen to send even more of their contingent presently in North Africa to the aid of the Greeks. Metaxas was unsure. Although the presence of air support was welcomed, his own men were putting up an adequate performance and the presence of Allied ground troops would only succeed in drawing the awesome firepower of an irate Hitler whose soldiers were suffering greatly due to the inadequacies of their footwear.

By the end of November 1940 three squadrons of Blenheim bombers and fighters had been stationed in Greece. Their brief, to defend Athens.

The political outlook changed at the end of January 1941 when Metaxas died suddenly and was replaced by Emmanuel Tsouderos who was well-disposed towards the Allies.

At a meeting in February, it was agreed the 1st Armoured Brigade, the 6th Australian Division and the 2nd New Zealand Division would be stationed in Greece to repel possible German aggression. With Bulgaria to the east rapidly

> **The Greeks were imbued with fighting spirit and managed to see off the Italians**

falling under the influence of Germany, and with Italy in the west, the fresh troops could plug defensive gaps left open by the Greeks fighting in Albania.

Neighbouring Yugoslavia, a country Britain failed to support, was feeling the Nazi pressure. The government were given an invitation-ultimatum in March 1941. Yugoslavia was to join the Axis powers. Prince Regent Paul was unable to secure aid from the British. With a heavy heart he finally gave his consent

Far left: *A ship unloading supplies for the Allies in Suda Bay comes to grief.*
Left: *Italian soldiers were held at bay when trying to invade Greece.*

EYE WITNESS

Howard Ganly was in the US 82nd Airborne Division. He was dropped behind enemy lines before D-Day to act as a pathfinder.

❝I was a little lost. They gave us the wrong maps. I made a few mistakes. I was shot at by my own men. They had got hold of some farmers' clothes and put them on, thinking they would be good disguises in German territory. Some of them were from my own company. I could have had them court martialled but I didn't. They stuck to me close for the rest of the war.

I was looking for open fields that weren't mined and didn't have big stumps stuck in the ground so they would be suitable for landing gliders. I would signal the gliders if it was OK to come in, with special lights and flares. We didn't dare use radios too much. I was very scared, I was just 19 years old. I came into the service when I was 17. The army kept pushing me around from one place to another. I didn't have any family, I spent most of my childhood in orphan asylums. I joined up to get a job and the money was good.

I survived D-Day but ran into trouble later on in Europe. I baled out in Holland behind enemy lines. A young Dutch girl put me in a barge and hid me from the Germans. She probably saved my life. I looked for her a few times after the war but never found her. I broke my leg and back in the fall. I have been disabled ever since. I was hospitalised for two years. I worked on and off but most of the time I have been crippled up.❞

and the Tripartite Pact was signed on 25 March.

Fury against the agreement among the Yugoslav people erupted immediately. There was an internal revolt which unseated the Prince Regent and put 17-year-old King Peter II in his place. On 27 March the pact signed with Hitler was ripped into pieces. The sombre mood in Belgrade was suddenly lifted, to be replaced with rejoicing.

HITLER OUTRAGED

The outbreak of anti-Nazism outraged Hitler. He resolved to teach the people of Yugoslavia a lesson. German commanders were told: 'Politically it is very important that the blow against Yugoslavia is carried out with pitiless harshness.' It made sense to combat the Greek problem at the same time so 'Operation Strafgericht' (punishment) against

Right: Germany soon won command of the skies over Greece, and this tipped the balance of the battle in their favour.

Yugoslavia and 'Operation Marita' against Greece were co-ordinated to begin on 6 April.

Hitler's campaign to break Yugoslavia into submission started with a dawn raid by the Luftwaffe. The sole declaration of war was the shower of bombs which hit Belgrade at 6am. The day-long assault claimed 17,000 lives and the grand buildings of the capital crumbled.

The day closed with another disaster, this time for Greece. The Luftwaffe wreaked havoc on Piraeus, the harbour of the Greek capital, which was crowded with ships from an incoming convoy. As the German bombs rained down destruction, one ship at anchor, SS *Glen Fraser*, had its 250-ton cargo of explosives ignited by a direct hit. The explosion that followed flattened much of the harbour, sank yet more vessels and even shattered windows in Athens some seven miles distant.

German armies began driving into both countries at the usual alarming rapid Panzer pace. Yugoslavia, which had a small army, held out for just 11 days. Much of its air force was knocked out on the ground by Luftwaffe attacks. The inglorious fortnight was compounded when Royal Yugoslav Air Force Hurricanes became embroiled in a dog-fight over Belgrade with some GBF-109s which unfortunately belonged to the very same air force.

RETREAT TO CRETE

The Greek army, too, was having difficulty fending off the advance. The fighting was gruelling. British commander General Sir Henry 'Jumbo' Maitland Wilson soon saw the hopelessness of the situation and ordered evacuation to the south. On 22 April Greece capitulated also. The initial destination of the fleeing Allied troops was the Peloponnese islands linked to mainland Greece· by a bridge at Corinth. Then it was onwards to the island of Crete.

Under fire from the Luftwaffe above, the Royal Navy came in to the southerly beaches on 26 and 27 April to hoist 26,000 men to safety. Left behind were 900 dead, 1,200 wounded and something in the order of 10,000 men who had

fallen prisoner to the Germans. Then there was the abandoned weaponry, amounting to more than 100 tanks, 400 guns, 1,800 machine guns and 8,000 vehicles. The RAF had lost more than 200 aircraft in total

On Crete there was chaos with hundreds of leaderless men awaiting an uncertain future

while the Royal Navy had had two destroyers and about 25 other ships sunk.

On Crete there was chaos with hundreds of leaderless men awaiting an uncertain future. The only thing of which they could be sure was that Hitler's men would not rest until Crete too fell into their grasp.

In command was Major-General Bernard Freyberg, a

Above: *Serbs in Yugoslavia were no friends of the Germans. Many fought as guerrillas against the invaders.*

pugnacious New Zealander who was ready to refuse the mantle of leadership until he discovered there was a sizeable number of his own men on the island – troops he believed had been taken back to Egypt.

His force amounted to two New Zealand brigades, about 7,750 men, plus an Australian brigade, two further battalions of Australians and a field regiment of artillery, with a combined total of 6,500. There were 15,000 British troops, too, comprising a brigade of infantrymen and part of the 1st Armoured Brigade, complete with two light tanks. Also at his disposal were about 10,000 Greeks. The Allies also had the support of

Above: *A Panzer division parades its might before the centuries-old Acropolis in Athens, after the city was overrun.*

the local population, many of whom would take up arms against the incoming Germans.

Freyberg, who won the VC in World War I, set about defending the island as best he could. He focused his forces at the three airfields, Maleme, Retimo and Heraklion, and the easily accessible Suda Bay.

From North Africa he received some tanks – less than two dozen but welcome nonetheless – and some rather war-worn artillery. There was a further injection of men, the 2nd Leicesters, who arrived on 16 May.

Crete – 136 miles long and an uneven 40 miles wide, and full of mountainous terrain – could hardly be adequately defended given the small number of men. Yet Freyberg was determined his men would give it their best shot.

From North Africa Freyberg received some tanks – less than two dozen but welcome

For Germany, the invasion of Crete posed some difficulties, not least in how to transport troops to the island. The Royal Navy had established a command of the seas. Already the shortcomings of the Italian navy had been shown up and the German command did not trust its ally's sailors with the lives of crack soldiers of the Third Reich. So an all-out

amphibious assault was deemed too dangerous.

Yet in the air the Luftwaffe was unrivalled. By 18 May only seven RAF aircraft were left on Crete, and these were promptly withdrawn to Egypt. An airborne assault might work. Airborne forces had been in existence since 1927 when the first was formed by Italy. The Soviet Union soon followed suit and the value of these sky-fliers was clear. They could be dropped into enemy territory either in small numbers for the purpose – of sabotage or in large numbers to begin an invasion.

There were, of course numerous hazards inherent in airborne operations, but until now the Germans had known only successes. Their use of paratroopers in Norway, Belgium

EYE WITNESS

Morley Pence, 71, from Los Angeles, served with the 26 Mobile Reclamation Squad of the 442 Troop Carrier Command. Based at Thatcham, near Reading, he built and tested CG4A canvas and wood gliders (capable of carrying six men or two men and a Jeep) for 'Operation Overlord'.

❝Before the invasion the whole of southern England was one big military camp. Everything was either painted green or under green canvas. It was like the civilians had all left for the summer.

It was such an unreal time. I remember us bringing aeroplanes through the centre of London on 40ft flat-bed trucks. There was absolutely no room for us to get round the corners so we just made room. No one seemed to mind. Actually, no one seemed to even notice.

When I see London now, this huge, busy bustling city, it brings it all back. I marvel at how the hell we drove those trucks anywhere.❞

and Holland during 1940 had brought striking results. The 55 men from the 'Granite' assault team who parachuted into Eben Emael, the strongest fortress in the world, on the Belgian-Dutch border, in May of that year,

The use of paratroopers in Norway, Belgium and Holland during 1940 had brought striking results

defeated 700 defenders in less than a day.

The Luftwaffe's airborne supremo was Kurt Student, a World War I fighter pilot and squadron leader. He had keenly studied the potential of airborne techniques in Russia during the 1930s and saw 'Blitzkreig' as an excellent opportunity to put theory into practice.

Not only did he have troops leaping from flying aircraft but also equipment-bearing soldiers carried in gliders, and 'air mobile' forces, men trained in the art of going into action straight from the door of a landed plane. He sought to use all types in the invasion of Crete.

'MERKUR'

'Operation Merkur', the German attack on Crete, was to be launched following days of heavy aerial bombardment, with the landing of 36 gliders whose elite troops would knock out anti-aircraft guns and capture key locations.

The men of XI Air Corps' 1st Assault Regiment were the next penned in to see action, capturing an airfield and other key locations. At the same time, men of the 3rd Parachute Regiment would drop further up the coast and the aim was for both prongs to battle to a reunion.

Then a second wave was planned in which the 1st and 2nd Parachute Regiments were introduced with heavier arms, while two further battalions arrived by sea in fast motor-cutters. More amphibious activity was planned when the island was in German control.

Right: General Kurt Student was the mastermind behind German paratroopers' triumphs – and their failures, like the ill-fated assault on Crete.

First hitch for the Germans came when too few planes were provided, forcing the commanders to cut the size of the airborne assault.

Student and his men believed only a few thousand men would be there to meet them when the attack on 20 May got underway. It was a catastrophic miscalculation.

As a swarm of aircraft receded into the distance, hundreds of parachutes billowed in the breeze. The troops on the ground had plenty of time to take aim and fire, relishing a chance to get revenge on the men who had so recently chased them out of Greece. The helpless paras were picked off one by one as they all fell virtually on

Above: German paratroopers were confident as they embarked for Crete, with good reason. Until then, they had only known success.

top of the defending Anzac and British forces. Olive groves and rocky escarpments were littered with bodies, many still strapped into 'chutes.

Some parachutists didn't even make it out of their planes. Ground fire penetrated the hulls of the low-flying aircraft, killing or wounding men while they were still inside.

The few that survived were compelled to seek cover and join up with their comrades as soon as they could. Only those who dropped away from their targets – and thus away from defensive fire – escaped being cut down. It was for them to fight their way across the rocky landscape and unite with other groups.

Communications were poor on both sides. With telephone lines down and radios suffering patchy reception, the Allied groups felt equally isolated from assistance and exposed to the enemy. It caused one New Zealand commander to withdraw his men from a commanding position in the heights above an airfield, leaving a vital foothold open to the attackers.

Groves and escarpments were littered with bodies, many still strapped into their 'chutes

There followed more bitter fighting, often at close quarters, with many Allied soldiers claiming victims at the point of a bayonet. Both sides vied for the airfields. There was an uncomfortable stalemate as both Allied and German commanders tried to land reinforcements. The Royal Navy sank the German transports while the Luftwaffe holed the British ships.

GERMAN VICTORY

At Maleme airfield brave German pilots began to land their transport planes, some coming to grief on the runway, others colliding with planes that had preceded them. Inside were well-trained, well-armed soldiers fresh and ready for the fight.

The New Zealanders at Maleme were finally overwhelmed. Germany had scored the first Victory in the battle for Crete.

It was a key triumph, for now that the attacking troops had control of Maleme airfield, the gateway was open for supplies and still more troops to be transported in.

OTTO SKORZENY

A scar-faced German captain called Otto Skorzeny was the action-man asked by Hitler to rescue Mussolini from imprisonment in September 1943. Skorzeny, who was frustrated in earlier plans to snatch the Duce to safety by the diligence of the Italian authorities who kept their prized prisoner on the move, planned for a German plane to land on a precarious mountain plateau while he in the company of other troops parachuted into the hotel hideaway where Mussolini was held. Italian guards at the mountain village of Assergi abided by his requests not to resist the bold German move. Mussolini was flown off in the tiny plane which battled to ascend from the plateau. On reaching Rome he was transferred to a Heinkel 111 for a flight to the safety of Vienna.

In less than a week, Freyberg assessed the situation as hopeless. He ordered the Allied troops, by now mentally and physically exhausted, to withdraw to the south where an evacuation was being launched by the Royal Navy.

Between 27 May and 31 May, about 16,500 Allied men were taken off Crete. Germany had sealed its Balkan front.

BALANCE SHEET

Both sides were left counting the cost, however. Left on Crete were 1,750 Allied soldiers killed in action, two thirds of them Anzacs, and 13,500 men now held as prisoners of war. The Royal Navy lost three cruisers and six destroyers in the rescue bid, along with about 2,000 sailors killed or taken prisoner. Also left behind were Greek, British and Anzac soldiers who turned guerrilla to fight a cloaked campaign against the occupiers. It was another inglorious rout for the Allies.

As for the Germans, nearly half the initial force were killed on Crete, amounting to some 3,700 men. Among them were

high-ranking officers including a divisional commander, and a colonel. The number of aircraft shot to smithereens by the Allies or junked on the island airstrips was also immense.

Hitler surveyed the results – and decided the price was too high. Matter-of-factly, he told Student afterwards: 'Of course you know, General, that we shall never do another airborne operation. Crete proved that the days of parachute troops are over.'

It was a gross over-exaggeration. Germany continued to employ parachute troops although never again in such numbers. Nevertheless, Hitler did decide to abandon plans to parachute men into Malta, the stepping-stone island in the Mediterranean. Had he won Malta, Hitler may have found victory in the North African campaign, and pushed into the Middle East and India to join hands with Germany's ally Japan.

The Allies observed the German experience on Crete but also decided in favour of using airborne troops in future engagements. Paratroopers played a pivotal role in the success of the D-Day operations in 1944.

'Of course you know, General, that we shall never do another airborne operation.'

Theirs was a precarious job, dropping behind enemy lines in darkness to act as pathfinders for the incoming gliders. Men of the US 82nd and 101st Airborne Divisions were charged with hindering the enemy advance towards to the coast. But the landings did not go as planned.

A combination of mistakes in navigation and inexperienced piloting had men dispersed over a huge area instead of being in a

Right: Captured Australian servicemen are a source of curiosity for their German guards.

Left: 'Pathfinder' parachutists are briefed before dropping into France, their task to direct airborne forces to landing points.

and unseen troops. One regiment in the 82nd Airborne Division managed to capture the town of Ste Mère Église.

British airborne troops were also seeing action as they seized vital bridges and knocked out a battery of guns aimed at the coast. For the British paratroopers, the ultimate test of endurance was to come later in the year at Arnhem in 'Operation Market Garden'.

concentrated group. Parachutists found themselves landing in some of the many engorged rivers in the region. Weighed down by their equipment they floundered for hours trying to get out. Others drowned in the struggle. Both Divisions were literally thousands of men short when they went into action. All

Weighed down by their equipment they floundered for hours trying to get out

the hazards of airborne operations, particularly those carried out at night, appeared to be coming in at the Americans.

Yet success bred out of disaster. Undoubtedly, the German defenders were thrown into confusion by the unexpected

Right: Horsa gliders lie in pieces after landing men in northern France in 1944. On these gliders the fuselage is split from the wings to unload.

ALLIED SUCCESS

Air superiority during D-Day became the key to Allied success. While it was thought that the Luftwaffe would sent up some 900 aircraft to make 1,200 sorties on D-Day, in fact only 100 were made in daylight and a further 175 after dark. By contrast the RAF alone flew 5,656 sorties on D-Day, about 40 per cent of the total made by the Allies.

Allied aircraft dropped a total of 4,310 paratroops and towed gliders containing 493 men, 17 guns, 44 Jeeps and 55 motorcycles without suffering harassment from enemy bombers.

As well as protecting troops and ships, Allied aircraft dropped 5,267 bombs against the coastal gun batteries.

The first German plane to fall victim on D-Day was a Ju 88, brought down by New Zealand Flying Officer Johnnie Houlton, one of 2,000 pilots in the Second Tactical Air Force who was in a Spitfire.

In the months which followed, three times as many bombs were dropped on Germany than in all the previous years.

Montgomery was eager to persuade Eisenhower of the wisdom of committing the ground troops to one hammer-blow into northern Germany. Eisenhower, however, favoured a fan-shaped attack instead.

'MARKET GARDEN'

'Operation Market Garden' was designed to capture key bridges in Holland through which Allied troops could be funnelled into Germany. The US 101st Airborne Division was charged with gaining land north of Eindhoven, the US 82nd Airborne Division was allocated two big bridges over the Meuse and the Wall rivers, while the British 1st Airborne Division had to seize bridges over the lower Rhine at Arnhem.

The men were carried to their targets in a total of 1,068 aircraft and 478 gliders. While the Americans experienced considerable success on their fronts, the British met enormous

German resistance en route to their target. Just one battalion, the 2nd, reached the bridge at Arnhem. Soon after, they were cut off.

Unfortunately for the British paratroopers, the Germans picked Arnhem as a focal point of defence and reinforced their lines with troops, including an SS Panzer corps containing two armoured divisions. All efforts by the British to reach the men isolated at Arnhem were repelled after fierce clashes.

At the bridge, the paratroopers were pushed back into a defensive margin. It took nine days for the men to establish an escape route across the Rhine. Just 2,200

It took nine days for the men to establish an escape route across the Rhine

men got out from a force which began with a strength of 10,000. Montgomery's plan to by-pass Germany's defensive Siegfried line had failed. The thrust continued as before.

Right: Troops taken by gliders into Arnhem in a bid to short-circuit the route to Berlin. The Britons had a grim fate in store.

WINGS OVER THE DESERT

The Western Desert Air Force was officially born on 9 October 1940 at Maaton Bagush in North Africa.

Here in the African desert, the theories of modern air warfare were established. For it was in North Africa that the principles of 'partnership' between air, sea and land forces were tried and tested for the first time, helping to put an end to decades of overt inter-service rivalry.

Co-operation of the kind enjoyed by air, sea and naval personnel among the Allies was unthinkable for their German and Italian counterparts, who not only fought a common enemy but were constantly embroiled in sniping against different factions on their own side. Indeed, there were plenty of hiccoughs along the way among the Allies with soldiers convinced the only worthwhile aeroplane was the one that flew protectively above their heads, regardless of the risk to the pilot and his inability to achieve results from that vulnerable spot.

The initial trials of tactical airborne operations were honed by the men of the Desert Air Force until they finally became adopted everywhere.

Lessons learned in the Desert Air Force now seem rudimentary and even naive. Yet aerial combat was still in its infancy when the war commenced. Fliers in World War I had the opportunity to make only elementary trials and errors. Little was done to advance the theory of warfare in the air after 1918 as most nations were concentrating on peace.

And until the conflict in the desert got underway, the Royal Air Force was from necessity concentrating primarily on defence.

To call it simply a Desert Air Force is to vastly over-simplify the case. The men who worked under its umbrella saw action in the skies above Egypt, Libya, East and West Africa, Greece, Yugoslavia, Palestine, and Italy.

This tremendous fighting force grew from an original nucleus of some 29 squadrons – a total of 600 aircraft. These were all that were available to Middle East Commander Air Chief Marshal Sir Arthur Longmore when hostilities with Italy commenced in 1940. Included in this total were a number of outdated biplanes and obsolete Blenheim bombers. That summer saw the Battle of Britain reach its momentous heights. So the chances of getting quality replacements were slim.

In addition, the airmen faced the same shortages that cursed the soldiers on the ground, those of water, fuel and spare parts to replace those worn by the inhospitable terrain.

Above: *Mussolini believed his air force could win the skies over Africa.*
Left: *Stalwart Beaufighters played a key role in the North African campaign.*

Against them was the Regia Aeronautica, the Italian air force, which had proved itself already in the Spanish Civil War and Mussolini's Ethiopian campaign in the mid-1930s. The Italians were flying home-produced planes like Capronis and Fiats. Unfortunately for the Italians, their early promise was soon dashed by the Desert Air Force.

MALTA ATTACKED

The Regia Aeronautica went into action for the first time on 11 June 1940, with 35 Savoia-Marchetti bombers attacking Malta. Pitted against them were four Gloster Sea Gladiators. By the end of the day, the Italians had launched seven attacks.

Responding to this, 26 RAF Bristol Blenheims attacked an Italian airfield in North Africa, eventually destroying 18 enemy aircraft on the ground.

Above: Despite their years of experience, Italian aircraft and pilots proved no match for the Desert Air Force.

There followed a number of skirmishes. Prime targets for the Italians were Malta, Gibraltar, the British base at Alexandria in Egypt and the British Mediterranean Fleet.

The action in Africa then forked, with General Graziani leading his contingent of Italians in the Western Desert against Wavell, while the Duke of Aosta led some 215,000 troops out of Italian East Africa and into a British dominion. To meet Graziani's men were the British 7th Armoured Division, soon to be joined by the 6th Australian Division. Meanwhile, the 4th Indian Division was dispatched to meet the threat in East Africa.

It was in the East African campaign that vital steps towards an orchestrated plan for close air support were made. At the outset in October 1940, the Italians in East Africa

were a formidable enemy. Their spirits were high, their maturity in desert warfare a major advantage. But much of their buoyancy could be put down to the fact that they enjoyed air superiority. Italy had 14 bomber squadrons or gruppi in East Africa, and five supporting fighter gruppi. The over-stretched British forces, comprising nine squadrons, were reinforced by a further eight squadrons from South Africa, flying Hurricane aircraft.

Soon the battle to win supremacy of the skies began to swing in favour of the Allies

Soon, the battle to win supremacy in the skies began to swing in favour of the Allies. Both sides fought bitterly, both on land and in the air, for command of Keren, a fortified hill top in Eritrea. At the end of eight weeks, however, the Italians were turfed out of their strong-

hold and, by April 1941, a corner in the war of East Africa had been turned. As the campaign toiled on, the South African Air Force formed a first Close Support Flight to co-operate with ground troops, achieving a good measure of success.

FIVE LESSONS

After the battle of Keren, one British observer noted five lessons to be learned. They were: the need for transport planes; the need for supplies to be dropped by air (which was to prove crucial in the jungle wars of Burma and the Pacific); the advantage lent by long-range fighters which could destroy the enemy's aircraft before they lifted off; the need for Red Cross air ambulances to evacuate the wounded; and the preference for dive bombers.

These were all points which would be brought home to subsequent senior air force officers. For now, only the immediate achievement of winning an

EYE WITNESS

Ern Stanton, from New South Wales, was 18 when he joined the Royal Australian Air Force and qualified as a flier on the Empire Air Training Scheme.

❛Of our EATS course in Canada, about 40 per cent were later killed. It was very sad and disheartening to hear about your mates dying in action but I was really too young and conditioned too much to death to realise the more serious aspects of war

I do particularly remember one little bloke in our squadron who would give away all his personal effects before he went on a mission because he was convinced he wasn't going to come back. When he did return safely, he would go around and get them all back. But he did finally get killed.❜

Below: *Hurricane pilots of 73 Squadron line up before a desert-worn aircraft in North Africa during 1941. The Hurricane was the RAF's first monoplane fighter.*

important initial victory was noted. As the Allies took greater command of the action, Italian commanders found themselves battling not only against the Allies but also against a sapped will among their own men. A proportion of their troops were native Africans whose loyalty was suspect.

The campaign in Eritrea was to end in a complete and resounding victory for the Allies by the middle of 1941. Yet short on success though the Allies were at this stage, there was little chance to celebrate. Much as the British commanders had feared, Hitler had sent German forces into the region to assist his floundering fascist soul-mate.

Early in 1941 it was clear the Luftwaffe were installing units of Fliegerkorps X in Sicily, a specialist branch of the air force which had cut its teeth in the Norwegian campaign and

specialised in picking off ships. The Mediterranean Fleet first felt its presence on 10 January 1941 when up to 40 aircraft attacked a convoy. In aerial warfare, the Luftwaffe quite simply outclassed the Italians.

At the same time, the conflict in Greece was intensifying. The

Early in 1941 it was clear that the Luftwaffe were installing units of Fliegerkorps X in Sicily

only assistance actively required by the Greeks at the start was an injection of air power. The expanding Allied air strength had little problem asserting its authority. In one battle which took place on 28 February 1941, 16 Hurricanes and 12 Gladiators were patrolling at 14,000 feet when they were attacked by 50 Italian Fiat planes. In the two-hour clash

which followed, the Royal Air Force fighters claimed 27 enemy planes for just one Gladiator lost.

The string of successes was a tribute to the ground crews who faced appalling winter conditions in the most primitive of airfields in order to keep the planes airborne. Spring saw further aerial reinforcements sent in by the British but the leaders in the field were uneasy. It was surely only a matter of months before Hitler made that battleground his own as well.

LUFTWAFFE ARRIVES

In April those grim predictions became reality. The Royal Air Force found its forces and those of its Greek and Yugoslav allies suddenly dwarfed by the arrival of the Luftwaffe. Its ranks included 430 bombers, 180

fighters, 700 transport planes and 80 gliders.

By 19 April the four Hurricane squadrons in Greece could rally just 22 operational aircraft between them. All were pulled down to Athens to lend air support to the evacuation of troops from Greece to Crete and North Africa. In the end there were only seven Hurricanes left.

On Crete they were joined by four Sea Gladiators and three Fairey Fulmars of the Fleet Air Arm. The abysmally small fighting force was virtually wiped out on the ground by the marauding Germans.

Added to the boiling pot was the Iraqi uprising against the British in May 1941. The Desert Air Force was by now staffed with Australian, New Zealand, Rhodesian and Free

Above: *German aircraft and pilots suffered the same difficult conditions as their Allied enemies.*

French units, as well as British and South African. But the ceaseless demands took their toll of its strength. And the menace from the Third Reich in

By April the four Hurricane squadrons in Greece could rally just 22 operational aircraft

the region did nothing to recede during that period. In fact, it gained momentum. Hitler was dallying with the idea of invading Malta. The little island which had found some relief when attacking forces were diverted to assist in the invasion of Greece, was once again at the top of the agenda for the Luftwaffe.

MALTA REPLENISHED

Its defences amounted to just four fighter squadrons as well as bombers and Fleet Air Arm forces based off the island. The succession of raids both by the Italians and increasingly by the Germans pared down the number of fighters. But the ranks were replenished on 15 June 1941 when 47 flew from the deck of the *Ark Royal*, and a further 64 were dispatched by similar means before the month had ended.

Below: SS Talbot *was one of scores of ships to fall foul of enemy planes in Malta's Grand Harbour.*

The hectic months ahead, saw the Malta-based fliers toiling to keep the convoys safe, and so deprive Hitler and Mussolini of the toe-hold they both sought. In addition, they attempted to destroy enemy convoys and hit targets in Italy – particularly Naples where, on 16 December 1941, 16 Wellingtons showered a torpedo factory with 4000lb bombs, the largest used in the Mediterranean to that date.

Between June and October 1941, 220,000 tons of Axis shipping was sunk en route to Libya, of which 115,000 tons could be marked down to the Desert Air Force, especially its Maltese division.

The fruits presented to Churchill by the frustrated Longmore were too few and far between to impress. Friction

On 16 October 1941, 16 Wellingtons showered a Naples torpedo factory with 4,000lb bombs

between the ground and air forces was still in evidence, never more so than when a reconnaissance flight reported enemy troops approaching a vital petrol dump in the North African desert. The dump was destroyed before it was discovered – the troops in question were in fact, British. Never mind

Above: On Malta, air strips like this one provided constant targets for Luftwaffe pilots.

EYE WITNESS

Post Office worker Arthur Helm was one of the first New Zealanders to sign up and fight for Britain following the outbreak of World War II.

❝ I had read a lot about the Germans and I knew how despicable they were. And I knew what I was letting myself in for.

I was a member of the First Echelon, the 6,607 men who first left New Zealand for Egypt. Later I was in northern Greece as a member of 4th Brigade Signals. After the invasion of the Germans, we moved to fight a rearguard action at Thebes. I saw the Acropolis about four hours before the Swastika was raised over it. At Port Rafti we held a two-mile stretch of coastline and two miles inland during the evacuation. We had to throw everything overboard except for our rifles, the clothes we stood up in and a small haversack.

Author Lawrence Durrell wrote that when everyone arrived in Crete they were dishevelled, dispirited and defeated – except the New Zealanders. They came up the beach with their rifles poised, their hats on and every one had a book under his arms. He was wrong – I had two books, a book of poetry and a Bible.

Spirits were high among the New Zealanders. We simply felt sorry for the Greek soldiers we left behind.

We expected the arrival of the Germans. I had just knocked off after 24 hours on duty and was having my breakfast when the first parachutes appeared.

There was a lot of deer-stalking and rabbit-shooting in New Zealand so most of us could shoot pretty straight. You knew when you had hit a parachutist coming down. He retracted his legs up as an automatic reaction.

Later I got involved at Galatas where we went in with bayonets after dark and drove out a bunch of Germans from the houses there. It was very nerve-racking but we got rid of them – even if we did have to retreat the next day.

I got out over the mountains to the harbour for evacuation. I met an English soldier at the side of the track and pointed out the way. He said: "I'm not going any further." I gave him some water and he told me he had been through Dunkirk but it wasn't a patch on this.

He just laid down on the hillside and died. He was done for, absolutely exhausted, and he had no will to live.

We lost Crete because the Germans had planes and we didn't. But we never lost heart. After being evacuated from Crete we went to Sidi Rezburgh. That was probably the worst campaign of the lot. ❞

that it was notoriously difficult to positively identify the nationality of soldiers from the air. The fighters on the ground had been deprived of valuable fuel for no reason. Longmore's repeated requests for more aircraft did little to endear him at home, either. Duly, Longmore was replaced by Arthur Tedder in May 1941.

AIR FLEET ENLARGED

The following month, Wavell was dispatched from North Africa by an irate Winston Churchill. Happily, his replacement, General Sir Claude Auchinleck, struck a harmonious note with Tedder which helped to end the bubbling army-air force discord.

Tedder, with support from the Air Ministry, helped to overhaul the repair and maintenance operations in the region which were proving so inefficient and therefore costly to the service.

Once he had enlarged the fleet of aircraft available to the Desert Air Force to beyond 1,000 in November 1941, Tedder turned his attention to the quest for new, well-trained recruits. There was a chronic shortage of training facilities in the Middle East. Tedder fell back

Two operations to relieve Tobruk, 'Brevity' and 'Battleaxe', had failed in the early summer of 1941

on his usual standpoint, which was to employ an expert – in this case Air Commodore B. Embry – who could devote his time and attention to the problem.

CO-ORDINATED ACTION

Two operations to relieve Tobruk, 'Brevity' and 'Battleaxe', had failed in the early summer of 1941 and once again it seemed that the relations between army and air force would be strained. It was in September 1941 that an adequate blueprint for co-ordinated action was finally drawn up to at last eliminate this problem. Drawing on the illustrations of the East African campaign, it set out the principles of close support of land forces by air forces, including pre-arranged and impromptu attacks on the enemy. Indirect air support was

defined as attacks on objectives other than the enemy forces in the battle proper.

An Air Support Control headquarters was created for each army corps. These were information exchanges linked by two-way radio to brigades in action. Representing the RAF at brigade was a team called a Forward Air Support Link. The RAF team could assess the action at close quarters and request air support if necessary. On receiving the request, the staff at the Air Support Control

Above: Air Chief Marshal Sir Arthur W. Tedder, Deputy Supreme Commander, Allied Forces Western Europe.

team headquarters could work out where best to send its aircraft during a battle for the most effective results.

The principles had already been put into practice on exercises in Northern Ireland as early as September 1940. A developmental Army Co-Operation Command had been set up by the RAF following Dunkirk when the air force received flak for not coming more visibly to the aid of evacuating soldiers.

In Africa, these close-support principles were put into action and adopted thereafter to the satisfaction of everyone involved.

THE END OF THE BEGINNING...

'This is not the end. It is not even the beginning of the end. But it is, perhaps, the end of the beginning.'

(Winston Churchill after the Allied victory in North Africa.)

REDS IN THE SKY

No one in Russia was ready for war when it came in June 1941, least of all the unwieldy air force.

Stalin boasted of a large body of planes. But like the sizeable French air force of 1940, the Red Air Force was ineffectively used and no match for the skill and experience of the Luftwaffe. Its sole four-engined bomber at the outset of the war was the TB-3, slow, under-powered and inadequately armed. It had ten squadrons of MiG, Yak and Lagg fighters. Yet these were far inferior to the Messerschmitts so elegantly handled by German pilots.

In addition, the Russians were part-way through a modernisation plan in which their outdated planes would be replaced by more competitive models. The Russian air force, like all branches of the establishment, had suffered its fair share of losses in the purges which Stalin organised to rid himself of potential opponents.

AID FROM BRITAIN

The pilots of the Red Air Force were trained to support the troops on the ground rather than enter into combat with

other aircraft. Many ended up frantically helping to evacuate Russian industry to the east, to save it from falling into German hands – reducing the aircraft available for other duties still further. Indeed, its fighter arm had never been put to the test. The summer and autumn of 1941 brought a succession of disasters for the Red Air Force.

Still punished by the Germans at home, the RAF still found the resources to send several squadrons of Hurricanes

Above: *Britain provided Hurricanes and know-how to the Russian air force, following the German invasion.*

to the aid of the Russians.

It was Churchill's wish that as much aid should be devoted to the beleaguered and reluctant new ally as possible – despite the fact he was a lifelong critic

The summer and autumn of 1941 brought a succession of disasters for the Red Air Force

of communism. In a broadcast shortly after Hitler's 'Operation Barbarossa', he explained how the hatred of fascism remained uppermost in his emotions.

'The Nazi regime is indistinguishable from the worst features of Communism. It is devoid of all

Left: *Much of Russia's air power was devoted to shipping industry east.*
Far left: *The TB-7 bomber that brought Russian minister Molotov to Britain.*

theme and principle except appetite and racial domination. It excels all forms of human wickedness in the efficiency of its cruelty and ferocious aggression. No one has been a more consistent opponent of Communism that I have for the last 25 years.

'But all this fades away before the spectacle which is now unfolding. The past, with its crimes, its follies and its tragedies, flashes away. I see the Russian soldiers standing on the threshold of their native land, guarding the fields which their fathers have tilled from time immemorial. I see them guarding their homes where mothers and wives pray ...

'I see advancing upon all this in hideous onslaught the Nazi war machine with its clanking, heel-clicking, dandified Prussian officers, its crafty expert agents fresh from the cowing and tying down of a dozen countries...

'I see the Russian soldiers standing on the threshold of their native land'

'I see the German bombers and fighters in the sky, still smarting from many a British whipping, delighted to find what they believe is an easier and safer prey.

'. . . if Hitler imagines that his attack on Soviet Russia will cause the slightest divergence of aims or slackening of effort in the great democracies who are resolved upon his doom, he is woefully mistaken.'

BRITISH TEACHERS

A British unit was sent with the aircraft to the Soviet Union to teach the Russians how to make and fly Hurricanes and to pass on tactical tips about the escort of bombers and general air operations.

Soon, the lessons of the visiting Britons and that of bitter experience began to sink in. Until the Russians became fully conversant with combat know-how and were better equipped,

Below: *Royal Air Force Hurricanes pictured in the air over the Russian countryside on their way back to base from escort duty.*

EYE WITNESS

Alexander Pokryshkin, the son of a bricklayer in Novosibirsk in Siberia, emerged as one of Russia's air aces. He flew 550 operational flights, fought 137 aerial battles and had 59 victories to his credit. He became the first member of the Soviet armed forces to be awarded the title 'Hero of the Soviet Union' three times, receiving his third Hero's Gold Star Medal in August 1944.

❝I was out with pilot Semyonov as my partner flying on a reconnaissance mission to Jassy where the Germans had an aerodrome. As we approached the town I espied five Messerschmitts flying towards us, three below us and two above. Here, at last, were live Germans. They spotted us. I rocked my wings as a signal to Semyonov that I was going to attack. There were five of them and only two of us.

I was flying a MiG-3. It is a sturdy machine and well armed. It behaves wonderfully at high altitudes when its speed and manoeuvrability increase. I had my plan of action all worked out in an instant. Semyonov was to cover me as we had previously arranged on the ground. I shot up into the clouds and kept on climbing until I ran into one of the two Messerschmitts coming towards me. The German zoomed almost in my face. I did a stall-turn and found myself on the tail of the yellow, blunt-winged craft. I fired at short range. The Messerschmitt burst into flames and plunged downwards. I watched it as it fell and that almost cost me my life. The other German had crept up behind me. White ribbons of his tracers shot by and then my plane shuddered. Its port wing had been torn by bullets.

I dived to zero feet and hedge-hopped all the way home and, feeling that my aircraft was losing stability all the time, with great difficulty got back to the airfield. I made a normal landing, taxied to a stop, shut off the engine and slumped against the armoured back of the seat. I needed a drink. My throat was parched. That was the first German I had bagged.❞

however, a handful of German pilots had a field day.

King of the skies at that time was Erich Hartmann, otherwise known as 'Bubi' Hartmann or the 'Blond Knight'. During World War II he scored a record 352 victories, or kills, all of which were validated, making him an 'ace of aces'. Most were made on the Eastern front.

Hartmann was born in Weissach, near Stuttgart, on 19 April 1922. As a boy, he lived in China where his father was a doctor. When the family returned to Germany Hartmann was encouraged by his mother, herself a pilot, to sample the joys of flight. First qualifying as a glider pilot and instructor, Hartmann then joined the Luftwaffe aged 18.

He revealed the secret of his success: 'My only tactics are to wait until I have the chance to attack the enemy then close in at high speed. I open fire only

---

During World War II Hartmann scored a record 352 kills, all of which were validated

---

when the whole windshield is black with the enemy. Then not a single shot goes wild. I hit the enemy with all my guns and he goes down.'

In his beloved Me-109, he knocked out seven Red Air Force planes above the Battle of Kursk on 7 July 1943. It wasn't unusual for him to return from a sortie with more than one kill to his credit. No Allied pilot even approached such a mighty score.

HARTMANN ESCAPES

Operating over Russia, his plane was once shot down. Although he was unhurt, he was taken prisoner by Russian soldiers – a fate dreaded by German airmen at the time.

He pretended he was injured and was placed on a stretcher in a truck. En route to find a doctor he sprang up, overpowered his guard and leapt under fire from the lorry into a field of sunflowers. Sleeping by day and walking by night, he finally reached the German lines where he was almost shot by one of the sentries.

His outstanding success and distinctly Aryan features made him a favourite with Adolf Hitler

Once he was even drunk enough to begin juggling with the Führer's hat but still remained a 'golden boy'.

HARD LABOUR

Erich Hartmann scored his last victory on the final day of the war, having flown 1,400 missions. He then came down to earth with a jolt, being captured by Russians. His sentence following the war was 25 years' hard labour – although he was offered freedom if he agreed to settle in East Germany and train their air force. He refused the deal and was finally released in 1956 following negotiations by Chancellor Adenauer of West Germany.

Hartmann resumed his air force career and learned to fly jets under the auspices of the

Above: Russian pilots are congratulated by their major after completing a mission on the Eastern front.

Below: Erich Hartmann was one of the most successful pilots of the war, scoring most of his victories over Russia.

who awarded him the Knight's Cross and later added the prestigious German military decorations of Oak Leaves, Swords and, then finally, Diamonds. Courageous not only in the air, he frequently had cross words with his German superiors.

ACE PILOTS

In the league table of wartime ace pilots, the first five places are occupied by Germans followed by two Japanese and a Finnish pilot. The first pilot from the West to appear in the league comes in 27th place, South African J. Pattle, who is followed by Richard Bong (below) and Thomas McGuire of the US and J. Johnson of Britain.

the conflict with Russia dragged on, and a final total of 200,000 men abandoned their air duties to become infantrymen. They were also to suffer from lack of aircraft and fuel and a diminishing training programme.

Worse was to come for the German air forces remaining on the Eastern front

Russian industry which had moved to the safety of the east produced supplies for the Red Air Force – which was further bolstered by American aircraft through the Lend-Lease Act.

Below: With much of Russia's powerful industrial muscle in the safety of the east, Stalin was able to provide his air force with vital replacement planes and components when Hitler could not.

Americans. He was married in 1944 to his wartime sweetheart Ursula Puetsch, and the couple had a daughter. Hartmann died in 1993, aged 71.

As 1941 closed, the prospects improved considerably for the Russians in the air war. The Luftwaffe having deployed the majority of its air power in the opening stages of 'Operation Barbarossa', its strength on the Eastern front soon waned as it became overstretched and struggled to maintain its operations on three fronts.

LUFTWAFFE SUFFERS

Worse was to come for the German air forces remaining on the Eastern front. Luftwaffe field divisions were created to back up the ground forces as

TIGER, TIGER, TIGER

By 1941, tensions were running high between the Americans and Japan. The United States government looked on uncomfortably as Japan sought to expand its empire by waging a brutal war on China.

Although Japan's leaders had pledged neutrality in the European war, alarm bells were sounding out across the Western world. Both America and its future allies aided the hard-pressed Chinese.

Seizing an opportunity in September 1940, the Japanese, pushed the boundaries of their empire back by moving into Indochina at the expense of Vichy France, the colonial rulers of the country. This was a move the European puppet state was powerless to resist. In retaliation the anxious and angry United States and Britain broke off trading relations, which meant a halt to the supply of vital oil to Japan. The exiled Dutch government did likewise. Australia was by now viewing the aspirations of Japan with trepidation.

Without oil, Japan could only survive for 18 months at the most despite the huge stockpiles it had imported during the 1930s. At stake was its considerable economic might. The hawks among the Japanese hierarchy quickly argued that time was running out for Japan and that a military strike to consolidate its position was needed sooner rather than later.

TRIPARTITE PACT

In the same month as the threatening manoeuvres in Indochina, Japan joined with aggressors Germany and Italy in the Tripartite Pact, which set out a code of co-operation between the three. There could be little doubt now that the Land of the Rising Sun was poised on the brink of war. But the question which troubled the

Americans was, just how would the inevitable conflict begin?

Japan had sound reasoning behind the desire to enlarge its lands. In 1939, its population reached 99 million and was increasing at the rate of five million a year. Its home islands were becoming overcrowded and overstretched. Britain, France and Holland all enjoyed the benefits of colonies. America, although ideologically opposed

In September 1940 Japan joined with aggressors Germany and Italy in the Tripartite Pact

Left: *An aerial view of the US Pacific Fleet's base at Pearl Harbor.*
Below: *Japan's foreign minister Matsuoka talks with Ribbentrop in early 1941.*

to colonialism, had its spheres of influence. Japan felt entitled to the same. It was not unreasonable, the Japanese felt, for their country to hold sway over the Pacific and China. Japan's transformation from feudal backwater to a burgeoning world power had been rapid. It was only in the latter half of the 19th century that Japan had come out of isolation. After that, the Japanese followed the British and American examples

The Japanese felt cheated, unable to trust the countries they had known as friends

and were set on a programme of industrialisation. This new breed of manufacturers struggled to compete on the same terms as the Westerners. Britain had tariffs which discouraged overseas trade while America also followed a policy of protectionism. Japan joined the Allies during World War I. Afterwards, the Japanese were anxious to be accepted as part of the New World

Right: Japanese pilots were hailed as heroes back home after their unannounced attack on the US Pacific Fleet's base at Pearl Harbor.

Order on equal terms with other nations. Failure was in store.

At the Paris peace conference, the Japanese proposed a clause of racial equality, with the aim of removing the discrimination they had felt. The emissaries from Japan assumed that there would be no controversy over the clause's acceptance.

JAPANESE ANGER

In the event, it was barred by none other than American President Woodrow Wilson, who went on to place a ban on Japanese people entering the US when immigration by other nationalities was rife. Australia, too, had a 'whites only' immigration policy. The Japanese felt cheated and angry, unable to trust the countries they had hitherto known as friends. Western powers seemed more fraudulent than ever when the Washington Treaty of 1922 was drawn up, limiting Japan to just three capital ships for every five run by both the US and Britain.

Left: Admiral Isoroku Yamamoto was the architect of the strike against Pearl Harbor. Yet he feared he had 'awakened a sleeping giant'.

The Japanese largely followed Western models of democracy. Although there was an emperor, he was bound by the decisions of his ministers. Its civilian ministers ran civil affairs. But there were ministers from the army and navy entirely responsible for military matters. Without the co-operation of those ministers from the armed services, the government fell. It meant they wielded huge power. To further complicate matters, there was an enormous degree of rivalry between the army and the navy and the two services could rarely agree.

Aside from these wranglings, there was also the sinister threat of assassination. It became a political tool increasingly used by young patriots. Those in power became cautious, corrupt and sly. There came a feeling among the Japanese that politicians could

PEARL HARBOR

On the morning of 7 December 1941, the Japanese attacked on Pearl Harbor. As the US naval base prepared for its day, Japanese carrier aircraft swept in and tore into the US Pacific Fleet at rest. The fleet's carriers were at sea, but the battleships were in. *Arizona*, *West Virginia*, *California* and *Oklahoma* were destroyed; *Pennsylvania*, *Nevada*, *Tennessee* and *Maryland* were damaged. The Japanese lost nine Zeroes, 15 'Vals' and five 'Kates'.

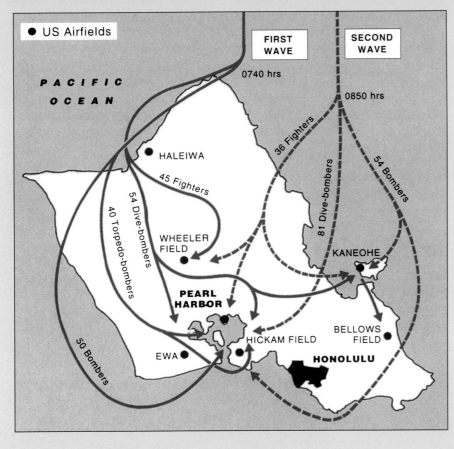

wealthy, precisely why they were incorporated into empires in the first place. Japan would become stronger than ever if only it could avail itself of the assets there.

With Japan's vast military might, the islands were easy enough targets. But the Japanese leadership rightly guessed that America was unlikely to sit back and watch as it established a thriving Pacific or Asiatic powerbase. It would send its big ships to trouble-spots. The answer, it seemed, was to knock out the American navy to obtain the freedom of the seas.

The answer, it seemed, was to knock out the mighty American navy

The pride of the US fleet was based in Hawaii, closer to Japan than the inaccessible mainland of the United States. And so the infamous attack on Pearl Harbor was conceived.

It was a brilliant short-term strategy drawn up by Admiral Yamamoto. Key to its success was the element of surprise. There was a summer of training for the pilots of the fighters, dive-bombers and torpedo-bombers which were to be shipped in for the pre-emptive strike. Most Japanese pilots had seen action in the war with China.

To ensure the action, code-named 'Operation Z', was effective, powerful six-inch naval shells were adapted for use by the aircraft, sufficient to plough through the armour of the US battleships. The Japanese also had a 24-inch torpedo known as the 'Long Lance', containing

not be trusted. Not only that, there was widespread fear about the encroachment of communism. Together with a growing admiration for the achievements of Nazi Germany, Japan swung towards militarism.

Japan, still cut out from overseas trade by the policies adopted by key trading partners Britain and America, began to feel the pinch during the Great Depression of the 1930s. Japan spent much of the 1930s meddling in internal Chinese affairs. When China became unwilling and belligerent, the two countries

finally went to war. In 1937, Japan withdrew from the League of Nations and denounced the Washington Treaty, privately planning to increase its naval strength to compare with that of Britain. And she sought to boost her empire.

YAMAMOTO'S PLAN

Japanese Military leaders realised the colonial outposts were now vulnerable, with the mother countries being embroiled in problems thousands of miles away. The remote islands were economically

Right: Japanese aircraft warm up on the deck of the carrier Hiryu before delivering their stunning blow to the US Navy at Pearl Harbor.

1,000 pounds of explosives; it was among the most powerful weapons in the world.

As early as 26 November 1941 the Japanese navy set off from its base, using an obscure route and maintaining complete radio silence. By 7 December it was in position, 270 miles north of Pearl Harbor in the Kurile Islands

'TIGER, TIGER, TIGER'

The fleet, under Vice-Admiral Chuiki Nagumo, comprised six aircraft carriers, with a capacity of 423 planes. In the attack 360 were used, the force comprising 104 high-level bombers, 135 dive-bombers, 40 torpedo bombers and 81 fighters. In addition, the escort force consisted of two battleships, three cruisers, submarines and supply ships.

In dock at Pearl Harbor were 96 American ships. Fortunately for the US, the base's two aircraft carriers were at sea. Their destruction may have altered the course of the war.

At Pearl Harbor, a new day day was beginning, clouded only by a general fear of war. Still, the beaches were silvery, the sun was warm and the majority of the servicemen based there were looking forward to a day of relaxation. Many were still in bed when the storm broke.

Although America had been forewarned that Japan was planning a major strike, it didn't

The ships in Pearl Harbor were undefended, their ammunition in lockers

know where or when it would take place. Most thought the Philippines the obvious target for Japanese aggression. The ships in Pearl Harbor were undefended, their ammunition safely held in lockers.

The only clue to the carnage to come came in the early hours when a periscope was spotted in the harbour mouth. A destroyer

Left: Pearl Harbor explodes under the onslaught of Japanese bombs. Fortunately, key fuel installations were left intact, so averting utter disaster.

PEARL HARBOR

US Losses
18 ships, including 8 battleships, sunk or badly damaged; 164 aircraft destroyed and 124 aircraft damaged; 2,403 men dead and 1,178 men wounded.

Japanese Losses
29 aircraft downed; 5 midget submarines sunk; 64 men dead or missing; 1 prisoner taken.

Below: US servicemen at Pearl Harbor were staggered at the sight that greeted them. Japanese aggression was dubbed 'treachery' around the Allied world.

duly went out to sink the unidentified submarine.

In fact, few people outside the navy top brass in Tokyo knew what was going on. Unwilling to announce its intentions and give its game away, Japan didn't deliver its declaration of war to America until Pearl Harbor was smoking.

At 6am the first wave of aircraft took off and headed to Hawaii. As they came within sight of Pearl Harbor Captain Mitsuo Fuchida, in command of the first wave, broadcast to his men, screaming 'Tora, Tora, Tora' – 'Tiger, Tiger, Tiger',

literally translated. The message informed them that the Americans were still unaware of what was to come. At 7.56am the first shots rang out.

As they came in sight, Fuchida broadcast to his men, screaming 'Tora, Tora, Tora'

In neat formations, the skilful, well-practised pilots made runs over the lines of vessels anchored along 'Battleship Row', the section of the harbour where the capital ships lay.

Far below them, braving the

tell-tale shallow waters of the harbour, were Japanese midget submarines, each one hoping to bag a battleship.

A stunned commander ordered them to take action, bellowing 'This is no drill!'

Ship after ship was blasted and soon the air was filled with thick, oily black plumes of smoke. As the flaming oil from one stricken vessel spilled into the sea, it set light to another. The second wave of Japanese bombers had difficulty locating targets through the smoke.

The *Arizona* was hit and exploded – 1,200 members of her crew died. The battleships *West Virginia*, *Oklahoma*, and *California* were also destroyed, and *Nevada*, *Maryland*, *Tennessee*, and *Pennsylvania* were damaged. Further casualties included the cruisers *Honolulu*, *Raleigh* and *St Helena*, and the destroyers *Shaw*, *Cassin* and *Downs*. These ships, all symbols of America's greatness, were left tattered wrecks.

In the midst of the chaos a contingent of American aircraft arrived. Their pilots must have gaped in disbelief at the scenes before them. What once was a landing strip had been set ablaze, along with most of the aircraft on it. Then they too were attacked. The same fate applied to the crews of dive-bombers from the absent carrier *Enterprise* returning to base during the attack.

29 PLANES DOWNED

At times the Japanese pilots screeched in so low they were clearly visible to the frantic Americans.

The men at Pearl Harbor responded to the onslaught with considerable zest. A stunned commander ordered them to take action, bellowing the words: 'This is no drill!' Despite the shock and disbelief, the Americans soon manned the guns as they had done before in training and claimed Japanese planes. Others raced to rescue comrades trapped in blazing ships or operated fire-

Below: *'Battleship Row' Pearl Harbor provided rich pickings for the carrier-borne aircraft of Yamamoto's strike force.*

Above: *Despite the suddenness of the strike, troops rushed to man the guns. A total of 29 Japanese planes – 9 Zeroes, 15 'Vals' and 5 'Kates' were downed.*

fighting equipment. Finally, there was calm. The surviving servicemen set about their grim tasks with one ear open for the return of the Japanese.

While the Pacific Fleet's base was extensively damaged, it was not crippled, since the fuelling and repair depots had escaped unscathed. However, it would take months, and in some cases years, to refloat and repair the shattered bodywork of the damaged ships.

The Japanese did not return to finish off the base, as was widely feared among US servicemen and their families. Well satisfied with the results of the operation, which went better than any of the Japanese commanders dared hope, Vice-Admiral Nagumo decided a quick, getaway was now in order, particularly as fuel was running dangerously low, and the US carriers *Lexington* and *Enterprise* might appear.

In America there was outrage and horror at the loss of life. US Secretary of State Cordell Hull was still in conference with Japanese negotiators when news of the attack reached him. They had already presented him with a document purporting to set out the area of debate.

A REPEAT OF 1904

Mr Hull furiously declared: 'In all my 50 years of public service I have never seen a document that was more crowded with infamous falsehoods and distortions on a scale so huge that I never imagined until today that any government on this planet was capable of uttering them.'

Although some took the opportunity to condemn President Franklin Roosevelt for his lack of readiness, most US citizens were determined to pull behind him in their fury at the Japanese action.

Ironically, the attack on Pearl Harbor mirrored a military move made by the Japanese against the Russians in 1904. Once again, without an official declaration of war, the Japanese navy carried out a surprise attack on a key Russian base. Back then, *The Times* of London hailed it as 'an act of daring' and praised the Japanese for their initiative and vigour.

In Britain, the *Daily Mail* now voiced the venom of many when it wrote: 'Not even Hitler has yet achieved the infamy of a stab in the back while his envoys were still ostensibly negotiating terms of agreement with his intended victim.

'This is an act which the world will never forget so long as the records of history are

> ## On 8 December, both America and Britain officially declared war on Japan

read. It will stand for all time as an example of the ultimate depths of deceit to which it is possible for any nation to descend.'

On 8 December, both America and Britain officially declared war on Japan. In response to the declaration and the wave of Japanese attacks around the region, the Royal Navy battleship *Prince of Wales* and battlecruiser *Repulse* sailed out of Singapore with an escort of four destroyers. Disastrously, 'Force Z', as it was known, ignored the threat of airborne action and left without the protection of an aircraft carrier.

EYE WITNESS

Kazuo Sakamaki was the commander of a midget submarine, one of five which was sent into action at Pearl Harbor.

❛Something went wrong. At the moment of release my submarine nearly toppled over into the water. The trim had not worked well. I feared that it we attempted to emerge hastily, enemy observers might spot the ship. I remembered that the opening of hostilities was to follow the handing of the notice of war to the US government. If by my own mistake the presence of the Japanese forces should be discovered it would create a grave problem. It would spoil the air attack and every other detail of the carefully worked-out plan. I could not cause such a blunder. No matter how dangerous the condition of my ship I could not let it emerge to the surface.

My aide and I crawled back and forth inside the submarine removing the lead ballast and filling the tanks with water to correct the trim of the craft. It had been our plan that by midnight all five submarines would be inside the harbour and would sink to the bottom and wait for the dawn. But when I looked at the watch it was midnight already. The ship righted itself.

I figured that as long as we entered the harbour during the night no damage would have been done. I drank a bit of wine and ate my lunch.

"Let's do our utmost." My comrade and I held each other's hands and pledged success. I took my position and moved forward with minimum speed.

After ten minutes I lifted the ship slightly to see through the telescope where we were going. To my horror, the ship was moving in the wrong direction.

Moving blindly because my gyrocompass was not working, the ship had gone 90 degrees off her course. If I could manage the ship with the help of the telescope we could get back on our course but this was clearly impossible.

"We must get to the mouth of the harbour" I repeated to myself. My hands were wet with cold sweat. I changed the direction three or four times, hoping against hope that somehow the ship would get going where I wanted to go. The speed was maintained at the minimum as before.

Time ticked away in complete indifference to my predicament. It was almost the moment for attack.

As we came nearer to the enemy ships guarding the entrance I was able to see the white uniforms of the sailors aboard. I concluded they were destroyers.

I pushed the midget submarine toward them, Suddenly I heard an enormous noise and felt the ship shaking. I was hit on the head and lost consciousness. This was my first contact with war.

I came to myself in a short while and saw white smoke in my submarine. I changed the speed to half gear and turned the ship around. I wanted to see if any damage had been done. My comrade was all right. My two torpedoes were all right. I did not want to waste my torpedoes on those destroyers which began again to charge against me. They threw depth charges at us. They fell near us but not as close as the first time. ❜

Their aim was to prevent the Japanese making landings on British-held territory in South East Asia. But the mission went wrong when the two British giants became targets for the Japanese Naval Air Arm flying out of Indochina.

The *Prince of Wales*, able to fire 60,000 shells every minute from its 175 anti-aircraft guns, was thought to be impregnable. Japan's pilots didn't think so.

On 10 December, both ships were sunk off the coast of Malaya within an hour of each other and 800 crew members were killed, although 2,000 were saved by the accompanying destroyers. Among the dead was the leader of the ill-fated squadron, Admiral Tom Spencer Vaughan Phillips. There were 34 high-level bombers and 51 torpedo-bombers coming at the ships from all directions. Winston Churchill heard the news by telephone from the Chief of Naval Staff. 'I never received a more direct shock,' he commented.

As militarily admirable as it might have seemed to the Japanese at the time, the long-term consequences of the attack on Pearl Harbor were clearly ill thought-out. Japan had a superb

Below: *Both Roosevelt and Cordell Hull were disgusted by the Japanese attack.*

navy, powerful enough to compete with that of America or Britain, with the most modern aircraft carrier fleet in the world.

A GIANT AWAKENED

Japan could not have hoped for an occupation of the US. It was a geographical and numerical impossibility. If the leaders of Japan hoped the action at Pearl Harbor would encourage the Americans to capitulate, they sorely misjudged their foe. The aim seems to have been merely to cause enough damage to keep America at bay while Japan built up its strength in the Pacific.

It is likely they were then hoping for a war of attrition in which America would compromise. Admiral Yamamoto clearly had an inclination of what lay ahead when he said: 'I fear we have only awakened a sleeping giant and his reaction will be terrible.'

Above: British newspapers joined the wave of indignation against the war-mongering Japanese after their opening strikes in the Pacific.

EYE WITNESS

A correspondent for the National Broadcasting Corporation gave this account of the bombing of Pearl Harbor.

'The most thickly populated air base was attacked by Japanese planes a little after 8am local time.

After machine-gunning Ford Island the Japanese planes moved to Hickman Field. Observers say that considerable damage was done there but a number of planes were brought down.

Three ships of the United States Pacific Fleet based at Pearl Harbor were attacked and the 29,000-ton battleship *Oklahoma* was set on fire.

All lines of communication appear to be down between the various Army and Navy aerodromes and the Army in the field. The Army has issued orders for all people to remain off the streets.

The first raiders carried torpedoes and did considerable damage to shipping in Pearl Harbor and off Honolulu. They came in squadron formation over Diamond Head, dropping high explosives and incendiary bombs. They came over Honolulu itself and were at once met with anti-aircraft from Pearl Harbor, Ford Island, Wheeler Field, Honolulu Municipal Airport, Hickman Field and the new Navy repair base. A terrific barrage was put up but all the points I mentioned appear to have been attacked.

The chief of fire services has reported that the fires were under control and were not as bad as expected.'

AERIAL WEAPONRY

Ripe for exploitation, bursting with potential, the aeroplane came of age during World War II. It could never win battles alone. But the aircraft of those years undeniably made the difference between triumph and wholesale military failure. While they would never replace ground troops, they did succeed in making giant battleships obsolete and changed the face of modern conflict.

Incredibly, following World War I, British politicians, including eminent figures like Prime Minister Stanley Baldwin, were all for scrapping military 'wings'. French Marshal Ferdinand Foch summed up the prevailing attitude when he said: 'Aviation is good sport but for the army it is useless.'

It was only the vociferous campaigning of Lord Hugh Trenchard, Marshal of the Royal Air Force during the 1920s, that kept the RAF in business. It was the same story across the Atlantic where sceptics failed to see a future in flight. William Mitchell, Assistant Chief of the US Army Air Service, faced similar negative reactions against the budding force. He managed to silence some of the critics with trial bombardments between 1921 and 1923 which sank six warships.

SHANGHAI BLITZ

German air attacks by Zeppelins and aircraft in south east England during World War I claimed 1,413 lives – paltry by comparison with the casualties on the Western front but sufficient to bring the war home to people in Britain. In reply, the British fliers killed 746 Germans in a total of 242 raids.

There was a school of thought which predicted dire consequences for Britain if it was the victim of a concerted air attack during the 1920s. But its voice was ignored by those who

Left: A pilot hauls himself from the cockpit of his Beaufighter, this one equipped with radar.
Right: An Italian Macchi aircraft.

funnelled their thinking and actions towards peace following the 'war to end all wars'.

Only when fighting broke out between China and Japan in 1931, and parts of Shanghai were reduced to rubble by Japanese bombers, did air power come back on to the agenda.

Still, the British government at the international disarmament conference of 1931 urged that military and naval air forces be abolished. The conference ended inconclusively – but not until 1934, by which time Britain was substantially behind in the re-armament race. Italy had begun to build up its military, and Germany, now led by Hitler, was doing the same despite limitations still in force from the Treaty of Versailles.

Then it was left to the people who flew for thrills to make the running in air technology between the wars.

Racing became the pursuit of playboys, which not only earned them accolades but won the infant industry some valuable knowledge. For example, the British Supermarine S.6

racing plane – a winner of the prestigious Schneider Cup – was transformed into the Spitfire fighter. In Germany, the Messerschmitt 109 set a speed record of almost 470 miles per hour in 1939 and went on to father some of the Reich's most effective planes.

In 1935 the first B-17 Flying Fortress rolled onto the runway

Although flying speed increased, the performance of many aircraft did not, due to a lack of fuel capacity. New faster trips were inhibited by the number of stops necessary for refuelling. Greater capacity was needed to increase their range.

Now it was the turn of the US to rise to the challenge. In 1935 the first B-17 Flying Fortress rolled on to the runway, with its ability to travel thousands of miles on one fuel tank. Meanwhile, the Douglas Aircraft Company unveiled the DC-3, with its top range of more than 2,000 miles. Both machines were winners.

Above: *By March 1936 an early version of the Spitfire – which was based on a racing seaplane – was flying, although it was modified before becoming a battle winner.*

Britain was seeing a revolution in air power of its own with the development at Rolls Royce of the PV-12 engine, the Merlin, in 1933. Aircraft manufacturers in 1935 had turned out the Hurricane, a stalwart fighter plane which even in those

In Germany the Luftwaffe was reborn on 26 February 1935 with a total of 1,888 aircraft

early days was capable of speeds of more than 300 miles per hour. In total, 12,780 were built in Britain and a further 1,451 in Canada.

The 1930s saw the development of radar in Britain, vital for both air and sea forces. After realising that aircraft interfered with radio signals, Sir Robert Watson-Watt of the National Physical Laboratory hit on radio detection and ranging, in which a travelling aircraft reflected a radio pulse and was thus visible on a screen linked to a radio receiver. Radar gave the Allies a vital leg-up during the opening phase of the conflict. Indeed, it took the Germans some time to understand how it was that their bomber and fighter formations so rarely escaped attack during the Battle of Britain. As the war progressed, radar was fitted to planes for use against aircraft carrying out night raids on Britain, providing at last an antidote to blitz bombers.

In Germany the Luftwaffe was reborn on 26 February 1935 with a total of 1,888 air craft and 20,000 officers and men. Powering the new air force were four companies – Daimler-Benz, Junkers, BMW and Siemens-Halske. It was the designers from Daimler-Benz who dispensed with the carburettor and introduced a multi-point fuel-injection system giving a pilot far greater control during rapid airborne manoeuvres, The rival Rolls Royce engine was prone to cutting out during dives.

BRITAIN LAGS

The arrival of the Luftwaffe caused consternation in Britain and was enough to spur the Air Ministry into action. New military aerodromes mushroomed on the east coast. Yet still there were crucial delays and hold-ups in the building of planes.

The Wellington bomber, designed by Sir Barnes Wallis, was prepared on paper by 1932. However, its first flight was not until June 1936 and it wasn't

EYE WITNESS

Tony Langdon-Down joined the Royal Air Force in March 1941 when he was aged 18.

❝I left school because the war started and began to read for the bar. As soon as I was 18 I joined the RAF – not for any particular desire to fly but I wanted to get into the services and there was a shortage of pilots,

For four months I was in Cambridge which is where I learnt to fly. Going solo for the first time was one of the highlights of my life. I completed my flying training and was operational by February 1942.

I was a defensive night fighter mostly serving with 219 Squadron. It was a tremendous way to grow up. After a few months I joined a Beaufighter squadron, flew out to Casablanca and from there we went to Algiers and Tunis. It was the first time I had been abroad.

We took part in the Sicily landings. I didn't see much action except for patrolling. When we returned to Britain, we left all our old planes to the Americans. They found them extremely difficult to fly.

I was an instructor when flying bombs started to fall. I volunteered to fly Tempests, single-seater night planes. The flying bombs came over on the back of Heinkels. I only shot down two. One blew up in my face which was rather unpleasant.

We didn't bring them down in built-up areas which made our job difficult. When they came to an end I rejoined a Mosquito squadron.

Although we did night flying we did tests on our aircraft in pairs during the day. I went out with another plane one day when it was very cloudy. We came down through the cloud and we were 500 feet over a port. The next minute all hell let loose. The port was Dunkirk where a pocket of German resistance remained. To my horror the other plane was shot down. We were hit but we were able to get back to Britain to land. The wife of one and the fiancee of another crew member were visiting the base for the weekend. Their deaths came as a terrible shock because there was no reason to suppose they were in any danger.

As the end of the war approached, my commanding officer asked me to make a small speech for VE day. I travelled to the BBC in London to record it. Sitting in the mess after Germany surrendered, we were listening to the radio when Princess Elizabeth made a short speech. It was followed by me. As you can imagine, there was uproar among my friends. I hardly recognised my own voice.

I didn't have a very glorious war. Flying wasn't the dangerous occupation when I joined that it had been. The main risk to me was my own flying ability. We did fly in some pretty fearsome conditions, though I remember taking off in thick fog when I was chasing flying bombs and wondering how I would ever get down again.❞

---

delivered for active service for a full two years after that.

Even as late as 1938 the Royal Air Force were ill-equipped. Sir Maurice Dean, Private Secretary to the Chief of Air Staff, pointed out: 'The re-equipment of Fighter Command had barely begun. The radar chain was half completed. Of the 45 fighter squadrons deemed necessary at the time, only 29 were mobilisable and all but five of these were obsolete. The five modern fighter squadrons could not fire their guns above 15,000 feet owing to freezing problems.'

The onset of hostilities did much to speed ahead technology and cast off caution.

When war broke out the pride of Britain's flying stock were Hurricanes and Spitfires.

Below: *German Messerschmitt 109s like this one caused plenty of headaches for Allied pilots.*

Above: *Boeing B-17 Flying Fortresses ready for action. The enormous capabilities of these classic aircraft were a tremendous boon to US airmen.*

At sea, the slow Swordfish still earned their colours despite their advancing years

However, there were also Fairey Battles, Gloster Gladiators, and Bristol Blenheims, all of which were hopelessly outdated. In September 1940 the first Bristol Beaufighters were introduced, complete with radar sets to combat night attackers. At sea there were slow Swordfish – which still earned their colours despite their advancing years, both in sinking the *Bismarck* and in the successful raid on the Italian fleet in Taranto.

During the war came the Handley-Page Halifax, which was progressively bettered, the subsequent Halifax Mark III, known for its versatility, and the heavy-duty Avro Lancaster. Best-loved of all was the wooden Mosquito, fast enough with its two engines to outrun many of its German adversaries on bombing runs.

ESCORT FIGHTER

Ranged against them were Henschels, old-fashioned but nevertheless effective, the Ju.87 'Stuka', an ideal Blitzkrieg weapon thanks to its terrifying siren wail, Junkers, Heinkels, Dorniers and Messerschmitts. One of the most successful late arrivals in the German air fleet was the Focke-Wulf 190, which preyed on bombers. However, the Germans never found a successful formula for a heavy bomber, preferring instead fast bombers like Heinkels.

The best of Japan's aircraft were carrier-borne. They included the Mitsubishi A6M, better known as the Zero, torpedo-armed Nakajimas and dive-bombing Aichis. It came as a mighty shock, but the Japanese, when they entered the war, had the best air force in the world both in terms of agility and range.

In their aircraft arsenal, the Americans had the invaluable Boeing B-17 Flying Fortress heavy bomber and the North American P-51 Mustang long-

EYE WITNESS

E. Rickman, who had been building model aeroplanes since he was a child, opted to join the Fleet Air Arm In April 1942. By 1944 he was based on HMS *Illustrious* and flew Grumman Avengers, US-made aircraft and the pride of the British fleet.

❝In January 1945 we were told the twin oil refineries at Palembang in Sumatra which provided the Japanese with nearly half the aviation fuel they needed in South East Asia had to be put out of action. One of the refineries was successfully bombed despite a barrage balloon protection. Three days later we were told the next one was our target.

During the briefing, our commanding officer Lieutenant-Commander Charles Mainprice, told us: "I consider this operation to be highly dangerous ... I consider this strike to be so dangerous that if anyone would prefer not to fly, I shall respect his wishes and I shall not, repeat not, think any the less of him for so doing."

The next day at about 4.45am as we approached Palembang, I could see the target ahead and the balloons. Just before I made our dive an enemy plane got on our tail. Suddenly, the Browning gun jammed. Fortunately, it was our turn to get in line for attack, I trimmed the Avenger for the dive and put the stick forward and the enemy plane broke off its engagement. There were three aircraft ahead of me. I could see one balloon cable between us and the pump house which was our prime target.

The commanding officer who went in first didn't see it. To my horror, he hit the cable with his port wing, cutting off two thirds of it as clean as a whistle. His plane went into a spin and exploded on impact seconds later.

The senior pilot next in line saw the cable and steered around it. But I could hardly believe my eyes when the third plane in line hit the same cable and suffered the same fate as the CO. I felt sick and angry but I didn't have too long to think.

It was my turn to go in. I went around the cable and met a huge smoke cloud which was obliterating the target. I had no choice but to go through it. The plane bucked in the turbulence and emerged from the smoke on its side at 500 feet. I levelled out, went to tree-top level and headed around the coast, blasting away with my front guns at any target I could see.

On my way back I saw another Avenger which looked all right. But before my eyes I saw it descend into a shallow dive and blow up as it hit the sea.

At the end of the attack we were told there were 18 direct hits on the target and we did not need to return again.❞

---

range escort fighter. On the other hand, they had problem planes, too. Captain Philip White was in a squadron of Brewster Buffaloes – heavy with armour plating and lightly armed – which was virtually wiped out by Japanese Zeros. He later wrote: 'It is my belief that any commander who orders pilots out for combat in a Brewster should consider the pilot as lost before leaving the ground.' The Australians were given 154 Brewsters with which to defend Malaya. Within three months every one was destroyed.

A welcome addition to the US ranks during the war was the P-51 fighters, which had enough range to protect bombers on long-distance missions deep into Germany. In the bomber fleet, as well as Flying Fortresses, there were Liberators, less effective but with the supreme advantage that one rolled off the assembly line every 50 minutes back at the Ford Motor Company in Michigan.

LACK OF TACTICS

At the start of World War II, British tactics were virtually non-existent. Planes would merely took off and headed in the general direction of their target. It was only when aircraft formations ascended in unison heading for a common target with the support of fighter escorts did the British find some success.

Aircraft design was refined to provide faster fighters and better bombers

Throughout the war, aircraft design was refined to provide faster fighters and better bombers. The latters' capacity for bombs was continually increased. Also, aircraft such as bombers that could act as transport planes or were able to fly low level missions to drop supplies, were in demand as aircraft took a broader role in the war.

Below: *Sir Robert Watson-Watt was a pioneer of radar, which became crucial during World War II.*

Fortunately for the Allies, the Luftwaffe fell into disfavour with Hitler and many new German innovations were scuppered. Nevertheless, Hitler maintained a lively interest – which ensured a financial life-line – in the development of rockets and jets.

From test centres of the Third Reich came the ME-163 Komet, capable of speeds of 600 miles per hour. Still in its infancy, it did not cause the headaches for the Allies that it promised.

Its fuel was a combination of C-Stoff (hydrazine hydrate in methanol) and T-Stoff (hydrogen peroxide and stabilisers). When the two fuels were mixed they transformed into an explosive hot gas, sufficient to kill any members of the ground crew who accidentally combined the two on the ground.

Below: *The military version of the Douglas DC-3, the C-47, entered service during 1941. The aircraft was known as the Dakota in the RAF.*

Inside there were only five engine controls for the pilot to consider. These were off, idle and thrusts one, two and three. His mind was often taken away from the business of flying by the incredible agonies of extreme G-forces not to mention the high possibility of death by fire should the plane explode.

In fact, the Komet was too fast to be effective against the much slower Allied planes

After the flight came the hazardous and problematic landing, done in a gliding skid on the undercarriage. In fact, the Komet was too fast to be effective against the much slower Allied planes. Swooping down on Flying Fortresses, for example, the target was only in range momentarily before the Komet shot past. They also became targets themselves for Mustang fighters who took to patrolling near Komet bases to pick them off as they landed.

Britain was not far behind. Sir Frank Whittle, an RAF officer, piloted its first jet-propelled aircraft as early as May 1941 but Britain failed in the race against the Germans to get it into service.

DEATH RAY

There were other ideas being knocked around in Britain which failed to come to fruition. One, originating in World War I, was to freeze the clouds and mount gun emplacements on them. Another was to freeze stretches of sea and use them as landing strips – which was a project taken seriously enough to be given a code-name, 'Habbakuk', Thirdly, there was the much-loved idea of the death ray. No matter how hard scientists tried, they found it only worked when the chosen victims had first been thoroughly poisoned.

Despite the odd flight of fancy, aviation science and skills moved on apace on both

Above: The Junkers Ju.87 'Stuka' dive-bomber was a terrifying aircraft.

sides during World War II. However, it can be assumed that the Germans were a step

German scientists were enticed to America...many on a 'no questions asked' basis

ahead of the Allied countries as far as technology was concerned. Many German scientists were enticed to America following the war, many of them on a 'no questions asked' basis. There was an outcry years later when it was discovered that people regarded by some as war criminals were harboured in the US.

EYE WITNESS

Hilda Richards, from Cardiff, Wales, joined the ATS in 1941 when she was 21 and worked on the radar which guided one of the biggest 'ack-ack' guns in London.

❛There were only three gun sites like us in the country. One was on Wimbledon Common, one in Regent's Park and ours was outside Eltham. Most guns measured 3.5 while this had a 5.25 specification. It came from an abandoned cruiser.

I was one of six girls on radar. I still keep in contact with four of them. There was a lot of comradeship. For most of us it was our first time away from home. I wouldn't have missed it for anything – even when we counted 108 buzz bombs passing over us in just one night.

We worked any time the sirens went off at a post about 100 yards away from the gun itself. Rotas were 24 hours on duty, 24 hours on standby and 24 hours off. It sounds tough but we got used to it.

If we were on standby we could get some rest until we heard the siren. Then we would slip our trousers and battledress over our army pyjamas and run. The majority of us smoked because we had to keep awake.

We were tracking in south east London and on the edge of the Kent fields on circular radar screens. We could recognise the Germans as our own used to carry a signal. Then we could take height, distance and bearing and relay these to the command post.

I can remember when Hitler's rockets came down. They didn't make a sound. They would land and two houses would suddenly be gone. Every man and woman who wasn't doing anything would run to pull people out. It was just an unwritten law.

Looking over towards Woolwich one night, I saw all the huge oil drums on fire after an air raid. It was like daylight even though it was miles away.

I was in London, my sister came to join me and my brother went over to Burma. I never even considered what my mother went through at the time until I had children of my own. ❜

FIRES IN THE NIGHT

While German bombers were pounding Britain during 1940 and 1941, the British people huddled night after night in stuffy, cramped shelters and comforted themselves that Royal Air Force bombers were delivering similar punishment to the citizens of the Third Reich.

Sadly, they were mistaken. While British bomber crews were full of sterling young men with an iron resolve, their success rate in the first half of the war was low – and for sound reasons.

Night bombing was far safer for the aircraft and crew, as the Germans had illustrated in their raids over London. RAF Bomber Command was keen to conserve these valuable assets too and favoured night-time bombing raids instead of exposing its forces to daylight risks.

But the Luftwaffe was operating from occupied airfields a short hop over the English Channel. For the Royal Air Force to strike at the heart of Germany, its pilots and planes had to fly many more miles than their German counterparts, in aircraft that were ill-equipped for long-distance flying or bombing. It took time and investment for new, heavier bombers to be commissioned for the task.

The limited resources of Bomber Command were stretched in many different directions. Not only were there the demands of bombing raids over enemy territory but Coastal Command was in constant need of planes to combat the U-boat menace in the Battle of the Atlantic. With Britain under threat of isolation if the U-boat peril was not seen to, the need to have planes available for maritime duties was paramount in 1940. In addition, the Middle East and North Africa required a quota of bombers, together with crews and parts – all of which required regular replacements. For a while, night bombing raids over Germany were abandoned so the force could focus on its duties elsewhere.

EARLY PROBLEMS

Operational shortcomings put the RAF at a disadvantage, too. For the first sorties were flown, rather informally, on an almost individual level. Following a joint briefing, each aircraft would depart at five-minute intervals following a course chosen by its own navigator to the target. Often, the crews would not catch sight of another plane until after their return. The effect of single bomb drops on

> **For a while night bombing raids over Germany were abandoned altogether**

the ground were, of course, much less than an orchestrated raid involving greater numbers.

Added to this, the navigational aids available on planes at the time were wildly inaccurate. Crews conforming to their instructions were sure their bombs were away right on top of the targets. It was not the case. While bomber crews scored hits on clear nights in easily located target areas, bombs dropped on blacked-out Germany often as not fell short. After the war it was discovered that 49 per cent of the ordnance released by British crews between May 1940 and May 1941 exploded in open countryside.

Navigators used maps, a sextant and a procedure of 'dead-reckoning' to work out their position, all of which could be fouled up by poor weather conditions. Precision bombing by the RAF at night could be successful only on clear, bright,

Left: *German planes on a daylight raid of London before night-time tactics were introduced.*
Far left: *The Renault works at Billancourt after bombing by the Allies.*

Above: A Wellington bomber and its crew prepare for an arduous night's work over Hitler's 'Fortress Europe'.

windless nights of which there were few. It took many months before the difficulties of finding targets under cover of darkness were resolved.

Bomber Command was bearing losses from the missions over Germany, in exchange for few results. It soon became clear a new tactic was in order.

The principles of precision bombing – almost impossible to execute successfully given the constraints of the era – were abandoned for 'area bombing'. A large factory making vital components in open countryside would be overlooked in favour of a smaller factory among other small factories and industrial workers' housing.

That way enormous damage could be caused for the same amount of effort and risk as was required in precision bombing. Not only was there the clear-cut

intention of halting Germany's industrial output, but the chance to demoralise the people by bringing the war to their doorstep, making them homeless or otherwise hampering their daily existence.

The concept was fostered by Air Marshal Sir Richard Peirse, in charge of Bomber Command during 1941. The failure of his forces to destroy three German warships, *Scharnhorst*, *Gneisenau* and the heavy cruiser *Prinz Eugen*, while they were in dock at Brest, northern France, did little for the reputation of the force.

BREST RAIDS

While these three sea monsters roamed, the British suffered terribly. Between them they were responsible for the loss of HMS *Glorious*, HMS *Ardent*, HMS *Acasta* and the armed merchant cruiser *Rawalpindi* and something in the order of 115,600 tons of merchant shipping.

In the spring of 1941, Bomber Command flew 1,161 sorties against the ships, scoring just four direct hits, none causing substantial damage. All this for the loss of 43 bombers. Even when the three ships left the dockyard to slip back to home

Below: Air Chief Marshal Sir Arthur 'Bomber' Harris, Commander of the RAF's Bomber Command.

ports, the 242 planes sent to destroy them failed to dent the pride of the German navy.

It signalled the departure of Peirse and the arrival of Air Chief Marshal Arthur Harris, who adopted the idea of area bombing as his own.

Afterwards, Harris summed up his position. 'I had to prove quickly, to the satisfaction of those who mattered that the bomber force could do its work if it was large enough and if its efforts were not frittered away on objectives other than German industry as a whole.'

The historic town was engulfed in a firestorm which swallowed up 200 acres

His first priority was to bolster the stocks of planes available to carry out attacks, particularly heavy bombers of which there were fewer than 70.

An opportunity to prove the ability of himself and his men came just a matter of weeks after he was installed at Bomber Command. On 3 March 1942, Harris sent a force of 235 bombers across to Billancourt, France, where a giant Renault factory was turning out tank components for the German war effort.

The planes set off in three waves and now Harris mimicked a successful German tactic. The first wave carried not only bombs but a large number of flares which would light up the target for subsequent attackers. With the River Seine acting as a brilliant marker, 223 of the aircraft found their targets within

SUICIDE BOMBERS

Germany formed its own squadron of suicide bombers known as the Sonderkommando Elbe. They first went into action in April 1945 and engineered mid-air collisions with laden Allied bombers. The 300 volunteers were told they could parachute to safety if possible.

the space of two hours. Enough machinery was put out of action to stop the factory working for several months.

Harris felt that Germany's industrial heartland of the Ruhr was his for the taking.

Five days after the Renault raid, 211 bombers took off and headed towards the city of Essen. Once again, the technique of using flares and incendiaries was employed. But this time, many had burnt out before the second wave of bombers had got the measure of the area. It finally bore the hallmarks of the haphazard raids which Bomber Command were now known for. Another three attacks made on ensuing nights also failed to produce the spectacular results Harris yearned for although there was widespread damage caused in the city.

Harris had to wait until the end of the month for the next feather in his cap, a raid carried out against Lübeck, a Baltic port comprising many ancient timbered buildings.

When almost 200 aircraft dropped 300 tons of high explosives plus 144 tons of incendiaries on the night of 28/29 March, the historic town was engulfed in a firestorm which swallowed up 200 acres.

ROSTOCK RAID

At the end of April another Baltic port, Rostock, was given similar treatment. The targets for the bombers were specifically a factory which produced the Heinkel 111 aircraft and the town itself. An estimated 70 per cent of the old town was turned to rubble with direct hits being scored against the factory too. Of the 168 bombers that set off for the mission, all but 12 returned safely.

Harris noted that, yard for yard, the destruction wrought in Germany by Bomber Command in those two raids equalled that caused by the Luftwaffe in Britain in 1940 and 1941.

Below: The Renault works at Billancourt was destroyed by Bomber Command.

The Nazi hierarchy was riled by the savage encroachment into the Fatherland. In a fury, Hitler ordered raids against Britain's historic cities to even the score. He picked the targets from a tourists' book of Britain called the *Baedeker Guide*. Among them were Bath and Exeter.

'MILLENNIUM'

For one daring raid against a factory producing U-boat parts, Harris was persuaded to return to daylight attack. New Avro Lancaster heavy bombers were brought in for the assault on Augsburg in southern Germany. Together with their fighter escorts they flew in low over enemy territory to avoid radar detection and then began a breathtaking roof-top scrap with Luftwaffe fighters before hitting their target. The cost was high. Seven out of 12 bombers were lost. The crews of the returning battle scarred aircraft were decorated for their bravery.

It confirmed the view that daylight raids were too risky given the aircraft available. In any event, Harris became far too preoccupied with his latest tactical trailblazer to consider further daylight sorties. The continued all-out efforts to obliterate the Ruhr were proving frustrating. With the lack of truly efficient navigation and the industrial smog it was impossible to co-ordinate a successful mission. He had pondered about pulling off a single operation which would earn the admiration of those doubters at home and the trepidation of the Germans.

The answer, he decided, was a thousand-bomber raid against a prime target in Germany. But, given that the most he had been able to rally for an attack to date was 235 bombers, it seemed this was nothing more than a flight of fancy. That was until Harris's deputy Air Vice Marshal Saundby got to work.

With the use of borrowed aircraft from Coastal Command and the entire stock of his reserves flown by trainee pilots and instructors alongside existing crews, it was conceivable that 1,000 bombers could be gathered for an epic raid.

Code-named 'Operation Millennium', the first thousand-bomber raid took place against Cologne on 30 May 1942. All the planes were to strike within an hour and a half.

The raid represented a new departure in aerial warfare. The largest force of aircraft dispatched to Britain at any one time had numbered 487 while the British had never been able to gather together more than 235 bombers at any one time.

Churchill was captivated by the idea of such a mighty strike. He

Below: An RAF Wellington bomber is loaded with bombs before setting off on another mission.

was under pressure from fellow politicians who saw the largely inconclusive night raids against Germany as a waste of time and effort. Stalin was also waiting in the wings, always demanding a decisive attack by the British against Germany. It was realised that there would be too

> ## Ground crews worked flat out on damaged aircraft to furnish Harris with the required number

few German fighters in the air to halt the impact of the raid. The possibility of collision was to be diminished by dividing the planes into three groups operating in parallel lines against different targets. Despite the immense commitment, it seemed the risks were calculated. The raid could not end up as the swan-song of Bomber Command.

1,046 BOMBERS

For some time, 'Operation Millennium' was under threat as Coastal Command refused to release the 250 planes it had promised. Its chiefs had got cold feet. They decided the risk of releasing their aircraft was too

great. A spell of poor weather which caused the operation to be postponed proved a saving grace. Ground crews worked flat out on damaged aircraft to furnish Harris with the required number. On the morning of 30 May the magic 1,000 was surpassed.

The 1,046 bombers departed from 53 airfields across Britain and assembled in a 70-mile convoy across the North Sea. Before them went 50 fighter planes ready to duel with the defending Luftwaffe.

Mechanical difficulties would account for 100 planes in the force even before it had reached the target and they turned back to base.

Still, the first bombs and incendiaries were dropped at 12.47am on 31 May. The rest of the operation went according to plan. Land-based defences and intercepting Luftwaffe fighters were overwhelmed and the last bomber dropped its load over Cologne at 2.25am.

As they flew homewards, rear gunners could see the city burning from 150 miles away. The night's work destroyed 18,432 buildings, killed nearly 500 people, injured 5,000 more

Above: Sir Barnes Wallis, inventor of the bouncing bomb, which proved a huge morale-booster in Britain.

and left almost 60,000 homeless. Forty bombers did not return, which meant the loss of 40 instructors and 49 pupils.

It was hailed as a triumph at home but the success in itself put pressure on Harris to produce more of the same. Now the British public expected many more raids of similar dimensions to lambast the enemy.

An attack on Essen on 1 June involving 956 bombers left key industrial centres unscathed.

It wasn't until 25 June that another large-scale attack was attempted, on Bremen. For the 1,046 bombers, it was a great success except for the higher number of casualties claimed by Germany. This time 49 aircraft didn't return.

The Luftwaffe quickly realised the intention of Bomber Command. It set about denying the British an opportunity to destroy German industry.

To combat the upsurge in Luftwaffe fighters and improve

EYE WITNESS

Dennis Golding, of Gosport, near Portsmouth, England, was a British rifleman with the King's Royal Rifle Corps. As a light infantryman he was engaged in hand-to-hand combat with German troops throughout the 1944 advance across Western Europe.

❝On VE day we marched into Hamburg to find everything devastated except the roads. The Germans had cleared them and stacked up all the re-usable bricks they could salvage. It was typical German efficiency and I suppose it also helped improve their morale.

The civilians were more or less glad to see us. There was certainly no hostility and, like our own people, they were just glad it was all over. We weren't allowed to fraternise with them at first. It you were caught you were put on a charge That rule soon broke down. When they spoke to you you felt you had to talk back.❞

the success of the night bombing raids, a Pathfinder force was created, led by Australian Group Captain D.C.T. Bennett, a first-class pilot and skilled navigator.

Their aim was to fly 'finder' aircraft over the target on parallel tracks two miles apart dropping flares, creating a 'runway'. Behind them came 'Illuminator' aircraft, dropping further flares picking out the target area precisely. Then came the 'marker' group starting fires with incendiaries to pinpoint the targets for following bombers. When it was cloudy the Pathfinders dropped 'sky-markers', parachute flares which lit up the target beneath the cloud cover. In response the Germans used fires on the ground as decoys in much the same way as the British did during the Battle of Britain. The Pathfinders proved a huge boon to the night bombing raids, with the additional attraction that their loss rate was a smaller-than-average three per cent.

At the end of 1942 Bomber Command diverted resources to the 'Torch' landings in North Africa and provided valuable support. At the same time it carried out some successful raids over Italy, finding the air defences there far lighter than those in Germany.

Still, Harris was determined to kill off German industry in the Ruhr. By March 1943 he was set upon a concerted attack on the region. The Battle of the Ruhr got underway on the night of 5 March with a 442 aircraft raid and continued for six weeks more or less none stop. During the battle the

Above: *A Lancaster of 617 Squadron, loaded with its 'bouncing bomb' before heading for the German dams.*

famous Dambusters raid was carried out. Although Harris himself was opposed to it, the Air Ministry favoured a plan to knock out three giant dams which would deprive the region of vital hydroelectric power. To succeed, Wing Commander Guy Gibson and his squadron had to drop new 'bouncing bombs', designed by engineer Barnes Wallis.

DAMBUSTERS

Each bomb weighed five tons, measured five feet in length and four feet across. Carried in a special cradle beneath a Lancaster bomber, it went into action with backspin imparted, which would cause it to skip along the surface of the water until it met the dam wall.

The targeted dams – the Möhne, the Eder and the Sorpe – were 150 feet high and their concrete walls were almost the same again in thickness. The skill required by Gibson and his crews was enormous. They had to fly in at low altitude to evade

German radar and drop their bombs at precisely 60 feet above the water and exactly 425 yards from the perimeter of the dam.

On the night of 16 May 1943 the 19 Lancasters took off in three waves. In the first wave of nine planes, headed by Gibson, one plane was lost to flak before three explosions ripped through the Möhne Dam and a flood poured down the valley.

In the second wave just one of the five Lancasters reached the Sorpe Dam, under the guidance of Flight Lieutenant McCarthy, an American serving with the RAF. His bomb load damaged the dam but failed to breach it. The third wave scythed a gap in the Eder Dam.

Eight of the Lancasters together with their 56 crew members failed to return. And, although it was a feat of undoubted heroism, the damage took the Germans just three months to repair. Perhaps it was

EYE WITNESS

George Funnell joined the 55th Kent Regiment in 1939 aged 17, after lying about his age. He witnessed the Blitz in London when he was stationed at an anti-aircraft battery – and later saw the destruction caused by air raids in Germany after fighting his way through Normandy, Belgium and Holland to Hamburg in 1944.

'In Hamburg there was mile after mile of devastation. I lived through the London bombing but it was nothing like as bad as that over Germany.

Even when we got to Hamburg, long after the air raids had taken place, there was still the stench of death coming from crumbled buildings. It took ages to find some of the buried remains.

On the streets we only found a few old men and young boys. The rest of the male population had been called up into the army. The vast majority of the people we met were women struggling to survive as best they could.'

most successful in capturing the public's imagination in terms of a morale-boosting coup and depriving the Atlantic Wall in northern France of some labour.

Harris continued his bombing campaign, targeting Hamburg. 'Operation Gomorrah' began on 24 July with the first use of aluminium foil, which was able to fog radar screens. The Air Ministry refrained from using as the same device could be used in retaliation. Germany also refrained from using it, for the same reason. Called 'Window', it was brought in to play on the orders of Churchill in a bid to counter the Luftwaffe defences.

HAMBURG HORROR

At midnight 740 bombers dropped 92 million strips of tin foil, blocking radar systems. The planes went on to deliver almost 3,000 tons of bombs. Subsequent attacks made by night and day virtually devastated the city's defences. Fine weather had left the city dry as paper. As new fires were sparked by existing blazes, the perpetual heating of the air which funnelled into the sky caused a firestorm, akin to a tornado with wind speeds of 150 miles per hour. Delayed detonators on some of the bombs wrought havoc among the rescue workers.

The melting temperatures achieved in the raid scorched buildings and bomb shelters, water mains and electric cables. Hamburg endured the horror for nine days by which time ten square miles of the city was laid waste. In total 2,630 bombers unleashed more than 4,300 tons of incendiaries and a similar amount of high explosives, creating three firestorms. The death toll was estimated at 42,000.

Harris continued to work through the list of German cities he hoped to destroy. His armoury now included a 12,000lb bomb and excellent new navigational aids and target-finders. Now his sights turned towards Berlin. The German capital was a far-distant target from British airfields across hostile territory. The Battle of Berlin opened in November 1943 and a further 15 attacks were launched against it. The demands on the participating crews of Bomber Command eased when airfields were opened in Europe following D-Day. Those raids cost no less than 587 aircraft together with 3,640 men killed or missing. When reconnaissance photographs proved little was being gained from the attacks, they were suspended.

If Harris had hoped to end the war with his tactics bathed in a blaze of glory, he was to be disappointed. Public opinion both in Britain and overseas began to question the wisdom of saturation bombing.

On 30 March 1944 a night raid by Halifaxes and Lancasters was sent awry by a strong wind which sent them into the arms of defending Luftwaffe fighters. Out of the 795 aircraft that set off, 95 failed to return and another dozen crashed in England. Night bombing raids afterwards came to an end.

Below: A reconnaissance photograph reveals the damage done to the Möhne Dam by Wing Commander Guy Gibson and his Dambusters.

CARRIERS AND KAMIKAZES

Americans were down in the dumps following the raid on Pearl Harbor. With the Imperial Japanese Army and Navy riding roughshod over the Pacific and South East Asia, there was no glimmer of optimism as the nation became preoccupied with the sight of its young men marching off to war.

Finally, on 18 April 1942, there came some small consolation for the folks back home. It was provided by a daring air raid into the heart of Japan itself. American airman Lt-Colonel Jimmy Doolittle, a veteran of glamorous pre-war air races, delivered a small but significant strike back against the aggressor.

The newly commissioned aircraft carrier *Hornet*, bearing 16 army bombers, in the company of fellow carrier *Enterprise* and a body of cruisers set off from Midway Island towards Japan. Some 650 miles short of the Japanese coastline, the fleet stopped so the B-25s could be launched. Despite the stiff wind, the planes took off at dawn, heading for Tokyo and other major cities.

At noon, 13 of the aircraft unloaded their cargoes of bombs over Tokyo. The other three dropped incendiaries on Nagoya, Osaka and Kobe. In fact, little was achieved in the exploit and many Japanese people remained unaware that it had even taken place at all. Its main effect was to shock the Japanese commanders who had until now considered themselves somewhat impregnable.

It now seemed vital to the Japanese to take control of Midway Island, a gap in the extended front line they had created in the Pacific. Those who had doubted the wisdom of pushing Japanese lines still further were persuaded that the vulnerability of the home islands warranted the new push.

As for the attacking American B25s, they did not have the range to return to the aircraft carriers which were by now high-tailing it for home. Their orders were to seek out friendly airstrips in China.

JAPANESE REPRISALS

All made it out of Japanese air space without a problem although one crash-landed in Russian Vladivostok. Only four of the planes actually touched down while the rest ditched after their crews baled out. Three of the men were captured by Japanese troops operating in China and shot.

A further five died but 72, aided by Chinese peasants, made their way to Chungking and eventual freedom.

When Japan realised the escape route taken by the fliers, troops exacted revenge against the native Chinese, slaughtering anyone suspected of aiding the airmen.

It was 30 months before Japan was once again in range of American bombers. This time the aircraft were far more fearsome, their capacity for wreaking terror far greater than in 1942.

Even from airfields in India and China in the summer of 1944, the American fliers found it difficult to carry out effective missions over Japan. The only island within their range was Kyushu, the southernmost Japanese home island.

It took victory in Saipan, freeing the Marianas Islands and their airfields, before a more comprehensive bombing campaign could begin. On 24 November 1944, 110 B-29s took off with the aim of knocking out Japan's aircraft industry in Tokyo, Nagoya, Kobe and Osaka. They were to drop 500lb bombs from high altitudes. But cloud cover obscured the targets and only one factory out of nine was struck.

Left: Lieutenant-Colonel Doolittle ties a medal to a bomb bound for Japan.
Far left: US Navy pilots receive a final briefing before a raid on Tokyo.

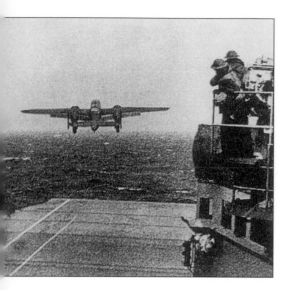

At the start of 1945 Major-General Curtis LeMay was brought into 21st Bomber Command. He had an inkling that the flimsy wooden shacks which filled Japanese cities were a major fire hazard. He pinpointed incendiaries as the best weapon with which to attack them.

On 4 February his theories were proved correct when a force of 70 Boeing B-29 Superfortresses dropped 160

To add to the effect of the bombs a fresh wind fanned the flames

tons of incendiaries on the centre of Kobe. A tenth of a square mile was burnt out and that included several factories.

The ploy was repeated on 25 February, this time against Tokyo. 172 B-29s dropped nearly 450 tons of incendiaries, devastating a square mile. An estimated 28,000 buildings were razed.

Right: Kobe, Japan's sixth-largest city, comes under attack with incendiaries dropped by US B-29s. Fires have already been sparked in the industrial areas.

Left: A B-25 heavy bomber takes off from the USS Hornet to deliver its load to Japan. The Doolittle Raid sparked Japanese reprisals in China.

Interrupted by the call for aid in Okinawa, LeMay had time to consider his options. The use of incendiaries had proved itself beyond question but the effect was far more widespread when the bombs were dropped from lower altitudes. It pointed to the need for night raids.

In advance, a single plane would pinpoint targets with marker bombs and the rest of the bombing party would follow at intervals of every couple of minutes.

On the night of 9 March 334 B29s took off and showered a 12-square-mile industrial area of Tokyo with 1,700 tons of oil incendiaries. To add to the effect of the bombs, a fresh wind fanned the flames until it seemed the entire city was on fire.

RAIDS CONTINUE

Anti-aircraft fire claimed 14 of the planes but their mission was an outstanding success. No less than 16 square miles of the city had been burned out, with 267,000 buildings flattened and 84,000 people killed. An official Japanese report noted: 'People were unable to escape. They were found later piled upon the

EYE WITNESS

Masuo Kato was a reporter in Japan throughout the war and detailed the terror by fire inflicted by US bombers.

❝For more than three years my small nephew Kozo Ishikawa, who was about five years old when the war began, held an unshakeable faith in Japanese victory. To his small world it was unthinkable that the Emperor's armies could suffer defeat or that the Japanese navy should endure any fate other than glorious victory.

After his home was burned to the ground during a B-29 raid, destroying almost every familiar material thing that had made up his existence, he told me with great gravity. "We cannot beat the B-29." The psychological effect of the loss of his home went deep. He had been one of the happiest and most carefree of children. He became thoughtful and serious and it was seldom that he laughed. He became ill and died shortly after the war was over. A nervous breakdown, the doctor called it.

The B-29s had brought the war to the Japanese people in a real and personal sense and each man had begun to form his own opinion on whether Japan was winning or losing. My nephew's experience was repeated many thousands of times in every part of Japan. To each family that watched its home and belongings go skyward in a rush of smoke and flame, the news from Okinawa, true or false, meant little. For them, their personal war was already lost.❞

bridges, roads and in the canals. We were instructed to report on actual conditions. Most of us were unable to do this because of horrifying conditions.

Two nights later 285 aircraft dropped 1,800 tons of incendiaries at Nagoya. Without the wind, the fires were more contained. One aircraft was lost and two square miles of the city destroyed.

On 13 March Osaka was the target for 274 B-29s. 13,000 people died, 135,000 homes were

Below: *A large area of Osaka was levelled by sustained fire-bomb attacks carried out by the Americans.*

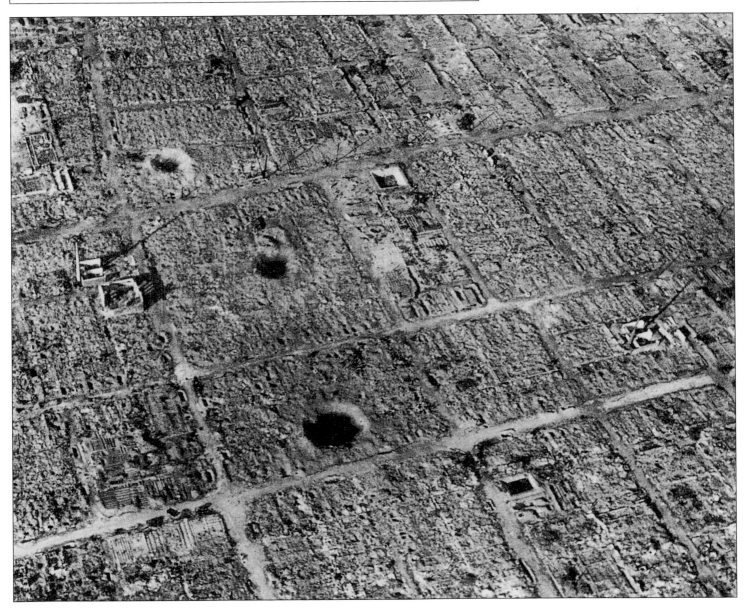

Above: *Tokyo became a patchwork city following the destruction delivered by the incendiary raids, with much of its industry and housing flattened.*

burned down and 119 factories were knocked out. American losses were light, with just two aircraft lost and 13 damaged by anti-aircraft fire.

The heaviest attack was made against Kobe on 16 March, using 2,355 tons of mixed oil and thermite bombs. More than 300 planes launched the onslaught and three were lost. At Kobe 2,669 people were killed, with 66,000 houses and 500 industrial centres eradicated. A fifth strike was made against Nagoya three days later, in which high-explosive bombs were among those used.

In 11 days 21st Bomber Command had notched up

Right: *Major-General Curtis LeMay (left) believed the policies of 21st Bomber Command – obliterating key centres – would bring about Japan's defeat.*

1,595 sorties and dropped in excess of 9,000 tons of incendiary bombs, proving that Japan was exposed to complete devastation. Equally as important to the Americans was the low level of losses the bomber command had sustained. Only 20 aircraft were destroyed, mostly by anti-aircraft fire and only one per cent of the crews were lost.

The rate of attacks was kept up, some made by day but those against Tokyo were at night. LeMay became involved

in psychological warfare, too, with the dropping of thousands of leaflets prior to the raids, naming 12 cities which were going to be hit and urging the civilian population to evacuate. This not only spread confusion but helped to demoralise the battered, war-weary population.

At the same time, 21st Bomber Command was involved in a minelaying programme to complete the blockade of Japan. Between the end of March and the middle of August about 12,000 mines were dropped into the waters around the islands. It meant that in May, mines were responsible for more losses to Japanese shipping than submarines were.

LEAFLETS DROPPED

Submarines were then able to move into the Sea of Japan, looking for the occasional ship which had escaped the blockade and also organising lightning sabotage raids.

With the Japanese Imperial Navy now completely impotent and the majority of surviving Japanese aircraft in hiding, American aircraft carriers also

EYE WITNESS

Geoff Michael, from Perth, was 18 when he joined the Royal Australian, Air Force in 1942 and trained under the Empire Air Training Scheme, launched in 1939 to train Allied pilots. He went on to complete 32 missions with Bomber Command and retired from the RAAF after 37 years' service, as Air Commodore.

'Even though it was a hectic and sad time, one is inclined to remember most of the good things – the great time I had on leaves etc.

But I also recall vividly having my aircraft shot up by ground fire and fighters. The fortunate part was that I was never wounded and never lost a crew member.

However, I did lose a close mate who was killed in a daylight raid over Germany. I saw the plane go down but didn't realise at the time it was my mate's plane.

It was a time when we were conditioned to death. Every morning you expected not to see the next one. So all you did was to read the operations board, see if you had been metered on a mission and, if your weren't, go out and relax and have a good time.'

DEVASTATION

In Japan itself the people were enduring appalling hardship. Homelessness caused by the effective incendiary strikes left many in dire straits. If their factories had also been destroyed they were in an even worse situation. There were few building materials on hand in the devastated city and little food. Inadequate rice rations were sometimes being boosted by sawdust. The wounded were also receiving scant attention. But if the population went to the countryside to scavenge food where it could, who would man the remaining factories and workplaces?

By August, Japanese ministers called for a collection of acorns to turn into food

Natural disasters, including extensive flooding, added to their problems. By July 1945 an estimated 25 per cent of all housing in Japan had been destroyed, leaving 22 million people homeless.

By August, Japanese ministers had called for a collection of acorns to turn into food. Yet, the people spoke of surrender only in whispers. An inherent will to serve the Emperor prevented an uprising. The Japanese would struggle on regardless.

LeMay was delighted with the success of his aerial bombing campaign and was convinced that it alone would bring Japan to the point of surrender. His confidence was somewhat premature.

sailed close to the home islands, their aircraft launching attacks at regular intervals. Freed by the end of the war in Europe, Royal Navy warships joined the US Navy in the waters off Japan, and combined attacks were launched, before the typhoon season made any air attack impossible.

In August a Japanese plan to launch 2,000 kamikaze planes on the 21st Bomber Command bases in the Marianas was

discovered. The carrier fleets moved to within range of the airfields on the northern island of Honshu where the heavily camouflaged planes were being gathered for the covert operation. For the first time since the end of the Okinawa campaign, a Japanese fighter counter-attacked and a kamikaze aircraft struck at an American destroyer. Still, the Japanese airfields came in for heavy bombing.

DAYLIGHT RAIDING

By the time America entered the war, the British had some fixed ideas about aerial combat.

The Royal Air Force had learned the hard way that aircraft employed on daylight raids were more vulnerable to the enemy, that bombers had a better survival rate when they were accompanied by fighters. Harris and the other British air supremos thought it best that the US fliers reinforced the existing night bombing expeditions being carried out by the RAF.

Novices at warfare in the air they may have been, but the Americans had thoughts of their own on the issue. US pilots were untrained for night missions. Not only that, they had a different bombing philosophy from that of their British counterparts, that of precision bombing.

FIRST ACTION

Given that their Flying Fortresses were, in their opinion, well defended and that the aircraft were equipped with a revolutionary new bombsight called the Norden which 'could drop a bomb into a pickle barrel from 20,000ft', it was their preferred plan to fly during the day. No amount of friendly persuasion from the British could dissuade the US air chiefs from their stated aims.

The Royal Air Force held Flying Fortresses in low regard. During experiments with the new aircraft in 1941, pilots felt they became large targets for German defences. For their part, the US air chiefs believed the RAF had used the Fortresses wrongly, sending them out in twos and threes instead of in a large formation when they performed best.

First taste of action for the US pilots came on 17 August 1942 when a dozen Flying Fortresses flew out of Grafton Underwood aerodrome, heading for Rouen, northern France.

With protection from four squadrons of RAF Spitfires, they made the flight, dropped the 18.5 tons of bombs on railway targets and returned home intact but for slight damage on two Fortresses caused by flak.

On the mission was Ira C. Eaker, a Brigadier-General, and superb pilot, who set up the headquarters for the US 8th Air Force in Britain and was soon given command of its European flight operations.

There followed a succession of small-scale bombing raids. The success of precision bombing was trumpeted by Eaker although, like the number of victories claimed against the Luftwaffe on such outings, the statistics had to be treated with caution. Nevertheless, in 13 missions, just two planes were lost – an enviable record.

The Norden bombsight 'could drop a bomb into a pickle barrel from 20,000 ft'

Still, their operations had been strictly 'local' on missions regarded as workaday 'milk runs' by the British pilots.

Left: *A US Flying Fortress carries out daylight bombing raid over Germany.* **Below:** *By 1942, US aircraft were a familiar sight in Britain.*

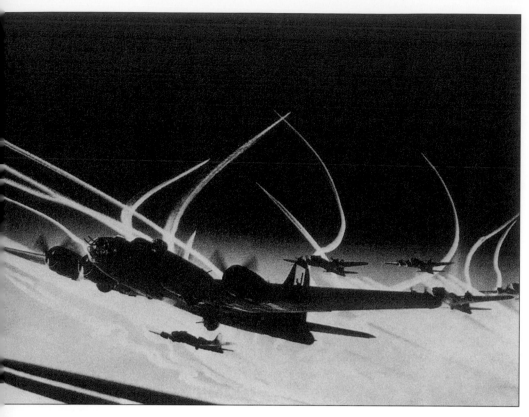

Above: US B-17s plough on towards their targets while fighter escorts fend off marauding enemy interceptors. The range of escorts increased during the war.

Then poor weather began to not only hamper the efficiency of the Norden bombsight – which had earned its colours in the cloudless skies above New Mexico and struggled in the cloud – and smog-filled heavens above Germany – but brought about the wholesale cancellation of planned raids.

Like the RAF, the USAAF had to do its bit for the 'Torch' landings in North Africa in late 1942, which cut aircraft and crew stocks by a third.

Then the Luftwaffe hit on a new tactic which took its toll among the American fighters. German pilots spotted the Achilles heel of the Flying Fortresses, which was head–on attack. There were no defences on the nose of the plane and the

Germans had enough guts to mount daring frontal assaults despite the obvious risk of a collision.

Churchill was among those who strongly objected to the Americans going their own way. He believed that precision bombing being executed by the Americans, which needed daylight to succeed, was the height of folly. Area bombing under the cover of darkness appeared a far better bet and might encourage the Americans to venture for the first time over German territory.

At the Casablanca Conference of January 1943, Churchill hoped to persuade Roosevelt that daylight bombing raids should be dropped in favour of night bombing operations by both air forces.

Eaker had one chance beforehand to convince Winston Churchill otherwise. Finally, it only took one sentence. His proposal in favour of the

continuation of daylight raids contained the words: 'By bombing the devils around the clock we can prevent the German defences from getting any rest.' The idea instantly caught Churchill's imagination. He vowed to give Eaker the opportunity to prove his point.

THE B-24 ARRIVES

The Casablanca Directive, backed orchestrated day- and night-time bombing raids and listed top targets, namely the centres of German industry.

On 27 January that year the US airmen were at last sent to Germany to produce the goods. Their target was Wilhelmshaven on the North Sea, where U-boats were made. By now B-24 Liberators had joined the Flying Fortresses in the ranks. Of the 53 which left for Wilhelmshaven, three were lost and the remainder had to battle at close quarters with Luftwaffe fighters while achieving only moderate success in their mission. The difficulties of daylight raids over hostile territory were crystallised for the Americans.

Danger from flak and enemy fighters was not the only problem to be faced by the Americans on their daylight raids. To stay out of reach of the enemy, they flew at high altitudes, usually above 20,000 feet. The chill of the air numbed their faces, crammed as they were in small cockpits. Tension mixed with boredom as another lengthy mission got underway. For a while each member of the crew remained vigilant for the enemy, but there were long hours when the Luftwaffe didn't

EYE WITNESS

Burdsall D. Miller, from Sacramento, California, joined the US Army Air Force, aged 24, following the Japanese raid on Pearl Harbor. Based in Sudbury, England, he became a colonel and flew 32 missions.

'I flew ten missions in a B-24 Liberator and then switched to B-17s for a further 22 raids. Most of them were daylight raids over Germany although we also hit Italy and Noway. I got shot up but never enough to bale out or crash land.

As command pilot, I sat in the co-pilot's seat and made all the decisions as far as the group or squadron were concerned that day. I was scared but I was trained to do a job. The thing that made the biggest impression on me was flying in formation and seeing a wing man shot down in flames. It was very upsetting.

But we all got fatalistic and figured when our time came we were going to get it. Perhaps that made us seem like we had nerves of steel. Otherwise we would not have lasted. We had some men who didn't last. They refused to fly, but It was very few out of a considerable number of men.

As soon as we dropped our bombs, we got out of the target area as most were heavily defended. As we turned we could see bombs hitting and we could usually tell if we had hit the target.

I have a big picture at home. It was taken on a raid over Germany on one of the most heavily defended targets. We had turned to start our bombing run. We just opened our bomb bay doors. To the left of us, another plane was doing the same when some flak went right into the bomb bay. The plane just exploded. Nobody got out alive. At the moment the plane blew up, my waist gunner took the picture.'

appear in which there was little to do but study the clouds.

Every US airman wore a steel chain vest to protect himself from flak. His flight suit was thick to protect him from the cold. Each wore a parachute and an oxygen mask, itself deeply uncomfortable. Despite the elaborate precautions, there was at least a one in ten chance of dying.

Americans adopted different flying patterns to suit the daylight nature of the raid. Up to 21 planes would form a box which was staggered vertically and horizontally for protection. Three boxes lined up in the air to form a combat wing.

To improve the accuracy of bombing, the most skilful men were placed in the lead planes and gave the signal for the rest of the aircraft in the box to drop their bombs.

Historically the US Army Air Corps was treated as the poor relation by the White House

On the ground, Eaker had his own problems. The US Army Air Corps, as it was first known, was treated as the poor relation by the White House. Priorities changed only slowly during the war and Eaker spent many fruitless hours harrying his bosses in America for extra planes and crews. It wasn't until mid-1943 that his efforts paid off. The US 8th Air Force could at last increase the size and effectiveness of its attacks.

DANGEROUS GAME

Perhaps the biggest bonus of all to the US airmen was when fighter aircraft increased their range, although it was late in the conflict when a combat aircraft, which could escort bombers into the heart of Germany and back, came into use.

Daylight missions were stepped up in 1943 and the heavy bombers recorded some admirable successes. Assisting their cause was the decision to scale down Luftwaffe defences in France by withdrawing two groups back to the Reich to improve air security there. The

Left: *Despite damage from a German rocket in the Battle of Berlin, this US B-17 still managed to land safely.*

Allies were now making a concerted effort to draw the Luftwaffe aircraft into the sky at every opportunity, trying to shoot down as many as possible. A considerable number of Allied planes fell victim while playing this dangerous game.

PLOESTI RAID

The US medium bombers fared less fortunately. A flight of B-26C Marauders which set off from Great Saling on 17 May was virtually wiped out during a raid on Haarlem.

And raids later in the year proved yet again the perils of daylight raiding. On 1 August 1943 the target was Ploesti, the oilfields in Romania which fed Germany's war machine.

The Americans had planned a surprise attack, keeping radio silence and flying at low altitudes to avoid radar detection. Their approach was to be over a lightly defended sector and their escape route was to North Africa. Alas, the planes were picked up in Germany as soon as they left the runway.

Navigational errors brought them in over the thickest of the anti-aircraft gunfire. Fifty three of the Liberators on the raid were shot down in enemy territory. A further 55 reached Libya in such appalling condition that they were fit only for scrap. The results were disappointing, with only a small dent being made in the oil production levels.

In the same month, the Americans tackled Regensburg and Schweinfurt, key centres for aircraft manufacturing and the production of that tiny but indispensible engineering component, the ball bearing. The raids would be without fighter escorts. So deep were the targets inside Reich territory the existing fighters did not have the capacity to fly there and back.

When the 146 Flying Fortresses dispatched for Regensburg crossed over the German border they met a hail of fire from a host of defending Luftwaffe planes. The German pilots were under no illusions. They were no longer the favoured elite. Hitler was once

again frustrated at the lack of success brought home by the Luftwaffe which once had seemed invincible. Now fewer resources were being ploughed into aircraft manufacture and the training of crews. Without this investment, the entire force would surely be strangled. Luftwaffe production chief Ernest Udet had committed suicide in despair at the plight of the force. The pressure was on to prove the worth of the air force before the unpredictable Führer sought his own revenge against it.

Those Flying Fortresses that had survived the arduous 90 minute flight to Regensburg dropped their bomb loads and made off in haste towards Algiers, saving themselves a possibly fatal return journey.

Now it was the turn of 230 Flying Fortresses to run the

gauntlet across Germany en route to Schweinfurt.

The fierce firepower of 300 Luftwaffe fighters battered the American planes. The Germans lost 25 fighters that day, the US bombers lost 60 and another 47 planes could not be salvaged.

The figures were bleak for the USAAF. In October 1943, 153 aircraft were lost in a single week. It led to the halt of bombing raids without fighter escort.

DROP TANKS

Fortunately the drop tank appeared, a suspended fuel tank which could be jettisoned when empty. This was attached under the wing to vastly increase the range of fighters. Hot on its heels came the P-51 Mustang, a fighter with an 850-mile range. It helped tip the balance of the air war over Europe in favour of the Allies.

By 1944 the Allies were producing twice the number of aircraft as the Reich was. The Luftwaffe's difficulties were compounded by the damage each fighter was sustaining which wasn't being repaired. Hitler was punishing the disappointing Luftwaffe by depriving it of essential materials to stay alive.

Yet the theories adopted by 'Bomber' Harris for the RAF and Eaker for the USAAF cannot be said to have been an outright success. Harris hoped to defeat the Third Reich by saturation bombing, destroying the will of the German people. The question of the morality of carpet-bombing civilian centres, including the ancient city of Dresden late in the war, raged long after the conflict had ended.

Eaker targeted industrial centres, certain that concerted bombing raids would cause Hitler's regime to topple. The principles were flawed. Hitler illustrated only too well over Britain in 1940 that air power by itself was not sufficient to win a war. Bombs from above failed to break the will of the Germans in just the same way as they had failed to crack the British. And damage sustained by industry could inevitably be repaired – particularly in Germany with the use of forced labour.

The liberation of Europe came with the arrival of the ground troops, albeit with priceless assistance from their colleagues in the air forces.

EYE WITNESS

Lieutenant Harmon Cropsey, a former state senator from Decatur, Michigan, served with VB110, a US Navy squadron, navigating, Liberators on 12-hour anti-submarine patrols into the North Atlantic. He was based at Dunkeswell In Devon under RAF Coastal Command.

❝One of my fellow officers was Joe Kennedy, John's elder brother. We used to moot quite regularly in the mess and swap notes He was flying the same aircraft as me.

It was Joe who volunteered for one of the most dangerous missions of the war. The idea was to strip everything out of one of the Liberators and pack it full of TNT. He was to fly this out over the North Sea to a prearranged navigational point and bale out. The plane would then be radio controlled to crash-land on its target – a 40-foot layer of reinforced concrete around some U-boat pens in Holland.

But something went wrong and the plane exploded in mid-air over England. We never found out what the problem was, and obviously there was nothing left of his body. He was a very brave man.

Our base lost a many airmen. The other two squadrons, 103 and 105, had around two-thirds of their crews killed in the first few months of our arrival in 1943. There was a German advanced training base at Brest and they were sending up the twin-engined Junkers 88 which had a 50-knot advantage on our planes. If you got caught out over the sea on a clear day you were a dead duck. Your only hope was to find cloud cover.

I know of only one plane, flown by a Free Czech crew, which made it home after being attacked. We were just fatalistic about it.

Every mission you were handed a top secret chart showing where all the Allied subs and ships should be. One day I'd got this thing spread out inside the plane with the door still open. Suddenly the engines start and the chart blows right out into a field. I chase after it and my flight suit gets caught on some barbed wire. As a result, I fall and dislocate my shoulder.

That incident extended my war. You could go home after 25 missions but due to my injury I stayed behind when all my chums left. Then they decided they needed an experienced navigator to show the new crews what to do. I ended up flying 42 missions.❞

THE ULTIMATE WEAPON

In Japan, the people were preparing for all-out war against invading Americans.

As early as November 1944 all Japanese men aged between 14 and 61 were conscripted. Women between the ages of 17 and 41 were on standby for military service. They were schooled in beach defences and guerrilla warfare. Those that were left unarmed – the vast majority – were told to practise martial arts skills as a form of defence. The message from the rulers of Japan was to be seen on giant posters hung around towns and villages. 'One hundred million will die for Emperor and nation!'

Key installations in Japan had been destroyed by the American bombing campaign. Much of the Japanese shipping had been sunk already by US ships, aircraft and submarines, which were now operating a blockade of the island coastlines. Japan was being starved of everything she needed to survive – yet still there was no sign of surrender.

The Japanese had explored through neutral sources for a negotiated peace, all cloaked in secrecy. Finally, the Japanese foreign ministry approached Russia to act as an intermediary. But Japanese demands were unacceptable to the Allies who would agree to nothing less than an unconditional surrender.

The lack of a cohesive war leader in Japan was keenly, felt. Emperor Hirohito was a figurehead who could apparently do little without the say-so of his government. Prime Minister Admiral Suzuki was eager to sue for peace but there remained in opposition hardliners who were willing to fight to the death. No one, it seemed, was in outright control and nobody dared utter the word 'surrender' without the prospect of assassination, political retribution or military uprising looming large. Japan struggled on in a vacuum of indecision.

The losses among the American troops in the landings around the Pacific islands had horrified and shocked the commanders. By now painfully aware of the Japanese resilience to attack and their reluctance to surrender, they viewed invasion of the home islands as a tall order. The estimates for the number of US casualties appeared virtually open ended.

When Truman met with Churchill and Stalin in Potsdam in July 1945, they discussed the inadequate peace overtures from the Land of the Rising Sun. Later, Truman confided that America had developed a new bomb which could finally end the war.

ATOMIC POWER

He was referring to the end result of the Manhattan Project, begun back in 1942, in which a band of élite scientists, the most admired brains of the free world, had got together to probe the possibilities of atomic power.

By December of that year, scientists under the leadership of Professor Enrico Fermi had made a significant breakthrough in understanding how to spark a man-made chain reaction.

At two big plants – Oak Ridge, Tennessee, and Hanford, Washington – work continued in the bid to extract the essential substance known as U-235 from uranium for the manufacture of plutonium.

It wasn't until 5.50am on 16 July 1945 that the theory was finally put into full-scale practice. In the scorched sands of the New Mexican desert the

Far left: Scientists knew they had created the ultimate weapon when it was tested.
Left: Truman confided in Churchill about the bomb at Potsdam.

Above: *A weapon similar to that detonated at Nagasaki. Its weight was 10,000 pounds and it was equivalent in power to 20,000 tons of TNT.*

Below: *Dr Albert Einstein (left) was the initial innovator. Dr Robert Oppenheimer (right) took up his theories and made them reality.*

plutonium bomb called 'Fat Man' was detonated. (It won the name by having a passing resemblance in profile to Churchill.) Observing scientists could barely hide their awe at the intense power man had created.

Dr Robert J. Oppenheimer, the physicist directing the project, instantly realised the shattering effect it would have on the world.

TRUMAN INFORMED

A telegram detailing the precise results of the 'Fat Man' experiment was sent to the Potsdam Conference for the consumption of President Truman – who himself had only found out in April the full scope of the Manhattan Project.

Two further atomic bombs were made and dispatched to the Pacific while the politicians pondered. Was the world ready for the atomic age? Once unleashed, would this mighty new force return to act as a Sword of Damocles poised over the heads of free and fair countries?

Churchill for one was in no doubt that it should be used. Afterwards, he wrote: 'To avert a vast, indefinite butchery, to bring the war to an end, to give peace to the world, to lay healing hands upon its tortured peoples by a manifestation of over-whelming power at the cost of a few explosions seemed, after all our toils and perils, a miracle of development.

'British consent in principle to the use of the weapon had been given on 4 July before the test had taken place. The final decision now lay in the main with President Truman, who had the weapon. But I never doubted what it would be nor have I ever doubted since that he was right.'

In his memoirs, Truman wrote: 'Let there be no mistake about it. I regarded the bomb as a military weapon and never had any doubt that it should be used.'

Still, there was debate about whether Japan should be warned about its terrible fate. A chain of events finally overtook these talks.

The Potsdam Conference finally closed on 26 July with an ultimatum for Japan. It called for unconditional surrender. In the absence of such a surrender, Japan would face complete destruction. Just two days later, Premier Suzuki announced his country would be ignoring the Allied threat.

Such belligerence was enough to confirm an order sent to Lieutenant-General Spaatz, Commanding General of the US Army Strategic Air Forces to prepare a B-29 to carry the newly fabricated atomic bomb.

On 6th August 1945 the first atomic bomb, called 'Little Boy', was released over Hiroshima.

Below: *Smoke rises more than 60,000 feet into the air following the explosion of the atomic bomb at Nagasaki.*

EYE WITNESS

Dr Michihiko Hachiya was at home when the first atomic bomb – 'Little Boy' – fell on Hiroshima from the bomb bay of B-29 'Enola Gay'. He recalls the moment of impact in his eye witness account Hiroshima Diary.

'The hour was early, the morning still warm and beautiful. Shimmering leaves reflecting sunlight from a cloudless sky as I gazed absently through wide-flung doors opening to the south.

Clad in vest and pants, I lay on the living room floor exhausted because I had just spent a sleepless night on duty as an air raid warden in my hospital.

Suddenly a strong flash of light startled me – and then another. I remember vividly how a stone lantern in the garden became brilliantly lit and I debated whether this light was caused by a magnesium flare or sparks from a passing tram.

Garden shadows disappeared. The view where a moment before all had been so bright and sunny was now dark and hazy. I could barely discern that a wooden column that had supported one corner of my house, was leaning and the roof sagged dangerously.

I tried to escape but rubble and fallen timbers barred the way. By picking my way cautiously I managed to reach the roka and stepped down into my garden. A profound weakness overcame me so I stopped to regain my strength. I discovered that I was completely naked. Where were my vest and pants. What had happened?

All over the right side of my body I was cut and bleeding. A large splinter was protruding from a wound in my thigh and something warm trickled into my mouth. My cheek was torn, I discovered, as I felt it gingerly with the lower lip laid wide open. Embedded in my neck was a sizeable fragment of glass which I matter-of-factly dislodged and with the detachment of one stunned and shocked I studied it and my blood-stained hand. '

any other description I can give it. It was black and boiling underneath with a steam haze on the top of it. Arid, of course, we had seen the city when we went in and there was nothing to see when we came back.'

On 8 August further pressure was exerted on Japan when the Soviet Union declared war and launched an invasion of Manchuria.

'We had seen the city when we went in and there was nothing to see when we came back'

A day later a further atomic bomb dropped, this time on Nagasaki. It came from the bowels of another B-29, this one christened 'Great Artist', under the command of Major Charles Sweeney. About 40,000 people died this time with a further 60,000 injured.

It is doubtful whether the introduction of atomic weapons had a huge effect on the people of Japan. The scale and horror of the previous bombing campaigns had claimed victims by the thousand and caused acres of destruction. Wholesale killing, burns and homelessness was nothing new for them. The only new aspect was the radiation sickness among the survivors, the wide-ranging effects of which were not immediately apparent.

For the rest of the world, the double bombing was like a

A mammoth 120 inches long and weighing 9,000 pounds, beneath its shell it contained the power equivalent to 20,000 tons of TNT. It was carried to its target in a B-29 called 'Enola Gay' which took off from the Marianas. In command was Colonel Paul Tibbets.

The uranium bomb exploded 2,000 feet above the centre of Hiroshima. Four square miles of the city was instantly wiped out. Those at the epicentre of the bomb were reduced to ashes along with buildings and cars. Beyond that immediate area, many more died and tens of thousands were horribly burned.

SHOCK WAVES

The authorities could only estimate the numbers of people who had perished in the ferocious cauldron. The final figure was put between 70,000 and 80,000 persons. Colonel Tibbets later described how his plane was shaken by the shock waves as it sped away and told of the scene of devastation he left behind: 'There was the mushroom cloud growing up and we watched it blossom. And down below it the thing reminded me more of a boiling pot of tar than

EYE WITNESS

Tsutomu Yamaguchi worked in the Hiroshima yard of the Mitsubishi shipbuilding company and was on his way to work when the bomb dropped more than a mile away.

❛Suddenly there was a flash like the lighting of a huge magnesium flare. As I prostrated myself there came a terrific explosion. I was lifted two feet from the ground and I felt a strong wind pass my body.

How long I lay in the road dazed, I don't know, but when I opened my eyes it was so dark all around me that I couldn't see a thing. It was as if it had suddenly become midnight in the heat of the day. When my eyes adjusted to the darkness I perceived that I was enveloped in an endless cloud of dust so thick it was black.

As the dust blew away and my surroundings became visible I saw what seemed to be thousands of tiny, flickering lamps all over the street and in the fields. They were little circles of flame, each about the size of a doughnut. Myriads of them were hanging on the leaves of the potato plants.

I looked toward the city and saw a huge, mushroom-shaped cloud rising high into the sky. It was an immense evil-looking pillar. It seemed to be reflecting every shade in the spectrum turning first one colour then another.

Feeling terribly weak and suffering intense pain from the deep burns on my face and arm, I stumbled into the potato field. There was a big tree out in the field and I headed for that. Sometimes I could only crawl, creeping from bush to bush. When I finally reached the tree I had no more strength to go on. And I had acquired a terrible thirst.

I saw a group of teenage boys unclothed except for torn underpants. As the boys came near I saw that they were pale and shaking severely. I had never seen such a horrifying sight as those five shivering boys. Blood was pouring in streams from deep cuts all over their bodies mingling with their perspiration and their skin was burned deep red like the colour of cooked lobsters.

At first it seemed strangely that their burned and lacerated backs and chests were growing green grass. Then I saw that hundreds of blades of sharp grass had been driven deep into their flesh, evidently by the force of the blast.❜

macabre sideshow with people riveted by the footage and photos of the vast mushrooming cloud that rose up some 20,000 feet as the bomb was detonated.

JAPAN SURRENDERS

In any event, it was clear that Truman's pledge to 'obliterate' Japan was no empty threat. Hirohito himself was sickened by the suffering among his people. Finally, he found the leverage inside his government to bring the conflict to an end.

The day after Nagasaki was bombed, Japan broadcast a willingness to surrender 'on the understanding that it does not comprise any demand which prejudices the prerogatives of the Emperor as Sovereign ruler.'

Yet still the hawks in the regime dragged their feet. A flight of US Navy carrier-borne planes flew over Japan on 13 August dropping leaflets which spelled out the surrender so the people would understand that it was all over.

The following day at 11pm the Emperor himself told his people the war was over. Even at this late stage, 1,000 militant soldiers stormed the Imperial Palace in a bid to prevent the surrender. They were beaten off by the Emperor's own guard.

VJ day was then declared on 15 August. The pockets of Japanese resistance around the Pacific and South East Asia surrendered through the following month, ending with Hong Kong on September 16th.

Left: The atomic bomb scarred the landscape of Nagasaki so deeply it was beyond recognition.

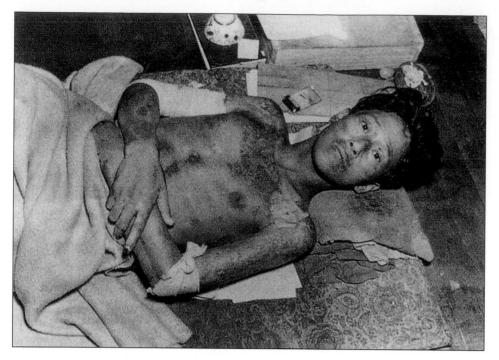

Left: The luckier victims of the atomic bomb blasts suffered burns to their bodies. The remains of many of the victims were never found.

In the meantime the official ceremony marking the outbreak of peace came on 2 September aboard the USS *Missouri* in Tokyo Bay. The Japanese delegation was led by the one-legged

'Let us pray that peace be now restored to the world'

Foreign Minister Mamoru Shigemitsu, who wore a top hat for the occasion. The military wing of the country was represented by General Yoshijiro Umezu. There to receive them were dignitaries from all the countries that had taken part in the war against Japan – America, Britain, Australia, New Zealand, Canada, China, France and Holland. Sailors squeezed into every available inch of the deck to witness the historic moment.

After the signing was over, General MacArthur gave a

Right: Servicemen greeted news of the atomic explosions with relief. The blasts probably saved thousands of US troops.

stirring speech opening the door to a new order.

'We are gathered here, representatives of the major warring powers, to conclude a solemn agreement whereby peace may be restored. The issues involving divergent ideals and ideologies have been determined on the battlefields of the world and hence are not for our discussion or debate.

PRAYER FOR PEACE

'Nor is it for us here to meet representing as we do a majority of the people of the earth in a spirit of distrust, malice or hatred. But rather it is for us both victors and vanquished to serve, committing all our peoples unreservedly to faithful compliance with the understandings they are here formally to assume. It is my earnest hope... that from this solemn occasion a better world shall emerge... a world dedicated to the dignity of man... Let us pray that peace be now restored to the world and that God will preserve it always.'

1939

MARCH

15: German troops cross the Czech frontier.

APRIL

28: Hitler rips up a non-aggression pact signed with Poland in 1934.

SEPTEMBER

1: Germany invades Poland.

3: Britain gives Germany an ultimatum to withdraw from Poland. At 11am Britain goes to war. Commonwealth countries also declare war on Germany. By 5pm France at war with Third Reich.

4: War Cabinet assembled with Winston Churchill as First Lord of Admiralty. SS *Athenia* sunk by a German U-boat. 112 fatalities.

9: German troops march into Warsaw.

17: Russia invades Poland.

18: Britain's aircraft carrier HMS *Courageous* sunk by U–boat – 500 sailors lost.

29: Poland surrenders.

OCTOBER

5: Hitler enters Warsaw, in triumph.

11: British Expeditionary Force – 158,000 plus 25,000 vehicles – shipped across Channel in just five weeks to defend France.

14: 800 men die when battleship *Royal Oak* torpedoed at Scapa Flow.

NOVEMBER

8: Hitler survives an assassination attempt in Munich.

13: First German bombs hit British soil in Shetland Islands.

30: Russia invades Finland.

DECEMBER

13: Battle of River Plate. *Graf Spee* limps into Montevideo with 36 dead, 60 injured and widespread damage.

17: Hitler orders scuttling of *Graf Spee*.

1940

JANUARY

1: Conscription in Britain for men aged 20 – 27.

8: Food rationing in Britain begins.

16: British submarines *Seahorse*, *Undine* and *Starfish* sunk operating in enemy waters.

21: War at sea intensifies – 81 lost when *Grenville* sunk.

22: British destroyer *Exmouth* sunk by U-boat with the loss of all hands.

FEBRUARY

10: In Czechoslovakia, Jews ordered to close shops.

20: Hitler orders U-boat commanders to consider neutral shipping as fair game.

MARCH

16: Scapa Flow naval base bombed by Luftwaffe.

27: Himmler, orders building of Auschwitz.

APRIL

3: Churchill asked to direct war effort.

5: RAF strikes at German ships in Kiel Canal.

8: Germany invades Denmark and Norway.

9: Germans take control of Oslo.

10: Battle of Narvik.

11: German cruiser *Blücher* sunk with loss of 1,000 crewmen.

13: Second Battle of Narvik. Allies victorious, sinking eight German destroyers and a U-boat.

15: Allies land in Norway.

24: British troops pull back after clashes with German forces.

25: Allied forces driven out of central Norway.

MAY

1: Trondheim evacuated by the Allies. Norway surrenders.

9: British conscription age limit raised to 36.

10: Germany invades Holland, Belgium and Luxembourg. Churchill made Prime Minister.

15: Dutch surrender.

19: British Expeditionary Force in France, withdraws to the English Channel.

25: British trapped on French coast.

26: Evacuation of British, French and Belgian troops from Dunkirk. by flotilla of small boats. In a week 338,226 men are taken back to Britain.

JUNE

3: Luftwaffe bombs Paris.

4: Germans seize Dunkirk.

8: Norway falls.

10: Italy enters the war.

14: Victorious Germans enter Paris while Rommel captures Le Havre.

15: Russian army occupies Lithuania.

17: French leader Marshal Pétain orders army to stop fighting and seeks 'honourable' peace terms with Germany.

22: French sign armistice.

23: De Gaulle announces French National Committee will continue to fight Hitler.

25: London hears air raid sirens for the first time. Germans occupy the island of Guernsey.

JULY

1: Jersey occupied by Germans.

10: Battle of Britain begins when Luftwaffe attacks English Channel convoys and Welsh docks.

AUGUST

4: Italy invades British Somaliland from Ethiopia.

11: Britain's coast under bombardment from Luftwaffe.

17: British warships attack ports in Italian-held Libya.

18: More Luftwaffe attacks over southern England.

20: Churchill pays tribute to the courage of the RAF. 'Never in the field of human conflict was so much owed by so many to so few'.

24: London Blitz begins.

25: RAF strikes Berlin.

27: Air raids over southern England.

SEPTEMBER

3: Hitler plans invasion of Britain on 21 September.

9: London hit by 350 Luftwaffe.

10: Buckingham Palace damaged.

11: Daylight raid on London kills

more than 100 people.

13: Italy moves troops into Egypt.

15: Largest air raid against London. British units strike at Italians in Egypt.

17: Hitler postpones invasion of Britain.

19: London and Brighton bombed.

22: Japanese land in French Indo-china.

24: London suffers 18th successive night raid. Southampton and Brighton also bombed.

27: Japan signs ten-year pact with Germany and Italy.

30: British civilian casualties in September number 7,000 dead and 10,600 injured.

OCTOBER

3: Chamberlain resigns.

7: German troops enter Romania.

9: Conservative Party elects Winston Churchill as leader.

12: Hitler postpones 'Operation Sealion' until spring 1941.

26: London suffers longest air raid.

28: Italians enter Greece.

29: British troops bound for Crete.

NOVEMBER

5: Franklin D. Roosevelt is re-elected as American President.

19: Greeks rout Italians.

DECEMBER

4: Greeks make headway in Albania.

9: British campaign in Africa begins.

12: British troops capture 30,000 Italians in Egypt.

1941

JANUARY

3: Australian troops assault Italian stronghold in Libya, taking 5,000 prisoners.

4: Allies capture 25,000 Italians

19: British forces enter Sudan and Italian-held Eritrea.

21: British and Australian forces capture Tobruk, in Libya.

FEBRUARY

14: Afrika Korps, led by Rommel, lands in Tripoli, Libya.

22: Rommel attacks British-held El Agheila.

MARCH

24: Rommel occupies El Agheila.

30: Rommel mounts counter offensive in North Africa.

APRIL

5: Allied forces enter Addis Ababa

6: Germany invades Yugoslavia and Greece.

10: Australian troops in North Africa pull back to Tobruk.

12: Belgrade surrenders. Allies pull back in Greece.

16: London suffers night raid with 500 planes dropping 100,000 bombs.

17: Yugoslavia surrenders.

21: Greece capitulates.

26: Tobruk under seige, Rommel makes headway in Egypt.

27: Germany enters Athens

MAY

2: British and Commonwealth troops withdraw from Greece.

4: British troops occupy airport and docks at Basra, Iraq.

10: Westminster Abbey, House of Commons, Tower of London and Royal Mint all hit in mammoth raid.

14: Singapore's defences boosted by Royal Navy and RAF

24: HMS *Hood* is sunk off Greenland.

27: Bismarck sunk off coast of France by cruiser *Dorsetshire*.

JUNE

8: Allies backed by Free French attack Syria. Vichy France outraged as Britain offers Syria independence.

12: RAF bombs Ruhr, Rhineland and German ports in a 20-night bombing campaign.

15: 'Operation Battleaxe', to relieve Tobruk, is launched.

16: Last Italians in Ethiopia surrender to British.

22: 'Operation Barbarossa' begins. Hitler invades Russia.

26: Finland declares war on Russia.

JULY

1: Germans seize Baltic port of Riga.

3: Stalin orders retreating forces to destroy everything as they fall back.

9: Russians defeated at Minsk.

10: Hitler encourages Japan to enter the war.

20: Britain adopts a 'V-for-Victory'.

28: Japanese troops land in southern Indochina.

SEPTEMBER

2: Fighting between Germans and Russians at Leningrad.

3: Gas chamber at Auschwitz in use.

6: Jews in Germany forced to wear yellow Star of David.

15: Siege of Leningrad begins.

18: Russians evacuate Kiev.

19: Kiev falls to Germany.

OCTOBER

16: Government leaves Moscow, Stalin remains.

18: Germans 70 miles from Moscow.

19: State of siege in Moscow.

NOVEMBER

6: German soldiers on the Eastern front experience frostbite.

13: German troops in Russia crippled by cold.

25: 8th Army attacked by Rommel.

27: American Pacific forces on alert.

DECEMBER

2: German troops close to Kremlin.

5: Hitler abandons for the winter his goal of seizing Moscow.

7: Pearl Harbor comes under attack from 360 Japanese planes.

10: Seige of Tobruk ends.

11: Germany and Italy declare war on America.

17: Rommel retreats in North Africa.

1942

JANUARY

2: Japan takes Manila.

11: Japan invades Dutch East Indies.

12: Kuala Lumpur falls to Japan.

15: Japan invades Burma.

20: Japan bombs Singapore.

21: Rommel launches another counter-attack in North Africa.

28: Rommel controls Benghazi.

FEBRUARY

9: Japan invades Singapore.

15: Singapore falls 9,000 dead and 80,000 Allied prisoners.

17: Japanese invade Bali in Dutch East Indies.

MARCH

27: Nazi U-boat base in western France wrecked by British commandos.

MAY

26: Rommel starts third offensive in Western Desert.

JUNE

4: Battle of Midway, between US and Japan.

21: Tobruk falls to Rommel. British forces fall back into Egypt.

JULY

6: British 8th Army sends Rommel into retreat at El Alamein.

AUGUST
7: US marines land on Guadalcanal.
12: Monty takes command in North Africa.

SEPTEMBER
5: Australians drive Japanese from Milne bay.
11: Japanese halted on Kokoda trail, Papua New Guinea.
23: Australians attack Japanese along Kokoda trail.

OCTOBER
14: Australian forces embroiled in fighting with Japanese.
23: Montgomery's 'Operation Lightfoot' begins at El Alamein.
26: Street fighting in Stalingrad.
27: Monty regroups 8th Army for second offensive at El Alamein.
30: Afrika Korps trapped by advancing Australians near Alamein.

NOVEMBER
2: 'Operation Supercharge', the second El Alamein begins.
6: Heavy rain hampers Monty's advance at Mersa Matruh.
8: 'Operation Torch' begins with Allied landings at Algiers, Oran and Casablanca.
13: Tobruk back in Allied hands.
15: Monty triumphs in second battle of El Alamein.

DECEMBER
1: Australians capture Gona, New Guinea.
8: Rommel's withdraws to Tunis.
25: 8th Army reach Sirte, but meet tough resistance from Afrika Korps.

1943
JANUARY
4: Japan evacuates Guadalcanal.
23: 8th Army moves to Tripoli
27: US 8th Air Force makes first bombing raid on Germany. RAF makes two day raids on Berlin.

FEBRUARY
4: 8th Army units enter Tunisia.
8: Russians liberate Kursk in USSR.
14: Chindits cross River Chindwin in Burma.
16: Himmler launches plan to eliminate Jewish ghetto in Warsaw.

MARCH
6: Rommel leaves Africa.
14: Strategic foothold of Kharkov in Russia is re-occupied by Germans.

APRIL
14: Rommel evacuates from Tunis.
15: 8,000lb bomb the 'Blockbuster'

is dropped on Stuttgart along with 4,000lb 'Factory-smasher' bombs.
20: Church bells are again permitted to be rung, now the Government believe that the threat of German invasion has past.

MAY
7: Tunis falls to Allies. North African campaign is over.
17: RAF Lancasters from 617 Squadron carry out the 'Dambusters' raid on Mohne and Eder dams.
30: Churchill and de Gaulle arrive in triumph at Algiers.
31: French 'provisional government' is established by Generals de Gaulle and Giraud in Algiers.

JUNE
7: Italy pulls out of Albania.
16: Japanese lose 100 aircraft over Guadalcanal.
19: Goebbels reports Berlin is 'free of Jews'.

JULY
10: Invasion of Sicily by Allies.
22: US 7th Army seizes Palermo, Sicily and heads for Messina.
25: Mussolini resigns and arrested.
27: A firestorm rages in Hanover after three days of continuous air raids.

AUGUST
2: A further raid by the RAF on Hamburg brings death toll to 40,000, with 37,000 seriously injured.
26: Russian forces assault German-held Ukraine.

SEPTEMBER
3: Invasion of Italy begins.
9: Allies land at Salerno in 'Operation Avalanche'.
17: British and American forces join up in Italy to push back the Germans.

OCTOBER
1: US 5th Army reaches Naples.
13: Italy declares war on Germany.

NOVEMBER
18: Massive bombing raid by the RAF on Berlin with 350 4,000lb bombs falling on the Reich's capital.
22: Churchill and Roosevelt meet with China's Chiang Kai-shek in North Africa.
28: Teheran Conference between Churchill, Rossevelt and Stalin.

DECEMBER
12: Rommel appointed Commander in Chief of German Atlantic defences.

24: Eisenhower is named Supreme Commander for Allied Invasion of western Europe.

1944
JANUARY
6: Russian forces move into Poland.
February
27: Leningrad seige ends after 900 days.
29: US troops land on Kwajalein, in the Marshall islands.

MARCH
1: Chindits enter Burma again.

APRIL
2: Russians enter Romania
5: Germany deporting Jews from Hungary.
9: de Gaulle is created Commander in Chief of the Free French forces.
16: Russian forces surge through the Crimea.

MAY
25: Chindits forced to withdraw under heavy counter-attack from Japanese.

JUNE
6: D-Day begins.
9: Allied armies meet in Normandy.
13: First V1 flying bomb lands in England.
15: US Marines land on Saipan, the Marianas.
18: Assisi is taken by 8th Army.
21: A thousand-bomber raid on Berlin staged by the US Army Air Forces.
26: 'Operation Epsom' to take Caen is mounted by British and Canadians.
29: Cherbourg liberated by US forces.

JULY
3: Russians recapture Minsk.
7: Caen is comprehensively bombed by the RAF.
9: Caen is taken by British forces.
17: 8th Army crosses the River Arno and is poised to take Florence.
US forces capture town of St Lô in Normandy.
Rommel is badly injured in an aircraft attack.
19: Russian troops enter Latvia.
21: US Marines land on Guam in the Marianas.
24: 'Operation Cobra' shatters the stalemate in Normandy.
25: Canadians force their way south of Caen.

26: Japanese counter-attack on Guam.
27: Guam is captured by Americans.
28: Red Army captures Brest-Litovsk on the River Bug.

AUGUST
1: Warsaw uprising begins as the Polish Home Army takes on the German occupying forces.
3: Germans leave the Channel Islands.
10: Japanese resistance in Guam virtually eliminated.
16: Canadian forces take Falaise in Normandy.
20: French troops liberate Toulon in south France.
23: Romania defeated by Russia.
25: Paris is liberated by Free French troops by General Leclerc. Romania declares war on Germany.
26: US and British forces head east of the River Seine.
28: Marseilles is freed.
31: Monty is promoted to the rank of Field Marshal.

SEPTEMBER
1: Canadian troops take Dieppe and Rouen. The US 5th Army takes Pisa.
3: The British Guards Armoured Division liberates Brussels.
8: The Red Army takes Bulgaria.
10: Prague falls to Russia. US troops enter Luxembourg.
15: Siegfried line is broken by the US 1st Army.
17: Allied troops parachute into Nijmegen and Arnheim.
24: British 2nd Army reaches the Rhine.

OCTOBER
2: Athens, is evacuated by Germans. British troops land on Crete.
9: Churchill visits Moscow for talks with Stalin.
14: Rommel commits suicide.
19: Germans pull out of Belgrade.
20: Aachen, the first German town to fall into the hands of the Allies.
27: Kamikaze attacks launched on American ships in the Philippines.
30: Mass exterminations end at Auschwitz.

NOVEMBER
2: Germans pull out of Greece.
12: Tirpitz sunk off Norway.
18: US 3rd Army enters Germany in force.
30: Churchill's 70th birthday.

DECEMBER
16: Battle of the Bulge, also known as the Battle of the Ardennes, gets underway.
22: German Panzers driven back from the Meuse.

1945
JANUARY
1: Luftwaffe tries to halt the Allied invasion with widespread bombing of French, Belgian and Dutch airfields.
17: Warsaw liberated by Polish troops.
27: Auschwitz concentration camp is liberated.
28: Battle of the Bulge ends. 120,000 Germans dead, injured or captive. Americans lose 8,600 troops with further 47,100 wounded and more than 21,000 missing.

FEBRUARY
1: US 6th Army pushes towards Manila in the Philippines.
3: Berlin is raided by 1,000 B-17 bombers.
4: Allied conference at Yalta, Crimea begins.
12: Yalta conference ends. The zones of influence around Europe and the world are drawn up.
13: RAF bombs Dresden with 800 Lancasters, causing 250,000 deaths.
19: US Marines land on Iwo Jima.
22: Allies paralyse German road and rail networks.
23: US Marines capture Mount Suribachi, the highest point on Iwo Jima, and raise the US flag.
27: Allies enter the German town of Mönchengladbach.

MARCH
5: The city of Cologne falls to Allies.
8: American troops move into Bonn.
19: Burmese city of Mandalay falls to 14th Army.
26: Japanese counter-attack on Iwo Jima. 216 Japanese prisoners taken from a force of 21,000. American casualties – 20,000 dead or wounded.

APRIL
1: US 10th Army lands on Okinawa.
6: Kamikazes attack 10th fleet.
7: Russian troops reach Vienna.
12: President Roosevelt dies. Truman takes over as President.
13: Allies liberate Belsen and Buchenwald concentration camps.
20: US 7th Army reaches Nuremberg.
23: US 8th Army captures Cebu in the Philippines. Hitler orders the arrest of Göring after attempts to take command of Germany.
25: US troops meet Red Army on the banks of the Elbe at Torgau.
26: Fighting continues on Okinawa.
28: Mussolini is captured and killed by Italian communist partisans.
29: Hitler weds Eva Braun.
30: Hitler shoots himself. His new wife dies at his side after taking poison.

MAY
2: Berlin is occupied by the Red Army. German forces in Italy surrender.
3: British take Rangoon.
4: Surrender of German troops in Holland, Denmark and north-west Germany.
5: Kamikazes claim 17 ships off Okinawa. Germans in Norway surrender.
7: The instrument of surrender of all German forces in the Allied HQ is signed at Rheims.
8: VE day.
9: Germany's surrender is ratified in Berlin.
10: Japanese forces west of the Irrawaddy River are isolated.
12: German forces on Crete surrender.
21: Belsen concentration camp is razed.

JUNE
1: Japanese forces retreat in Okinawa.
10: Australians invade Borneo.
20: Japanese surrender in Okinawa.

AUGUST
6: First atomic bomb dropped on Hiroshima, killing 80,000 people and injuring 80,000.
9: Second A-bomb dropped on Nagasaki. Death toll 40,000 with 60,000 injured.
14: Japan agrees to an unconditional surrender.
15: VJ Day.
28: Japanese surrender in Rangoon.
29: Allied occupation of Japan begins.

SEPTEMBER
2: Formal surrender document signed by Japan.
5: British return to Singapore.
7: Shanghai surrendered by Japanese.
12: Admiral Mountbatten receives surrender of all Japanese forces in South East Asia.
13: Japanese forces surrender in Burma.
16: Japanese forces surrender in Hong Kong.